Accessibility and Quality of Health Services

AF166014

Mario Jorge Ferreira de Oliveira (ed.)

Accessibility and Quality of Health Services

Proceedings of the 28th Meeting
of the European Working Group
on Operational Research
Applied to Health Services (ORAHS),
Rio de Janeiro, Brazil
July 28th – August 2nd, 2002

PETER LANG

Frankfurt am Main · Berlin · Bern · Bruxelles · New York · Oxford · Wien

Bibliographic Information published by Die Deutsche Bibliothek
Die Deutsche Bibliothek lists this publication in the Deutsche
Nationalbibliografie; detailed bibliographic data is available in
the internet at <http://dnb.ddb.de>.

ISBN 3-631-52016-6
US-ISBN 0-8204-6560-7

© Peter Lang GmbH
Europäischer Verlag der Wissenschaften
Frankfurt am Main 2004
All rights reserved.

www.peterlang.de

PREFACE

The EURO Working Group on Operational Research Applied to Health Services (ORAHS) was created in 1975 as part of a programme for developing special interest groups within the European branch, EURO of the International Federation of Operational Research Societies (IFORS). The group has at present members from 25 countries, mainly in Europe but also from overseas. The group gets together every year, each summer, for one week, in a different host country. Meetings are open to any person with a quantitative background and an interest in the subject area, although numbers may be limited to guarantee that open debate is practicable. The objectives of the group are communication of ideas, information and know-how concerning the application of Operational Research (OR) approaches and methods to problems in the health services area, mutual support between members, cooperation on joint projects, assistance with regard to approaches and posture in the field of applied OR.

The 2002 meeting took place in Brazil. The main theme for this, the 28th ORAHS International Conference was "Accessibility and Quality of Health Services". The Federal University of Rio de Janeiro, from July 28th to August 2nd, hosted the forum with support from COPPE, the Instituto Alberto Luiz Coimbra de Pós-Graduação e Pesquisa de Engenharia. The conference incorporated ten sessions on Quality Health Care, Emergency Services, Evaluation of Health Care, Scheduling Personnel, Location of Health Units, Performance Assessment, Decision Support Systems, Admission Systems, Information Systems and Performance Measurements. A selection of 20 of the 37 papers readily available at the sessions is presented in this book, after a review process, thus continuing the series started with the 21st meeting in Maastricht, The Netherlands, 1995.

The opening session was set up to welcome the participants from 19 different countries and to discuss issues of the Accessibility and Quality of the Health Services in Brazil. The participants of the round table included: Prof. Dr. Carlos Lessa - Rector of the Federal University of Rio de Janeiro; Prof. Dr. Mauro Marzochi - Health Secretary of the Municipality of Rio de Janeiro; Prof. Dr. Luiz Pinguelli Rosa - Director of Instituto Alberto Luiz Coimbra de Pós-Graduação e Pesquisa de Engenharia (COPPE); Prof. Dr. Flávio Fonseca Nobre - Head of Biomedical Engineering Program of COPPE and member of the Scientific Committee of the conference. The opening remarks was placed by Prof. Dr. Jan Vissers from Eindhoven University, The Netherlands - Head of the ORAHS working group and Prof. Dr. Mario Jorge Ferreira de Oliveira - Chairman of the ORAHS 2002 conference, gave the foreword as regards the meeting.

The conference included a debate on "Accessibility and Quality of Health Services". The event was open to the public. Members of the medical and scientific communities have been invited to attend. The following speakers at the table: Dr José Leôncio Feitosa - Health Secretary of the Rio de Janeiro State; Cel. Dr. Jorge Alberto Soares de Oliveira - Civil Defense Secretary of the State of Rio de Janeiro; Dr Edson Paixão - Director of Miguel Couto Hospital; Prof. Dr. Amâncio Paulino de Carvalho - Director of the Federal University of Rio de Janeiro Hospital; Prof. Dr. Luiz Fernando Loureiro Legey – Vice Director of COPPE/UFRJ; Prof. Dr. Duncan Boldy - Curtin University of Technology, Australia; Prof. Dr. Marten Lagergren - Stockholm Gerontology Research Center, Sweden; Prof. Dr. Jan Vissers - Eindhoven University of Technology, The Netherlands.

We are grateful to the session chairpersons (Arjan Shahani, Marten Largergren, Marco A. Lavrador, Keisei Tanahashi, Jan Schreuder, Harald Buhalg, Tom Bowen, Kevin J. Leonard, Jan Vissers and Flávio F. Nobre) and to the reviewers (Adriana B. de Moraes, Ludmila Gabcan, Antonio A. Goncalves, Rosimary T. de Almeida, Saint Claire dos S. G. Jr, Fatima M. H S. P. da Silva, Jaime Bellido, Leila C. M. Gomes, Luiz G. Acosta Espejo, Lupe N. P. Toscano, Patricia Oliveira and Hugo Ribeiro da Silveira), the appreciation for their most valuable comments on the papers submitted for this book. Many thanks are due to Paulo R.F. de Oliveira, Regina Sarandy, Silvia de Oliveira and Daniel de Oliveira for their assistance in organizing the conference. Late, but not least, we express gratitude to our assistant Vanessa Kelly Saavedra Frederico for her determination and competency in organizing the articles and designing the layout of the book.

Rio de Janeiro, September 2003

The Editor:
Mario Jorge Ferreira de Oliveira
Universidade Federal do Rio de Janeiro
Instituto Alberto Luiz Coimbra de Pós-Graduação e Pesquisa de Engenharia
Instituto de Matemática da UFRJ, Departamento de Matemática Aplicada
Cidade Universitária
Centro de Tecnologia, Bloco F sala 105, Rio de Janeiro, Brasil
Caixa Postal 68507
Email: mario_jo@pep.ufrj.br

CONTENTS

8

QUALITY HEALTH CARE

QUALITY IN RESIDENTIAL AGED CARE:
THE RESIDENTS' PERSPECTIVES

DUNCAN P. BOLDY[1], SHU-CHIUNG CHOU[1, 2], ANDY H. LEE[1]
[1]Curtin University of Technology, Australia
[2]Harvard School of Public Health, USA

Abstract

The paper describes a comprehensive approach to "assessing the residents" view in residential aged care facilities, with interview and self-complete alternatives, and outlines the results from the structural equation modeling of relationships between resident satisfaction and facility, staff and resident factors. Focus groups and interviews with residents, interviews with staff and management, consultations with relevant consumer groups and aged care "industry" representatives, were initially conducted, involving over 400 residents throughout Australia. The self-complete resident satisfaction instrument developed was then used, in conjunction with other instruments, in a total of 70 aged care facilities, involving 983 staff and 1146 residents. Whilst satisfaction with staff care was found to have a significant positive impact on all aspects of resident satisfaction, staff satisfaction itself is also particularly significant. Indeed, this latter aspect appears to have more influence on resident satisfaction than actual care hours provided, adjusting for resident dependency.

Key words: resident satisfaction, aged care, staff factors, modeling

1 Introduction

Recent "scandals" and a relatively new accreditation system (managed by an independent aged care standards and accreditation agency) [1] have placed the residential aged care sector in Australia firmly on the political agenda. Homes were required to comply by 2001 for them to continue to receive central government funding.

The accreditation process places a particular emphasis on "continuous quality improvement", within which resident satisfaction is considered a key outcome indicator. This poses the question as to how best to measure "resident satisfaction", in an institutional environment such as a nursing home or hostel (similar to a residential home in the UK). Further, if homes are to "continuously improve", it is fundamental that they gain an in-depth understanding of the key influences on the satisfaction of their residents.

This paper first outlines the development of a systematic approach to eliciting the views of the residents of nursing homes and hostels. Following this, the paper will describe the modeling of relationships between measures of resident satisfaction and measures of facility, staff and resident factors. Some brief results are presented with some illustrative comments. A more in-depth account of Australia's system of regulating quality in age care residential facilities, together with an assessment of its relevance to the UK, is contained in a recently published paper [2].

2 Methods

An earlier paper [3] has documented some of the key issues concerning the measurement of consumers' views in general and residents' views in particular. Apart from specific issues related to measurement instruments themselves (e.g. validity, inter-rater reliability, balance between quantitative and qualitative information) there are particular issues related to the nature of the institutional setting (e.g. fear of retribution if criticize services or staff) and its present clientele (e.g. increasing physical and mental frailty, ready acceptance of relatively low standards). Our approach does not claim to tackle all such issues, but it does attempt to address each of them.

2.1 Eliciting the Views of Residents

Whilst two instruments were developed, i.e. an interview schedule and a self-complete questionnaire, this paper is more concerned with the self-complete version and its subsequent use for modeling purposes. Those particularly interested in the interview approach, and its use by an aged care organization, can consult Boldly and Bartlett [3] and Walkerden and Campbell [4], respectively. For both instruments, in cases where residents are not able to participate directly (e.g. due to dementia), versions to use with resident representatives (e.g. close relatives or friends) have been produced.

Developing the instruments involved an extensive review of relevant literature, extensive consultations with residents and their representatives (25 focus groups in 11 homes involving 129 persons, covering a range of "types" - size, location, etc.) and consultations with other stakeholders (home managers and staff, consumer organizations, relevant researchers). The dimensions and issues identified formed the basis of a draft questionnaire, the self-complete version of which was structured as a series of three or four point Likert rating scales, with opportunity provided to add comments.

These scales covered the key dimensions of: moving to the home ("settling in"); resident's room; the home; passing the time; social life; links with the community; resident services; staff care; and resident involvement.

The instruments were tested in 35 different homes throughout Australia, a wide range of 159 residents being involved in the self-complete questionnaire version, which also included reliability testing [3].

2.2 Modeling Factors Influencing Residents' Satisfaction

The conceptual framework of Figure 1 summarizes the initial hypothesized relationships between the three groups of factors mentioned earlier, namely those related to the facility, to the staff and to the residents. The framework suggests that whilst all three groups affect resident satisfaction directly, facility and resident factors also influence resident satisfaction through their specific influence on staff factors.

A cross-sectional survey design, as described in Chou, Boldy and Lee [5], was employed, with over 1000 residents and nearly the same number of staff from 70 different residential aged care facilities in Western Australia, being surveyed between April 1998 and April 1999. The sample included a range of residents (e.g. by dependency), and staff, from a range of facilities (e.g. by size, level of care and location).

Resident satisfaction was scored using twenty-four items of the self-complete questionnaire [5], which covers six aspects of resident satisfaction (i.e. room, home, social interaction, meals service, staff care and resident involvement) derived from the components listed in Figure 1. For resident dependency, a composite score was created from three items: a resident classification scale (RCS); "how much assistance do you need from staff with your everyday activities?" (1 = a lot of assistance, to 4 = no assistance at all); and "who filled out this questionnaire?" (1 = assisted by others, 2 = resident only). For details see Chou, Boldy and Lee [6].

Staff satisfaction was measured as a composite score, using the Measure of Job Satisfaction (MJS) questionnaire [7], as modified by Chou, Boldy and Lee [8]. This covers five aspects of job satisfaction, namely personal satisfaction and satisfaction with workload, team spirit, training and professional support, derived from those listed in Figure 1 [9]. Other data collection instruments were designed to cover the range of remaining variables illustrated in Figure 1.

Structural equation modeling [10] was used to explore the relationships illustrated in Figure 1. Because of the considerable difference in the dependency and staff mix between nursing homes and hostels [6], [9], [12], separate models were produced for each. A full account of this analysis is contained in the doctoral thesis of Chou [11] and is covered in a forthcoming paper [12]. Qualitative analysis of the comments of residents was undertaken using NVivo software and some illustrations are included.

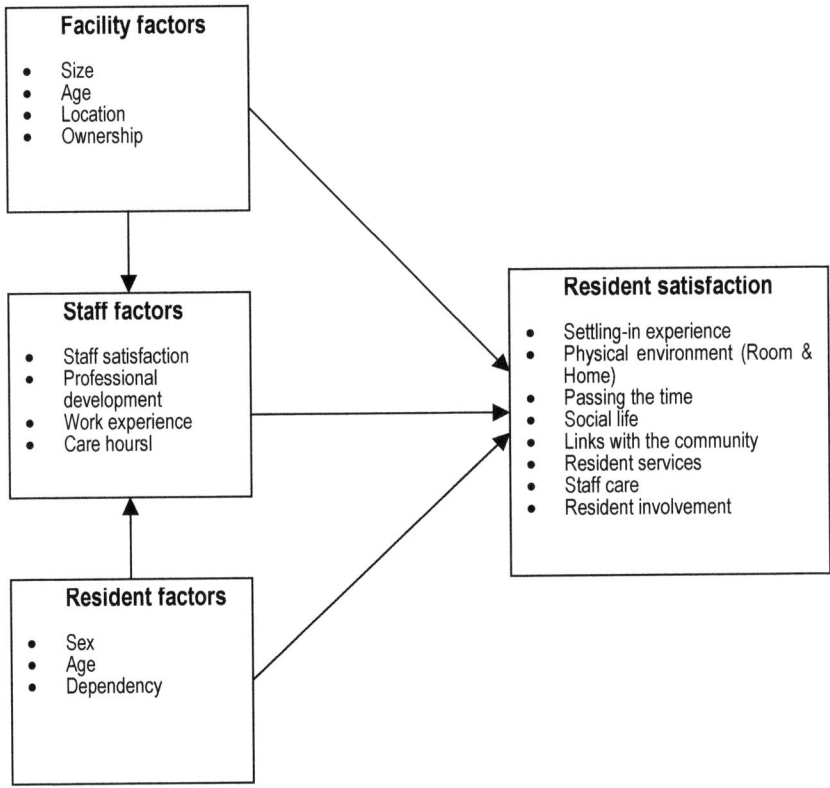

Figure 1: Conceptual framework of factors influencing resident satisfaction

3 Main Results

3.1 Facility Factors

Size has a positive impact on social interaction for hostels but not for nursing homes, suggesting that larger facilities tend to provide more social opportunities for relatively more active hostel residents. However, residents were less satisfied with involvement in larger hostels or nursing homes, probably because smaller facilities provide a more "homely" environment. As might be expected, residents in older facilities were less satisfied with their room. Issues commented on by residents related to older facilities included: the inappropriate positioning of call bell and a preference for an alarm buzzer worn around the neck; the positioning and inadequacy of storage space; the need for a separate entrance for each resident (24 year old nursing home).

3.2 Resident Factors

Older residents were more satisfied with staff care, possibly because either they were more accepting or because they felt more reluctant to criticize than the younger residents did [13] (e.g. "considering I am a bit of a nuisance they are very good"). Higher dependency residents were less likely to be satisfied with their room. As their room largely defines their "world", this probably reflects the greater level of importance they attach to it.

3.3 Staff Factors

Professional development of staff contributed to higher levels of resident satisfaction in hostels, mainly indirectly by increasing staff satisfaction, whilst the reverse was found for nursing homes. A possible explanation is that staff finds it easier to implement what they have learned from a variety of professional development activities in the more independent environment of a hostel. Higher care hours, adjusted for resident dependency, were found to be associated with a higher level of resident satisfaction with staff care. However, this relationship is relatively weak. In contrast, a strong positive association was found between staff satisfaction and resident satisfaction. More specifically, higher levels of staff satisfaction directly or indirectly lead to higher levels of all aspects of resident satisfaction for nursing home residents and increased satisfaction with social aspects, meals and involvement for hostel residents.

4 Conclusion

There are a number of general and specific issues, which provide challenges for those wishing to assess the views of residents in aged care facilities. This paper has described one such approach, followed by outlining the modeling of the relationship between aspects of resident satisfaction (as measured by a self-complete questionnaire) and factors concerning the facilities themselves, the residents and the staff.

The most important result is that the greatest potential for increasing the satisfaction of residents appears to be by attending to the factors, which influence staff satisfaction, especially in nursing homes. This is particularly significant and will not be easy, given the current difficulty in Australia and elsewhere in recruiting and retaining staff in this sector. This is related to the fact that nursing staff in aged care facilities has "lower status" and is typically paid considerably less than their colleagues in the acute hospital sector.

References

[1]   Aged and Community Care Division. Standards and guidelines for residential aged care Services manual, *Department of Health and Family Services*, Canberra, (1998).

[2]   H. Bartlett and D. Boldy, Approaches to improving quality in nursing and residential homes: recent developments in Australia and their relevance to the UK, *Quality in Ageing*, 2, (2001) 3-14.

[3]   D. Boldy and H. Bartlett, Residents' views and quality improvement in homes for older people, *Managing Community Care*, 6, (1998) 200-206.

[4]   S. Walkerden and T. Campbell, Seeking residents' views in homes: a user's perspective on an approach, *Managing Community Care*, 7, (1999) 35-37.

[5]   S.C. Chou, D.P. Boldy and A.H. Lee, Measuring resident satisfaction in residential aged care, *The Gerontologist*, 41(5), (2001) 623-631.

[6]   S.C. Chou, D.P. Boldy and A.H. Lee, Resident satisfaction and its components in residential aged care, *The Gerontologist*, 42(2), (2002) 1-11.

[7]   M. Traynor and B. Wade, The development of a measure of job satisfaction for use in monitoring the morale of community nurses in four trusts, *Journal of Advanced Nursing*, 18, (1993) 127-137.

[8] S.C. Chou, D.P. Boldy and A.H. Lee, Measuring job satisfaction in residential aged care, *International Journal for Quality in Health Care*, 14(1), (2002) 49-54.

[9] S.C. Chou, D.P. Boldy and A.H. Lee, Staff satisfaction and its components in residential aged care, *International Journal for Quality in Health Care*, 14(3), (2002) 207-217.

[10] B.M. Byrne, *Structural equation modeling with LISREL, PRELIS and SIMPLIS: basic concepts, applications and programming*, Mahwah, New Jersey: Lawrence Erlbaum Associates, (1998).

[11] S.C. Chou, *Factors influencing resident satisfaction in residential aged care facilities*, Unpublished PhD Thesis, Curtin University of Technology, Perth, Western Australia, (2000).

[12] S.C. Chou, D.P. Boldy and A.H. Lee, Factors influencing resident satisfaction in residential aged care facilities, *The Gerontologist* (2002) (submitted).

[13] J.A. Hall and M.C. Dornan, Patient sociodemographic characteristics as predictors of satisfaction with medical care: A meta-analysis, *Social Science & Medicine*, 30, (1990) 811-818.

A SIMULATION MODEL CONCERNING FUTURE NEEDS OF LONG-TERM CARE OF ELDERLY PERSONS IN SWEDEN

MARTEN LAGERGREN

Stockholm Research Center of Gerontology, Sweden

Abstract

The increasing number of elderly persons to be expected in the coming decades raises serious questions concerning the resources that will be demanded for provision of long-term care of the dependent elderly. Clearly, there is a need for augmented resources. However, simplistic calculations based upon the assumption that future needs of care will be proportional to the number of old persons per age group seem to lead to substantially exaggerated results by failing to take into account the positive health development of the elderly. A previous model developed by the author showed that the expected increase in the period 2000–2030 was reduced from 60% to around 20%, assuming that prevailing health trends should continue.

In an effort to corroborate these results and make possible further analysis of different factors pertaining to the estimation of future needs of publicly financed long-term care of the dependent elderly, a new model has been developed. The model makes it possible to analyze the impact of different factors on the future resource needs, such as the distribution of the elderly population according to age, gender, marital status and the balance of institutional versus non-institutional care. By varying control parameters the impact of prioritization between different groups and forms of care can be estimated. The model also contains a retrospective part, which shows how the consumption of different forms of care services for the elderly in Sweden developed during the period 1985–2000 with respect to the dependency, age, gender and marital status of recipients.

Data for the model are derived from different sources – longitudinal studies, local surveys of recipients of care, etc. An important source of data in the future will be the recently started Swedish National Study on Ageing and Care (SNAC) study.

Key words: projection, simulation, model, long-term care, elderly, costs

1 Introduction

The rising number of elderly persons to be expected in the coming decades creates serious questions concerning the need for increased resources for provision of long-term care of the dependent elderly. However, simplistic calculations based upon the assumption that future needs of care is proportional to the number of old persons per age group seem to lead to substantially overstated results by failing to take into account the positive health development of the elderly. In fact, a simple model earlier developed by the author shows that the expected increase in the period 2000–2030, is reduced from 60% to around 20%, assuming that prevailing health trends should continue [1].

In an effort to substantiate these results and make possible further analysis of different factors pertaining to the estimation of future needs of publicly financed long-term care of the dependent elderly persons, a new model has been developed. The model consists of two parts: The retrospective part shows how the consumption of different forms of care services for the elderly in Sweden developed during the period 1985–2000, with respect to the dependency, age, gender and marital status of recipients. The prospective part calculates a forecast, for the same development, during the period 2000–2030, under different assumptions. The model makes it possible to analyze the impact of different factors on the future resource needs, such as the distribution of the elderly population according to age, gender, marital status, the health development in different sub-groups and the provision of long-term care services in relation to care needs. Among others the balance of institutional versus non-institutional care can be analyzed. By varying control parameters the impact of prioritization between different groups and forms of care can be estimated.

The basic idea of the model is to describe the provision of care for different subgroups in the population and then calculate the impact – in terms of costs - of different assumptions concerning the development of these subgroups. The retrospective part this description is based on data derived from different sources: longitudinal studies, local surveys of recipients of care, etc. An important source of data in the future will be the recently started SNAC-study [2]. In the prospective part the calculations are based upon different trends that are estimated from earlier developments and prolonged into the future.

The need for a retrospective part of the model arises from the fact that available official statistics in Sweden are not sufficient for understanding the development of the long-term care system. From official data it is possible to deduce that, in the year 2000, a smaller proportion of the elderly received long-term care services compared to 15 years earlier. It is also possible to observe that the proportion of persons receiving more intensive services has increased. However, since there is no connected measure of the needs development it is impossible to tell, whether the reduction and concentration of the services is a reflection of decreasing needs due to improved health and functional capacity among the elderly or a real decrease in the level of provision of services.

Also the official statistics is flawed in many ways. The reporting from the municipalities is unreliable, the concepts that are used to describe the service provision are indistinct and there is no subdivision of the statistics according to the civil status of the care recipients. In fact, as shown by separate studies [3] civil status is a very important predictor of care provision, as married persons in Sweden tend to receive much less public elderly care services than single living. As result of these statistical deficiencies there has been a severe lack of solid facts to guide the public debate in Sweden concerning the recent developments of the elderly care system. The crucial question: "Who will get which care? " cannot be answered by the official statistics.

2 The ASIM III-Model

Without a clear view on how elderly care services are provided according to needs it is difficult to make forecasts of future developments, since these must be based upon clear assumptions concerning the needs development. The ASIM III-model[1] aims at solving both problems mentioned above by providing estimations on the amount of public long-term care services provided per age group, gender, marital status and degree of dependency both retrospectively for the period 1985-2000 and prospectively according to the same terms for the period 2000–2030. This is achieved by combining different data sources: the official national statistics on the provision of long-term care, the national surveys on living conditions and different local studies, namely the ASIM-studies in Solna municipality 1984–1994 and the SNAC study at Kungsholmen, Stockholm in 2001. The data sources will subsequently be improved, making the estimations of the past and future development more accurate.

The basic structure of the ASIM III-model consists of a subdivision of the Swedish population 65 years and above into subgroups according to age groups (65 –74, 75 –84, 85 +), gender, civil status (with or without spouse) and degree of ill health or dependency (six classes, cf. below). For each subgroup is denoted the number of persons that receive public long-term elderly care services according to four different levels:
- **Community care**: home help
    - 1 hour per day;

---

1 The model is the third in a series of models developed by the author starting in 1985 [5].

- o   1 –2 hours per day;
- o   2 hours per day;
- **Institutional care**: round-the-clock, residential or nursing home.

The prevalence of ill health or dependency for each subgroup (age, gender, and civil status) in the population is estimated using the Swedish National Survey of Living Conditions (ULF). These interview surveys have been performed nation-wide in Sweden since the end of the 1970's with a sample size around 8000 persons [4]. Among others, participants are asked questions concerning health conditions - subjective health status, restrictions in functional capacity, mobility restrictions. From the answers to these questions a health index with four degrees is constructed – full health, slight ill-health, moderate ill-health and severe ill-health.

The sample size of the ULF surveys does not permit direct estimation of the ill-health distribution in a local setting as a municipality. However, it is possible to estimate the local ill-health distribution in a certain area using age, gender, civil status and income as predictors by using multiple regression analysis. A limitation of the ULF-studies is that there is an upper age limit of 84 years (with the exception of one ULF-survey, 1988/89). This means that the ill-health distribution of the over 85-age group has to be estimated. This has been done using logarithmic extrapolation for each of the years 1985, 1990, 1995 and 2000. The result has been checked against the actual results of the 1988/89 surveys with good agreement.

The ASIM-data collected in Solna municipality 1984–1994 and the SNAC-data from Kungsholmen 2001 involves only recipients of care. In these studies all recipients of elderly care living in the area have been registered. The registration involves, among others, care services provided (in same terms as above) and dependency measured according to the so-called ASIM index [6]. This index summarizes information on functional capacity, mobility, incontinence, anxiety and dementia as denoted by the responsible care staff. Using that index a subdivision of the recipients of care into four classes of dependency can be made: Low, medium, high medium and high. The relation between the ill-health ULF-index and the dependency ASIM-index has been estimated using different data sources. Using this relation it is possible to construct the ULF-index in the Solna-Kungsholmen micro data.

Since the ULF-index is an ill-health measure of the full population and the ASIM-dependency class only involves recipients of care their distribution differ considerably. In fact all the three lower ULF index categories fall into the ASIM "Low"- class. As a consequence six ill-health/dependency categories in the population result:

- Full health;
- Slight ill-health;
- Moderate ill-health;
- Relatively severe ill-health (= medium dependency);
- Severe ill-health (= high medium dependency);
- Very severe ill health (= high dependency).

3 Calculation Method - Retrospective Part

Using the ULF-data (1985, 1990, 1995 and 2000) and population data (including income) for Solna and Kungsholmen (2000) an estimate is made of the distribution of the elderly population on age group, gender, marital status and dependency groups (six groups, cf. above) for each of the above years. The Solna ASIM-data (1985, 1990, 1995) and the Kungsholmen SNAC-data (2000) give – after construction of the ULF-index – the provision of care services to the same population groups in terms of number of persons on each level of services (cf. above). Using these data the proportion of persons in each sub-group receiving each level of services can be calculated. The resulting proportions are aggregated over marital status and dependency group and compared with the corresponding data from the national official statistics and calibrated to agreement[2].

Using again the ULF-data, the national distribution of persons is calculated on age group, gender marital status and ill-health groups (according to ULF). By subdividing the highest ULF-group into the three higher ASIM-groups of dependency, the corresponding distribution on dependency classes is obtained. The final step consists in multiplying the above proportions per service levels with the population data, in order to achieve the national distribution of persons for each year over age-group, gender, marital status, dependency and level of services. The result is a series of matrices (one per age group, gender, and marital status) for each of the years 1985, 1990, 1995 and 2000. In each matrix is denoted the number of persons per level of care services and class of dependency. An example of this kind of matrix is given in Table 1.

---

2 As described above the national data does not provide the level of detail that is given in the local studies (supported with the ULF-data). The calibration assumes that the relative differences between the local areas Solna/Kungsholmen and the whole country regarding the proportion of persons receiving services at a certain level are the same irrespective of marital status and dependency.

	Full Health	Slight Ill-health	Moderate Ill-health	Rel. Sev. Ill-health	Severe Ill-health	Very Sev. Ill-health	All Groups
Community							
Living without public help	15323	21799	14986	7486	2571	1785	63950
Living with help (1 hr/day)	79	2398	4568	2881	360	0	10286
Living with help (1-2 hr/day)	0	0	520	0	0	89	609
Living with help (2-1 hr/day)	0	0	85	262	87	0	435
Total number living with help	79	2398	5174	3144	448	89	11331
Institutionalized	0	131	209	787	787	1931	3846
Total number with public help	79	2529	5383	3931	1234	2020	15176
Total number of persons	15402	24328	20369	11416	3805	3805	79126

Table 1: Example of model matrix: Married women, aged 75 to 84, per class of dependency and level of care services, 1985

Using standard costs for the respective level of services, the resulting yearly costs per age group, gender, marital status and class of dependency can be easily calculated. These costs are then aggregated and compared with the actual costs the corresponding year. This has shown good agreement (If agreement is less than perfect an obvious correction is to adjust the standard cost).

4 Calculation Method - Prospective Part

In order to forecast future costs of the care services one needs a population forecast (according to age group, gender, and civil status) and assumptions concerning the development of ill health and dependency. It is then assumed that the provision of services according to gender, age group, civil status and class of dependency is unchanged[3]. The development of ill-health group (according to ULF) is extrapolated from the development between 1985 and 2000 using logarithmic extrapolation[4]. The subdivision of the "severe ill-health group" into ASIM-dependency classes (rather severe ill health, severe ill health, very severe; cf. above) is assumed to be unchanged. Forecasts are then made for the years 2005, 2010, ..., 2030 simply by multiplying the estimated number of persons in the population per sub-group (age group, gender, marital status and dependency

---

3 This is the default assumption in the model, which can be adjusted at will.
4 This assumption can also be changed at will and some other assumption introduced.

class) each year with the proportion of persons receiving services on the respective levels in 2000.

The ASIM III-model is implemented in EXCEL (2,8 Mb). The above results are aggregated to totals per age group, gender, and marital status and dependency class in order to facilitate comparison and analyses of results. Diagrams showing different aspects of the developments are automatically derived from the calculated data. Different parameters can be used to control priorities. In this way it is possible to adjust the result to budget constraints and calculate the implications for different sub-group of the applied priorities.

5 Results

The ASIM III model can be used for many different types of calculations concerning developments in the period 1985–2000 and forecasts for the period 2000 – 2030. In the sequel a few examples will be given of both kinds of results. One very important issue in the current public debate in Sweden on the development of the public care services for the elderly care concerns the question of which groups of the elderly have suffered reductions in the service level. Figure 1 shows the model estimation of the development in the period 1985–2000 of the proportion of the Swedish elderly population that received care services per degree of ill health (according to ULF, cf. above).

It can be seen clearly from Figure 1 that the severe service reductions in the years 1985–1995 mainly affected the group with moderate or mild ill health. Those with severe ill health were more or less shielded from the reductions. In the period 1995–2000 the service reduction halted and the distribution between the ill-health groups was partly restored.

Another type of application of the model concerns forecasts for the period 2000-2030 under different assumptions. Figure 2 shows the projected development of the total yearly costs for the long-term care services for the elderly per age group assuming unchanged health after the year 2000 (millions Swedish crowns).

The Swedish elderly population is expected to grow considerably in the coming decades. The growth in the period 2000–2015 concerns mainly the younger elderly and thus does not have a large effect on the costs for the elderly care services. The main thrust comes after the year 2020 and it can be clearly seen from Figure 2 that the main part of the increase in the period 2015–2030 comes from the oldest age group, assuming unchanged health after 2000.

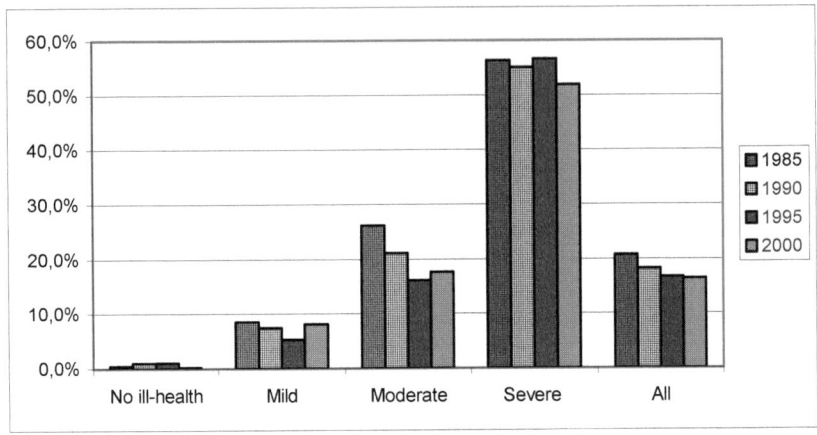

Figure 1: Proportion of elderly population that received care services per degree of ill-health, 1985 –2000

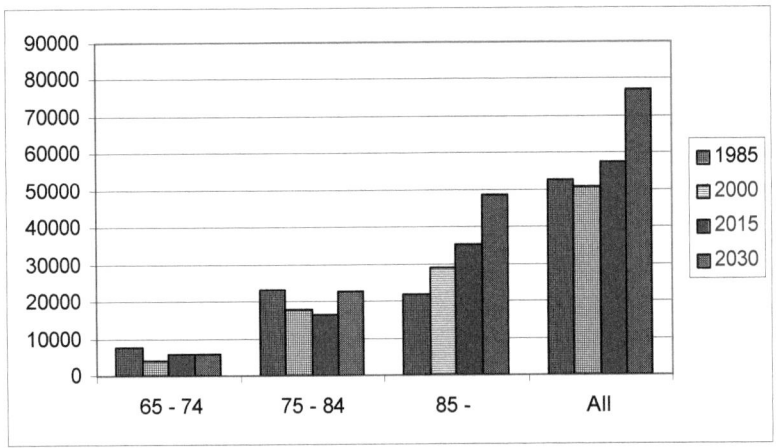

Figure 2: Projected development of the total costs for the long-term care services for the elderly, per age group

However, assuming unchanged ill-health in the population after the year 2000 is a questionable assumption since according to health surveys the trend since several decades in Sweden as in many other countries is towards improved health among the elderly. Figure 3 shows the development of the same total costs per age group assuming that current health trends persist during the whole period.

As seen in Figure 3 assuming continuing health trends among the elderly results in a lower expected cost increase. There is still a substantial cost increase for the 85+-group but this increase is by and large offset by the expected cost decrease in the younger age groups. The total cost increase from 2000 – 2030 in this case amounts to less than 10% compared to more than 50% in the former case with unchanged health. Assuming continuing health for another 30 years is probably too optimistic, but the model calculations show clearly the very large impact assumptions concerning the health development among the elderly have on the cost projections.

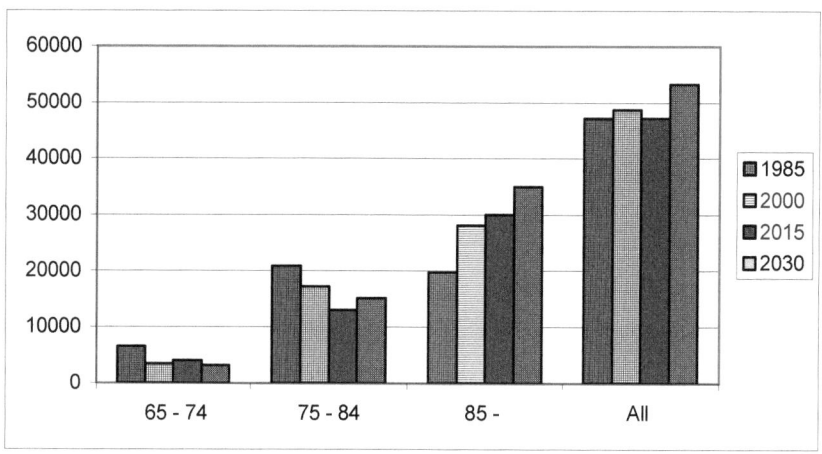

Figure 3: Projected development of the total yearly costs for the long-term care for the elderly per age group (millions Swedish crowns)

6 Discussion

As pointed out above the ASIM III model serve two purposes: As a tool of analysis for better understanding the development of the elderly care system in the last decades and as an instrument to forecasting future developments of the system under different assumptions. The public system of care for the frail elderly in Sweden has undergone many changes since 1985 [7]. Partly this has to do with organizational change: the so-called ADEL-reform and partly with economic pressures due to the severe economic crisis that happened Sweden during the early 1990's. The ADEL-reform moved the responsibility for institutional long-term care from the county councils to the municipalities. As a consequence the housing of the long-term ill elderly improved a lot and more people were able to stay and receive long-term care in there own homes. The economic crisis resulted in a much stricter prioritization. The number of persons receiving public services declined. The model calculations basically confirm the general observations made with the aid of official statistics and different local investigations. However, the model makes it possible to look at the development in much more detail and in a clearer and more systematic way.

The results of the forecasting part of the model also tally well with earlier, simpler calculation [1]. Again, however, the model facilitates a more detailed look at the development and simplifies the study of the effects of a broad set of different assumptions.

As described above the model uses a combination of different data sets in a novel way. Obviously there are critical issues in the calculation method, which need to be addressed in order to evaluate the reliability of the results. The local data sets from Solna and Kungsholmen are judged to be essentially representative of Sweden. They are calibrated to nation level with respect to gender, age group and service levels, but the distribution of care services according to marital status and class of dependency might of course differ in a way that is difficult to foresee. The data sets for the years 1985 and 1990 are pretty comprehensive being based upon three surveys each (1984–1986 and 1989–1991 respectively). The 1995 and 2000 data sets, however, are smaller and thus more prone to random variations. New data from other municipalities are now available for the year 2000 and this will improve the reliability for that year.

The most critical limitation of the ULF-surveys is that they do not include (except for the year 1988/89) the age group 85 years and older. The method to extrapolate the distribution of ill health from the age trend in lower age groups has been tested on data from surveys in other countries, among others the US NLTC-survey [8] and seems to be reliable. However, there are indications that the ULF-survey underestimates the prevalence of ill health in the over-80 group and this might affect the results. New surveys that will make it possible to improve the model database are now underway in Sweden. New data collected in the SNAC-study also give a stronger empirical base for the crucial translation between the ULF index of ill health and the ASIM index of dependency.

As pointed out above the ASIM III-model is essentially a tool for analysis. It provides answers, under given assumptions to different questions of importance for policy formation in the area of long-term care for the frail elderly. The structure of the model makes it possible to successively improve the basis for the calculations. In this way it is hoped that the model will be able to serve a useful purpose in the coming years of public debate concerning how to meet the growing care needs of the elderly persons in our populations.

References

[1] M. Lagergren and I. Batljan, Will there be a helping hand, *Annex 8 to The Long-Term Survey 1999/2000*, Fritzes, Stockholm, (2000).

[2] M. Lagergren, SNAC - The Swedish national study on ageing and care, in: M. Rauner and K. Heidenberger (Eds). Quantitative Approaches in Health Care Management, *Proceedings of the 27th meeting of the European Working Group on Operational Research* (ORAHS), Peter Lang, (2002) 71-76.

[3] M. Szebehely, Care supply from the wife or from the social services? In: *Swedish Council for Working Life and Social Research*, Everyday life in social services for the elderly, (1998) 73–88.

[4] Statistics Sweden (SCB), *The Swedish national survey of living conditions, 1975–1997*, Stockholm, (1999).

[5] M. Lagergren, Disability development and the structure of care: some results from simulation of an area based system of long-term care for elderly people, *Health Policy,* Vol: 29, (1994) 229-246.

[6] M. Lagergren, *The ASIM system: A tool for monitoring, evaluation and planning of the long-term care for elderly and disabled people*, Doctoral thesis, Karolinska Institute, Sundbyberg, (1994).

[7] M. Lagergren, The system of care for frail elderly persons the case of Sweden, *Aging Clinical and Experimental Research*, 14 (2002).

[8] K.G.M. Manton and G. XiLiang, Changes in the prevalence of chronic disability in the United States black and non-black population above age 65 from 1982 to 1999, *Proc. Natl. Acad. Sci.*, Vol: 11, (2001) 6354-6359.

EMERGENCY SERVICES

PLANNING THE EMERGENCY AMBULANCE SERVICE IN THE CITY OF ROME BY A MIXED INTEGER LINEAR PROGRAMMING MODEL

VANDA DE ANGELIS[1], GIOVANNI FELICI[2], GIOVANNI STORCHI[1]

[1] *Università "La Sapienza", Italy*
[2] *IASI - Consiglio Nazionale delle Ricerche, Italy*

Abstract

In this paper we address the optimal design and management of an emergency ambulance service in a large city characterized by high-density population and traffic congestion. We define a measure of the service quality level in terms of target access time and probability that at least one ambulance is available when a call arrives. Two integer linear programming models are formulated to provide a decision support tool for an efficient location of the ambulance stations and assignment of ambulances to the stations. An application of the proposed method to the city of Rome is presented.

Key words: emergency, decision support systems, ambulance services

1 Introduction

The Italian Health Emergency System (HES) operates since 1992, as a centralized system. A telephone number (118), which can be dialed throughout the country, calls the headquarters of the corresponding area to evaluate the gravity of the case and choose the type of action that follows. Our work refers to the case when a Basic Life System (BLS) ambulance should be sent. The goal of the HES is to make sure that a BLS ambulance will be on the spot within eight minutes in urban areas and twenty minutes in the countryside. This requires a continuous monitoring of the distribution and frequency of the calls and the necessary time to perform the emergency service. A very careful location of the ambulance stations in the territory and the assignment of a sufficient number of ambulances to each station are essential to guarantee the availability of an ambulance when a call arrives.

Our attention is focused on the service supplied in the area inside the "ring road" that surrounds the periphery of the city of Rome. In order to tackle the problem of improving the BLS ambulance service, we have defined a measure of the service quality level and identified two main targets that have to be taken into account in order to offer a decision support tool. The aim is determine the number and location of ambulance stations and the number of ambulances for each station in order to:

1. Minimize the cost for a given quality level of the service;

2. Maximize the quality level of the service at a given cost.

Solving the first problem provides the cost of the service for the desired quality level. If the budget of the system is too tight to afford the desired quality level, the second problem produces the best service that can be offered with the available budget. By interactively modifying the budget and/or the service level, the management can evaluate the different options and eventually adopt the best solution for the given constraints.

The paper is organized as follows: in section 2 we present the methodology that we used to develop our study; in sections 3-7 we describe the various phases in details, while the application and conclusions follow in section 8.

2 The Methodology

Our work is developed through seven phases:
- Data collection on the present performance of the emergency ambulance service and on the demand and service characteristics;
- Review of the literature concerning the location of emergency facilities;
- Construction of a graph representing the road system of Rome, with the addition of special nodes that are conventionally considered as demand origin points;
- Definition of the measure of the quality level of the service;
- Construction of mathematical programming models for the best choice of service points, location of ambulance stations and demand allocation to them;
- Solution of the model through available mathematical programming software;
- Analysis of the solution and validation of it through simulation.

3 The Data

The available data refer to:

- **Calls**: date and time of arrival of each call, place of the accident (home, work, road, etc.), pathology and color code representing the seriousness of the case (red, yellow, green, white);
- **Times**: ambulances departure from the station, arrival at the accident scene, departure from the scene, arrival at the hospital and return to the station.

4 The Literature Review

Emergency services, by definition, must be quickly accessed. Often, it is the time elapsed between the occurrence of the emergency and the arrival of the specialized staff and facilities that determines life or death for the people involved in the emergency situation. The definition of target access time, that is the maximum acceptable span of time that can elapse between the occurrence of the emergency and the arrival of the "specialists", is of fundamental importance in designing and managing an emergency service. There should be a sufficient number of specialized staff teams and facilities, well located on the territory. Ideally, such teams should be everywhere. But costs would be prohibitive and compromises must be made between what is ideal and what is real.

In order to tackle this problem in a proper optimization scheme, the two classical models, named Set Covering Location Problem (SCLP) and Maximum Covering Location Problem (MCLP) are of fundamental importance, notwithstanding their limits. In the first one, the minimum number and the position of the ambulance stations are determined, in such a way that any demand point may be reached within a given target access time [4]. In the second case, the position of ambulance stations is determined, given a maximum allowed number, in a way that the greatest number of calls may be reached within target travel time [1, 4]. While the first model gives the same importance to all demand points, independently from the frequency of calls that they generate, both models neglect the point that there may be no ambulance available at a station when a call arrives, due to the engagement in previous calls.

The Expected Maximum Covering Location Problem (EMCLP) [4] introduces the probability that at least one ambulance is available when a call arrives, based on a generic probability of an ambulance being busy. In a subsequent model [4, 5] a different value of such probability is used for each demand node. Both models use simple probabilistic models. Based on these results, we turned our attention to the construction of a different model where the probability that at least an ambulance is available when a call arrives is calculated by using queuing models.

5 Graph Construction

Our initial graph was the simplified road system graph currently used by the Rome municipality. The emergency call service has adopted the Rome A-Z Street Atlas that is currently the most updated and detailed road map available, to route the ambulances and to classify the area from which the calls are coming. Since the calls are classified according to the page they belong to in the A-Z Street Atlas, we defined a set of 92 special nodes, or centroids, that are assumed to ideally represent the origin points of the calls arising in the zone corresponding to the A to Z page. Each centroid is linked by an arc of length zero to the node, which occupies the most central place in the page, giving us a graph with 852 nodes and 2992 arcs. The weight attached to each arc represents its length.

The centroids represent the demand points. The set of candidate locations for the ambulance stations is assumed to coincide with, or to be a subset of, the set of demand centroids. Using the obtained graph $G=(N, A)$, we computed the distance between the couples of candidate station centroids and demand centroids, by a shortest path algorithm. Then, making an assumption on the average ambulance speed, it was possible to compute the access time between potential station centroids and demand centroids and identify, for each demand centroid, the subset of potential station centroids from where it can be reached within target access time.

6 Definition of the Measure of the Quality Level

The fundamental requirement for our service is that an ambulance must reach the client within a certain target access time d. Once d is chosen, it becomes a strict requirement on the location of the ambulance stations. For each demand node, there must be an ambulance station node such that the access time from the station to the demand node does not exceed the length d. This is not a necessarily sufficient requirement to offer a good service. In fact, ambulances might not be available in a station when a call arrives, because they are all engaged in serving previous calls. Therefore, we focus our attention on the probability that at least one ambulance is available when a call arrives. We set such probability value to α and require that at least one ambulance be available with probability α. The service quality depends on the values of d and α. It increases when α becomes larger and when d becomes smaller. However, the cost of the service will also increase.

7 The Mathematical Programming Models

We have constructed two integers linear programming (ILP) models of station and ambulance location and of demand allocation. The first model, that we call α-LSCP, is based on the LSCP and calculates the minimum number of ambulances necessary to cover all calls within target access time d with probability α. The second one, that we call α-MCLP, is based on the MCLP and maximizes the quantity of calls satisfied within target time d with probability α, given an upper bound on the number of ambulances allowed by the budget restrictions.

Both models take as input, for any number of ambulances allocated to a station, the value of the maximum call rate that can be served in such a way that at least one ambulance is available with the desired probability α, when a call arrives. Such value depends on d, α, and on the time an ambulance spends away from the station in order to satisfy a call. In situations that can be described by a $M/M/k$ queuing model, we can use existing formulas to calculate them, as we are going to show; otherwise, in more complicated situations, we may have to use a simulation program. This section contains:

- Preliminary calculations to determine the minimum necessary number of ambulances to guarantee availability with probability α in a $M/M/k$ model;
- Definition of sets and parameters involved in the model definition;
- Definition of the variables involved in the model formulation;
- Formulation of the two models.

7.1 Preliminary Calculations for the $M/M/k$ Model

We assume that, for a candidate ambulance station at node j, we know $\bar{s}_j$, that is, the average elapsed time between the ambulance departure and return at station node j, and an upper bound m_j on the number of ambulances that can be located at such station.

Then, for any number $k_j \le m_j$ of ambulances located at station j, we want to compute the maximum call rate $b_{jk_j}(\bar{s}_j, \alpha)$ in such a way that, when a call arrives at station j, there is at least one ambulance available with probability α. In the following formulas, λ_j represents the call arrival rate at station j.

If we call $P_{jn}, n = 0, 1, \text{K}$ the probability that n calls for node j are present in the system, we know, under the hypotheses valid for the $M/M/k$ model, i.e. that the calls arrive according to the Poisson process and the service time follows the exponential distribution, that:

$$P_{jn} = \frac{k_j!(1-\rho_j)}{k_j!(1-\rho_j)\sum_{n=0}^{k_j-1}\frac{(\lambda_j \bar{s}_j)^n}{n!} + (\lambda_j \bar{s}_j)^{k_j}} \qquad n=0$$

and:

$$P_{jn} = P_{jo}\frac{(\lambda_j \bar{s}_j)^n}{n!} \qquad 1 \le n \le k_j$$

The probability that at least an ambulance is available with probability α when a call arrives is:

$$R_j(\lambda_j, \bar{s}_j, k_j) = P_{jo} + K + P_{jk_j-1}$$

We can therefore calculate the maximum values

$b_{j1}(\bar{s}_j, \alpha), b_{j2}(\bar{s}_j, \alpha), K, b_{jm_j}(\bar{s}_j, \alpha),$ here called $b_{j1}, b_{j2}, K, b_{jm_j}$ for simplicity, such that:

$$R_j(\lambda_j, \bar{s}_j, 1) \ge \alpha \qquad\qquad if \qquad \lambda_j \le b_{j1}$$

$$R_j(\lambda_j, \bar{s}_j, 2) \ge \alpha \qquad\qquad if \ b_{j1} < \lambda_j \le b_{j2}$$

....

$$R_j(\lambda_j, \bar{s}_j, m_j) \ge \alpha \qquad\qquad if \ b_{jm_j-1} < \lambda_j \le b_{jm_j}$$

The following Figure 1 can help us to better understand the meaning of the values $b_{j1}, b_{j2}, K, b_{jm_j}$.

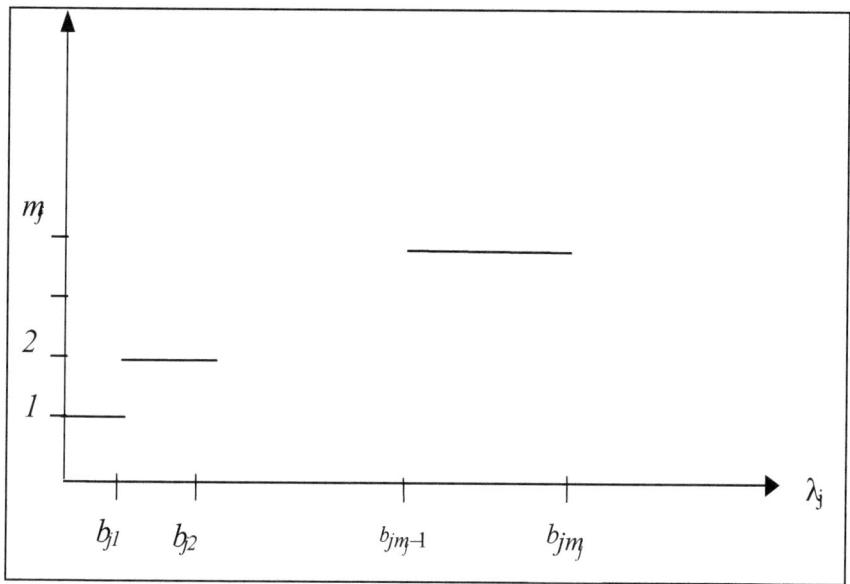

Figure 1: Minimum number of ambulances necessary to satisfy call rate λ_j with given availability probability

7.2 Definition of the sets and constants used

Let:

- N be the set of ambulance demand nodes;
- P ($\subseteq N$) be the set of nodes that are candidate ambulance stations;
- d be the target access time;
- a_i be the average daily call rate of node i, $i \in N$;
- P_i, $i \in N$, be the subset of P that contains only nodes j such that the distance d_{ji} between node j and j is such that $d_{ji} \leq d$;
- Q_j, $j \in P$, be the subset of N that contains only nodes i: $d_{ji} \leq d$;
- c_j^s be the fixed cost of an ambulance station at node j, $j \in P$;
- c^a be the fixed cost of an ambulance;
- m_j be the maximum number of ambulances that can be assigned to node j, $j \in P$, if it becomes an ambulance station;
- $\overline{s}_j$ be the average busy time of an ambulance positioned at node j, $j \in P$, i.e. the time elapsed between departure to serve a call and return of the ambulance to the station;

- α be the requested lower bound of the probability that at least an ambulance is available at a station when a call arrives;
- β be the lower bound on the fraction of demand to be satisfied;
- Let b_{jr} the maximum call arrival rate at node j, $j \in P$, that can be met by r ambulances in such a way that at least one ambulance is available at the station with probability $\geq \alpha$ when a call arrives, for $r=0,\ldots, m_j$.

7.3 Definition of the Variables Involved in the Model Formulation

Let our variables be:
- f_{ij} (≥ 0): average number of daily calls generated by node i, $i \in N$ and assigned to node j, $j \in P_i$;
- y_j (binary): indicator equal to 1 if an ambulance station at positioned in node j, $j \in P$; equal to 0 otherwise;
- δ_{jr} (binary): indicator equal to 1 if r ambulances are assigned to node j, for $j \in P$ and $r=0,\ldots, m_j$;
- w_{jr} (≥ 0): weight assigned to b_{jr} in order to express the average total number of daily calls assigned to node j as a convex combination of the values b_{jr}, for $j \in P$ and $r=0,\ldots, m_j$.

7.4 Formulation of the Two Models

7.4.1 α-LSCP Model

In this model, the least cost ambulance location is obtained in such a way that the total demand is satisfied within target time, and at least one ambulance is available with probability α

$$\text{minimise} : z = \sum_{j \in P} c_j^s y_j + \sum_{j \in P} \sum_{r=0}^{m_j} c^a r \delta_{jr}$$

$subject$ to:

$$\sum_{j \in P_i} f_{ij} \geq a_i \qquad\qquad \forall i \in N$$

$$\sum_{i \in Q_j} f_{ij} - \sum_{r=0}^{m_j} b_{jr} w_{jr} = 0 \qquad\qquad \forall j \in P$$

$$\sum_{r=0}^{m_j} w_{jr} = 1 \qquad\qquad \forall j \in P$$

$$\sum_{r=0}^{m_j} \delta_{jr} = 1 \qquad\qquad \forall j \in P$$

$$\sum_{r=1}^{m_j} \delta_{jr} \leq y_j \qquad\qquad \forall j \in P$$

$$w_{jr} - \delta_{jr} - \delta_{jr+1} \leq 0 \qquad \forall j \in P, r = 0, K, m_j\text{-}1$$

$$w_{jm_j} - \delta_{jm_j} \leq 0 \qquad \forall j \in P$$

$$f_{ij} \geq 0, \forall i \in N, \forall j \in P_i; \ w_{jr} \geq 0, \ \forall j \in P, r = 0, K, m_j\text{-}1$$

$$y_j binary, \ \forall j \in P; \ \delta_{jr} binary, \ \forall j \in P, r = 0, K, m_j\text{-}1$$

7.4.2 α-MCLP Model

In this model, a fixed number m of ambulances is given, and the best location of ambulances is obtained maximizing the demand satisfied within target time in such a way that at least one ambulance is available with probability α when a call arrives. The goal is achieved by minimizing the gap between the maximum theoretical demand b_{jm_j}, that an ambulance station j could satisfy if it was built and equipped with the maximum number m_j of ambulances, and the demand that is assigned to the station. Such objective function aims at satisfying the demand while keeping the number of ambulance stations (and their total cost) as low as possible.

$$\text{minimise}: z = \sum_{j \in P} b_{jm_j} y_j - \sum_{i \in N} \sum_{j \in P_i} f_{ij}$$

subject to:

$$\sum_{j \in P_i} f_{ij} \geq \beta a_i \qquad\qquad \forall i \in N$$

$$\sum_{j \in P_i} f_{ij} \leq a_i \qquad\qquad \forall i \in N$$

$$\sum_{j \in P} \sum_{r=0}^{m_j} r \delta_{jr} \leq m$$

$$\sum_{i \in Q_j} f_{ij} - \sum_{r=0}^{m_j} b_{jr} w_{jr} = 0 \qquad \forall j \in P$$

$$\sum_{r=0}^{m_j} w_{jr} = 1 \qquad\qquad \forall j \in P$$

$$\sum_{r=0}^{m_j} \delta_{jr} = 1 \qquad\qquad \forall j \in P$$

$$\sum_{r=1}^{m_j} \delta_{jr} \leq y_j \qquad\qquad \forall j \in P$$

$$w_{jr} - \delta_{jr} - \delta_{jr+1} \leq 0 \qquad \forall j \in P, r = 0, K, m_j - 1$$

$$w_{jm_j} - \delta_{jm_j} \leq 0 \qquad\qquad \forall j \in P$$

$$f_{ij} \geq 0, \ \forall i \in N, \ \forall j \in P_i; \ w_{jr} \geq 0, \ \forall j \in P, r = 0, K, m_j - 1$$

$$y_j \ binary, \ \forall j \in P; \ \delta_{jr} binary, \ \forall j \in P, r = 0, K, m_j - 1$$

8 Application

In our application to the city of Rome, we set $P=N$, with $|N|=92$, $d=8$ minutes, $\alpha=.95$. For simplicity, we assumed $\bar{s}_j = \bar{s}$, $\forall j \in P$, and, from the historical data of June 2001, when 13878 calls needed a BLS ambulance, we obtained $\bar{s}=35'27''$. As a consequence, also the values $b_{jr}(\bar{s}_j, \alpha)$ are independent of the node and all equal to $b_r(\bar{s}, \alpha)$. We then computed the average call rate per hour originating from each one of the 92 demand centroids in the same period and formulated our first problem. Our optimal solution for the α-LSCP model identifies 10 ambulance stations and allocates 28 ambulances. Since it uses fewer resources than the present system, we did not proceed to solve also the α-MCLP.

Our models are simple to use, even if we consider situations different from the $M/M/k$ model applied here, because, as we said before, the values b_{jr} can always be evaluated through the simulation, as a function of the number of ambulances r allocated to the station node j and the time that elapses between the departure and the return of an ambulance. However, various approximations are still present in our application, such as the call rate independent of the time of the day (calls are more frequent between 12:00 and 18:00 than between 0:00 and 6:00), and the ambulance speed constant in all areas and time of the day. Realistically, the number of ambulances in active service does not need to be the same through the 24 hours of the day.

The results obtained at the current stage of this project are only a first answer to the problem; several additional aspects need to be addressed, and special attention needs to be placed on the quality of the data used in the optimization. A promising strategy that we are considering, to validate the results of the optimization models before their actual implementation, is to set up a simulation system that reproduces the solutions and provides feedback on their validity and, more importantly, on their robustness [2, 3]. Other relevant issues that are considered for future research relate to the on-line management of the ambulances, that is, how to relocate optimally the ambulances on-line and which is the best on-line strategy to assign ambulances to calls.

References

[1] B. Adenso-Diaz and F. Rodriguez, A simple search heuristic for the MCLP: Application to the location of ambulances bases in a rural region, *Omega*, Vol: 25, 2 (1997) 181-188.

[2] V. De Angelis, G. Felici, P. Impelluso, Integrating simulation and optimization in Health Care Centre Management, *European Journal of Operational Research*, Vol: 150/1, (2003) 101 - 114.

[3] O. Fujiwa, T. Makjamrven and K.K. Gupta, Ambulance deployment analysis: a case study of Bangkok, *European Journal of Operational Research*, Vol: 31, 1 (1987) 9-18.

[4] C. Revelle, Review, extension and prediction in emergency sitting models, *European Journal of Operational Research*, Vol: 40 (1989) 58-69.

[5] C. Revelle and V. Marianov, A probabilistic FLEET model with individual vehicle reliability requirements, *European Journal of Operational Research*, Vol: 53, (1991) 93-105.

AN EMERGENCY DECISION SUPPORT TOOL BASED UPON QUALITY OF CARE PARAMETERS

LUPE N.P. TOSCANO[1], MARIO J. FERREIRA DE OLIVEIRA[2]

[1]*Universidad Nacional de Ingeniería, Peru*
[2]*Universidade Federal do Rio de Janeiro, Brazil*

Abstract

The decision making process involved with the medical emergency care is extremely complex. Because of the health risks involved a wrong decision means, in most cases, the difference between life and death. The process should act with quick, efficient and effective response. The appropriate configuration of the available human and material resources is one of the key factors that determine quality of the service. This paper introduces a model that points to the satisfactory emergency medical staff configuration based upon previously defined value parameters, which are set according to the urgency level of the case. Four emergency levels are studied and the main aspects of the procedures required, skill and practical experience are considered in the making-up of the medical team. It is argued that the proposed tool can be used to improve the quality of care.

Key words: emergency, quality of care, simulation, decisions support system

1 Introduction

Emergency services are facing new challenges after recent disasters happening at the beginning of the new century. Cities are vulnerable to new types of emergency situations that could become visible. Some are complex, either natural or caused by man, and our authorities will need a training device to be prepared to meet these challenges [1]. It is now desirable the availability of an adequate number of professionals to ensure a good hospital medical emergency care. There is a remarkable quantity of publications in the field of emergency management over the last few years [2 to 9]. Most of the earlier studies concentrate on management considerations and administrative issues such as the demand for services [10], evacuation planning [11], location of vehicles [12], [13] and other interesting problems that arise from this broad subject. Emergency arrivals are usually regarded as an unknown process and few studies contemplate the importance of short-term predictions of the emergency demand and its value to help planning.

Simulation is a decision support tool, which offers the possibility to perform a previous evaluation of the dynamic behavior of a particular system without interference in the real life. Previous research shows that simulation is one of the most important management analysis and operative tool [4], [7], [14].

A process simulation model is described in this paper, with the objective to determine the appropriate number and configuration of the medical staff to offer quality medical care to four different emergency levels. The model concentrates on the emergency hospital admission system of public hospitals and is part of a project that aims to the development of an Integrated Emergency Decision Support System (SISDE) for the public health care sector of the Rio de Janeiro City [15]. The project starts with a general study of the care process of the emergency room of different public hospitals, with the objective of modeling the existing problem [16].

2 The Modeling Environment

The models presented here focus on the actual demand behavior, the medical practice and the team building work of two different hospitals: the Hospital Antonio Pedro (Rio de Janeiro-Brazil) and the Hospital Cayetano Haeredia (Lima-Peru). A macro simulation model is developed inside the framework of a process simulation environment. The examples presented here are taken from the study of the general medicine specialty of both hospitals. An emergency event is considered in the model when the 'patient' arrives at the 'emergency room'. The admission process starts when any initiative towards 'medical assistance' is completed.

3 The Simulator

The simulation approach is patient-oriented [3]. The real-life objects, represented by entities and their attributes are stored in a register field. The occurrences, in a specific time, are modeled as events. The functioning of the system is modeled as a process. The process encompasses a series of events. The process and events are basic routines that can be linked to one or more entities. The execution and management of process and events, accordingly with specific rules is the function of the simulator. There is an internal clock that controls the time mechanism and points to the next steps or marked events. The Lehmer multiple congruency technique is used to generate the pseudo-random numbers. The software has a function library to produce random variables following the most popular statistical distributions, such as uniform, normal, exponential and gamma.

4 The Model

The patient is a temporary entity created in the "patient arrival" event (see 6.1). According to the observed behavior of the emergency room, the arrival pattern follows the Gamma distribution with two parameters: average arrival time and a constant k [16]. The used criterion to select patients is the urgency of the case. The classification follows the international standard of triage. An extra class (urgency level 4) is considered in this paper, in order to contemplate all the cases observed in the hospital [17].

All patients are initially classified in one of the three most usual urgency levels. Eventually, a fourth level is considered. That is the case of a patient showing, for example, an unexpectedly breath stop or some another life risk sign. That is the situation when this case the patient is re-classified as an urgency level 4. The minimum required number of staff necessary to take care of each of urgency levels is shown in Table 1. The data was obtained by observation at the emergency department of the two hospitals.

Staff Urgency	Senior Doctor	Doctor	Nurse	Assistant
1	0	1	1	1
2	1	1	1	1
3	1	1-2	1	1-2
4	1	2	1	2

Table 1: Minimum staff required for each urgency level

In order to achieve the quality measurements of the emergency care, the most important medical requirements are modeled and implemented in the model [18]. The following teamwork policies are implemented:

1. The health professionals of the emergency department are supposed to provide the necessary care to any patient. The right number of medical personal should be available in specific periods of the day, in order to build teams and there should always be appointed an experienced physician in the team for important decision making. Sub-teams carry out the care to each patient and each of them should be able to cope with more than one patient at the same time;

2. The care policy is implemented according to the degree of urgency of the arrivals. Patients classified as urgency level 3 and 4 have to be immediately taken care. Patients urgency level 1 and 2 would wait, a while, for the appropriate care. The "care event" begins when the patient is taken care by the staff;

3. Because of ethical and medical considerations all patients should receive a standard care. However, if a patient arrives with death risk and there is no possibility to build an exclusive team, then member other teams that are involved with lower priority tasks may occasionally be called up. As far as the simulation model is concerned, this mean that the event that represents care is placed on a waiting status while the higher risk activity is carried out. It is clear that the quality measurement will be affect by that action;

4. In the situation of the arrival of a serious case and the impossibility to find a complete team because the staff is busy with patients of equal seriousness, then the first available staff member in the neighborhood would be called. The staff should be able take care of more than one patient at a time. Only in extreme cases the staff may interrupt the care of the most serious cases.

Figures 1, 2 and 3 show the composition of teams for different urgency levels. The arrow that goes from the physician to the patient, in Figure 1, indicates a one-to-one relationship and the arrows in one of the physician's head of Figure 2, represents the decision making process involved with the urgency level 2.

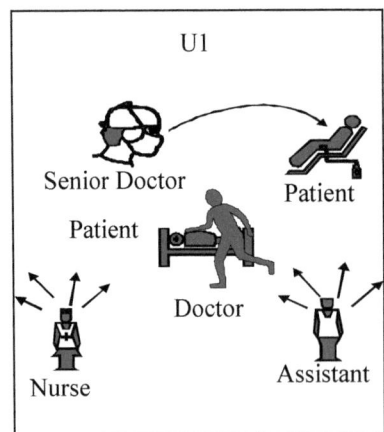

Figure 1: Staff for urgency level 1

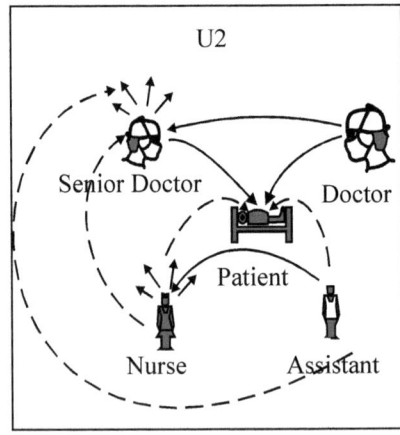

Figure 2: Staff for urgency level 2

Figure 3 shows the composition of teams for levels 3 and 4. It can be seen that the composition of the team requires one senior doctor, two doctors, a nurse and two assistants.

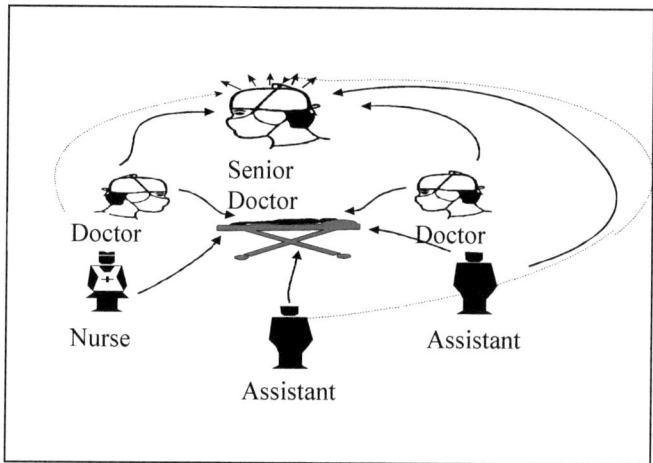

Figure 3: Staff required for urgency level 3-4

5 The Care Process

5.1 The Events

The 'patient arrival' is an event, which is characterized by its begin and end. It keeps up a correspondence to the entrance in the emergency area of the specialty. The simulator uses random variables that follow well-known statistical distribution that fits the data collected in the hospitals. Pseudo-random numbers are generated and tested by internal routines that produce the data used to simulate the arrival process, the demand and the duration of the services.

The 'primary care' and the 'triage' are basically a series of events. The primary care process comprises all the usual activities that are carried out in any emergency room. Triage is a brief and immediate evaluation of the case to establish priorities according to the gravity of the case and the medical procedures required. The triage is planned and approved by the general practitioner of the actual team in the room. These activities have duration of time, which is limited by the start and the end of the events. If the entities required to carry out a particular activity are unavailable then patients might wait. The waiting lists are organized according to the needs and priorities of the cases. The waiting time is one of the quality measures used to evaluate the performance of the service.

Depending on the case, the 'medical procedure' event and 'observation' event is scheduled. The beginning and end of the events is also modeled. The observation process starts if the patient remains in the observation room. It requires further medical care and extra time. The quality of this service can also be evaluated. The staff availability and the number of patients in observation can impose limits to the service. The medical procedure varies from case to case and the performance is measured by the attainment of its right sequence. Finally, the event 'stop simulation'. After a pre-established time this event is activated and it discontinues the arrival of new patients. The executive module of the simulator calculates and registers variables that will be used to evaluate the quality of the care.

5.2 The Entities

The main entities and their attributes are created. The most important entities involved in this experiment are: the patient, the doctor, the assistant, and the nurse. The patient is a temporary entity having the following attributes:
• The care time required;
• The treatment time;
• The observation time;
• The urgency level;
• The arrival pattern.

For the other entities, only the number and the state (free or busy) are modeled.

5.3 The Quality of Care Parameters

Quality, however defined, is considered as an attribute of the care. In order to attain quality, it is required a continuous and systematic observation and assessment of all activities involved in the patient's care [23]. A constant evaluation of medical practice is necessary to measure how far the current practice is from the pre-defined goals. The usual method of evaluating quality in public hospitals is quantity and costs. However, this may cause irreparable errors to the health status of a large number of patients.

The structure of the current emergency medical care is studied and its process is examined in detail. Patients are classified in one amongst four emergency levels according to the gravity of the case. The staff required for each emergency level is defined, using a scoring system for the desired standard of the medical practice. The quality measures are:

- The correct sequence of medical procedures;
- Achievement of the desired medical team and
- The reduction of patient's waiting times.

5.4 The Information Required

Three important pieces of information are necessary to handle the simulation:
- The number of people in the team for a quality care;
- The ability of professionals of each team;
- The arrival pattern.

The services required, the configuration of the staff and the medical team previously defines the care process. Figure 4 shows the flow of patients with urgency levels 1 and 2.

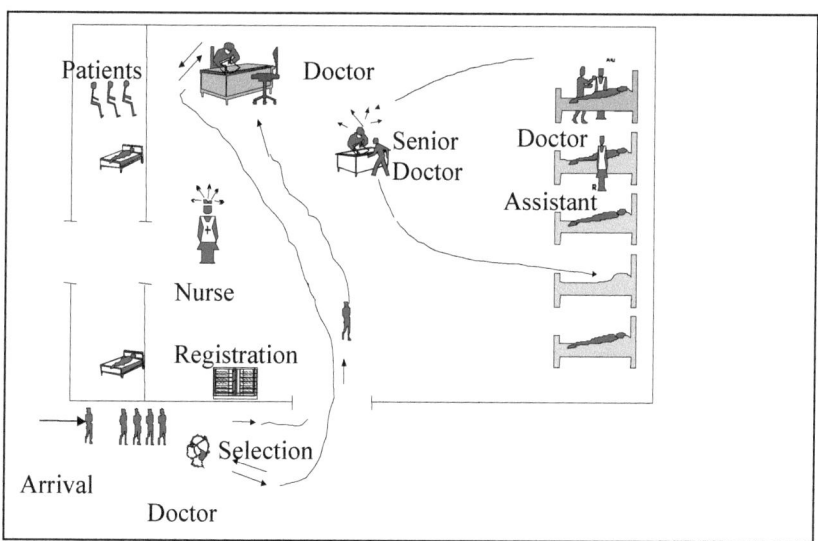

Figure 4: The Patient arrival in the emergency room for Urgency Patients 1-2

It can be seen that there is the possibility of a waiting line outside the room. The patient arrives, enters and goes through to the reception where a first evaluation of the case is made. Figure 5 shows the arrival flow of urgency levels 3 and 4 patients. The arrows indicate the situation where the attention is focused on the care to life risk patient.

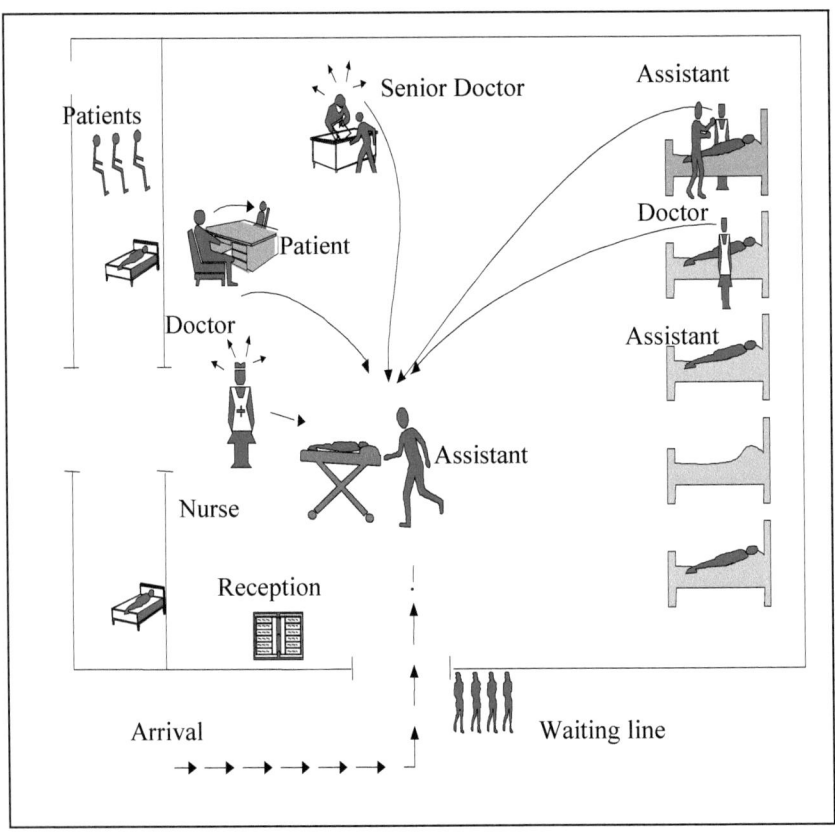

Figure 5: The Patient arrival in the emergency room for Urgency Patients 3-4

5.5 The Required Staff

The simulation is carried out based on a model that involves four urgency levels named U1, U2, U3 and U4. The calculations consider the distinctive care requirements based upon the following considerations:

1. The primary needs of U1 and U2 are based on information obtained from the work pattern of the intensive care unit. The data with requirements for the U3 and U4 are gathered from the observation of the medical team at work in the emergency sector;

2. The estimated number of professionals, essential to the provision of quality care to each of the four urgency levels are upon the medical literature [19 to 22]. The duration of time required by each process involving patients is programmed is studied and modeled separately. The duration of the primary care is estimated directly from observation in the emergency area. The duration of time for the process treatment and observation are estimated from information emergency inpatients.

After observation the time required by each process, the data is adjusted with functions of random variables in order to estimate the time requirements for the care of each type of patient, according to the medical procedure involved in the simulation model.

6 The Simulation Experiment

The configuration of the staff was made in terms of the number of doctors, nurses and assistants. The simulations calculate, for each urgency level, the percentage of quality achieved. A series of trials for surgical and medical specialties can be found elsewhere [16]. Figure 6 shows a sample of results from a 30-hour period simulation of a medical specialty [15].

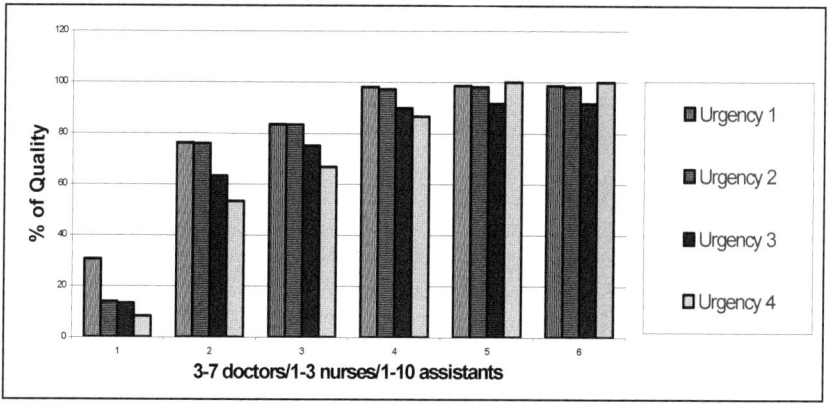

Figure 6: Percentage quality achieved by urgency level and staff configuration

The results of the experiment show that it is possible to choose the right configuration of the staff according to attention level and/or reduction of the patient waiting times. For example, a minimum of three doctors, two nurses and five assistants are required to improve quality.

7 Conclusion

The main contribution of this paper is a model that should be used to support the decision making related to the emergency care of the two hospitals studied. It points to course of actions that would improve the quality of care. The model deals not only with the flow aspect of the system, but also with the Doctor/Patient connect and the work pattern of the medical teams, towards integration of the efforts. The simulation experiment allows one to obtain coherent results as far as the patients' necessities and the expectations of the medical teams are concerned.

Quality will actually be reached if there are further initiatives towards an integrated emergency health care system, which grants access to anyone and improve the standard of services from the rescue operation to patient discharge. The contribution from this paper tackles only part of a complex problem related with the accessibility and quality of health services in developing countries such as Brazil and Peru. There is more to do in this direction than meets the eye, for the implementation of such a system depends on social, technological and political measures that are beyond the scope of this study. Accessibility and quality of health services is a broad subject and the theme of this conference.

References

[1]   S.F. Deslandes, O atendimento às vítimas de violência na emergência: Prevenção numa hora dessas? *Ciência & Saúde Coletiva*, 4(1), (1999) 81-94.

[2]   M.J.F. De Oliveira, 3D visual simulation platform for the project of a new hospital facility, in: V. de Angelis, N. Ricciardi, G. Storchi (Eds.), *Monitoring, evaluating, planning health services*, World Scientific Publishing Co. Pte. Ltd., (1999) 39-52.

[3]   M.J.F. De Oliveira, A patient-oriented modeling of emergency admission system of a Brazilian hospital, *Paper presented at EURO XIII*, Glasgow, July 19-22, (1994).

[4] F. Mcguire, Using simulation to reduce length of stay in emergency departments, *J. Soc. Health Syst.*, 5(3), (1997) 81-90.

[5] L.N.P. Toscano and M.J.F. De Oliveira, Models of the emergency attention to patients, *World Congress on Medical Physics and Biomedical Engineering*, Chicago-USA, July 23-28, (2000a).

[6] L.N.P. Toscano and M.J.F. De Oliveira, An integrated emergency information support system, *World Congress on Medical Physics and Biomedical Engineering*, Chicago-USA, July 23-28, (2000b).

[7] M.A. Washington et al., Computer simulation in health care, *Annual Quest for Quality and Productivity in Health Services Conference*, IIE, Norcross-USA, (1997) 201-210.

[8] M. Lagergren, What is the role and contribution of models to management and research in the health services? *European Journal of Operational Research*, 105(2), (1998) 257-266.

[9] M. Largergren, Modeling as a tool to assist in managing problems in health care, In D. Boldy, J. Braithwaite and I. Forbes (Eds.), *Evidence based management in health care: The role of decision support systems*, Australian Studies in Health Service Administration, No. 92, (2002) 17-36.

[10] M.J.F. De Oliveira, 3D visual simulation of hospital admissions, in: J. Riley (Ed.), Planning *The Future: Health, Service Quality and Emergency Accessibility*, Proceedings ORAHS 2000, Glasgow Caledonian University Press, (2000) 77-96.

[11] M. Pidd, F. N. de Silva and R. W. Eglese, A simulation model for emergency evacuation, *European Journal of Operational Research*, 90 (3), (1996) 413-419.

[12] J. Chaiken and R. Larson, Methods for allocating urban emergency units: a survey, *Management Science*, 19, (1998) 110-130.

[13] E. Savas, Simulation and cost-effectiveness analysis of New York's emergency ambulance service, *Management Sciences*, 15 August, (1969).

58

[14]   B. Lehaney and R.J. Paul, Use of soft systems methodology in the development of a simulation of out-patient services at Watford General Hospital, *Journal of the Operational Research Society*, July, 47(1), (1996) 864-870.

[15]   M.J.F. De Oliveira and L.N.P. Toscano, Emergency information support system for Brazilian public hospital, In: M.S. Rauner and K. Heidenberger (Eds.), Quantitative *approaches in health care management*, Peter Lang, (2003) 235-251.

[16]   L.N.P. Toscano, *Uma ferramenta integrada de suporte a decisões em casos de emergências médicas hospitalares*, Dsc Thesis, Federal University of Rio de Janeiro, (2001).

[17]   C.Y. Morales and E. Escalona, Triage extra e intrahospitalario, Manual de Urgencias y Reanimación Fundación Lucas Sierra, Viña del Mar, Vol: 1, 4, (1990-1991) 14-29.

[18]   I.P.M. Merino, I.C. Becerra, A.C. Garrido and M.D.L. Fernández, Sistemas de Garantia de Calidad en urgencias y emergências, *Cuidados Críticos y Emergencias,* Centro de Salud de Las Lagunas, Málaga, Spain, (http://www.medynet.com/usuarios/jraguilar/joserra.html).

[19]   C.S.M. Sheryl, Medical staff management: forms, policies, and procedures for health care providers, *Aspen Publishers, Inc.*, Book and Disk edition, (1996).

[20]   R. Ordner and J. Weitl, Calculation of nursing personnel for intensive care stations, *Krankenpflege (Frankf)*, Jul-Aug, PMID: 8377453, 47 (7-8), (1993) 452-4.

[21]   M.I. Cuthbert, Prediction, calculation and allocation of staff required for patient care, *J. A. Nurses*, Sep., PMID: 6557809, 13(3), (1983) 48-51.

[22]   R.W. Smallwood, M.J. Sando and R.B. Holland, Medical staff needed in a hospital to service anaesthesia and intensive care, *Anaesth Intensive Care*, Feb., PMID: 7258596, 9(1), (1981) 3-14.

[23]   M.M. Mellum and M.K. Sinioris, Total quality management: The health care pioneers, *American Hospital Publishing Inc*, USA, (1993).

TOWARDS AN INTEGRATED APPROACH TO IMPROVE THE EMERGENCY ADMISSION SYSTEM

LUIZ R.T.A. COSTA, ROGÉRIO A.C. PENNA, SÉRGIO L. HOEFLICH

Federal University of Rio de Janeiro, Brazil

Abstract

This paper intends to contribute to the accessibility to the public health services, considering many actors involved in the admission system of a municipal hospital, which is reference in emergency services in the Rio de Janeiro City. This work is part of an integrated project that aims at improvement and integration of the pre-hospital and the hospital admission system with more benefits to the patients, the society and to the public health care. A simulation model is designed in order to study the performance of the military fire brigade as an official emergency rescue service. The model is used to understand the structure of the system, to evaluate alternatives that can aggregate significant value to the patients' health, to examine the effects of the initiatives and to advancement of the emergency health care system as a whole.

Key words: emergencies, admission systems, simulation, rescue operation

1 Introduction

This paper focuses on the emergency admission system of the Miguel Couto Municipal Hospital (HMMC), which is a major public hospital in the Rio de Janeiro City. The hospital is a reference in emergency and its services are available 24 hours a day and 7 days a week. The central point is the arrival of patients via the emergency and rescue group of the military fire brigade, called Grupo de Socorro e Emergência (GSE).

The impact of the changes in the GSE's service upon the patient arrival at the hospital will be herein evaluated. The arrival pattern analyzed here concentrates on the basic operation of the GSE, which is beyond the organizational limits of the HMMC. Although it is important to stand out of the hospital, there is no need to further details of the other operations of the rescue groups, but only the steps of the pre-hospital care that are relevant to the evaluation of the hospital admission system.

The development and presentation of the work is divided into four parts. Firstly an observation of the system is performed. Secondly the data collection scheme is discussed. A Simulation model is developed based upon the data and processes observed. Six operational alternatives of the GSE operation are evaluated. Finally, the results of the simulation are discussed and additional questions with regards to possible courses of actions are considered.

2 The Data

As the rescue system acts outside the boundaries of the hospital, it is necessary to analyze the pre-hospital operation of the GSE. Besides preliminary information obtained at the corporation, statistical data provided by the HMMC are used to evaluate its operation [1]. Due to the requirement of a formal request, the data was available near to the deadline for the preparation of this paper. Therefore, statistical data previously summarized by the GSE are used here. Standard distributions are used to represent the arrival pattern and service times. It is clear that the accuracy of the data affects the quality of the results. However, it does not influence the comprehension of the operation pattern.

2.1 The Rescue System

The GSE provides most of the pre-hospital care on the streets and public places of the city of Rio de Janeiro. All the staff is well trained and protocol is strict. They provide rescue service to several hospitals. An incident in a public place creates a demand for one or more rescue units. The distribution of vehicles is made according to the placement of the headquarters. The number of vehicles, however, is a problem [2].

The activities of the pre-hospital operation are:
- **Calls:** 22.658 calls, in the HMMC area, in the period of 6 months. The percentage of calls effectively taken is about 62%;
- **Displacement:** the displacement time follows a log-normal distribution with average of 6 minutes;
- **Scene:** the average time for on-scene primary care follows a Weibull distribution with average of 10 minutes;
- **Removal:** the removal time to the HMMC follows a lognormal distribution with average of 8.7 minutes. The removal to other destinations, in the hospital area, follows a lognormal distribution with the same average.

From the services made inside the hospital area that requires further hospital care:
- 68% of the cases are directed to the HMMC;
- 25% are directed to other hospitals;
- 07% others (attendance refusal, death, etc.).

Delays are observed upon arrival of the rescue team to the HMMC hospital. The admission system is usually congested, for many reasons. The demand is very high and is basically composed of:
- Patients living, or not, in the hospital area that requires an evaluation;
- Transfers from other public and private facilities;
- Uninformed people looking for outpatient services.

The immediate consequence is the existence of long queues at the reception and at the medical triage. It is clear that not all the patients that arrive trough the GSE have to wait for emergency care. The most serious cases, of course, are immediately taken to the Intensive Care Unit (ICU) of the hospital. In all cases, however, previous bureaucratic procedures are necessary to be made for the delivery, before the ambulance crew is released. The average waiting time at the hospital before liberation follows a lognormal distribution with average of 12 minutes.

2.2 Simplifying Assumptions

This work is inspired on a paper written by the HMMC hospital administration [1]. This paper clearly identifies a series of problems that the administration of the hospital wanted to deal with. The complexity of the system is expressed in a previous publication [5] that formulates the problems, evaluates some of them and points to the direction of further development. This work provided the basic information to subsidize other studies that have been carried out simultaneously by other researchers [3,4].

The simulation model presented here is prepared with the available data at the time of this publication. Therefore, some simplifications have to be made, in order to reduce the scope of the research and focus only on the most important patterns of the operation of the rescue service.

The original intent of the present work is evaluating the overall performance of the rescue team, rather than the admission system itself. A deeper analysis of the hospital admission system can be found made elsewhere [4,5,6]. The original assumptions of the model presented here are based on the available information when this paper was presented at the conference. The basic assumptions are:

1. The transport time is the same for every patient and independent of the region where the rescue is made from. It is clear that distinct resources may be needed when the attendance is made outside the hospital area. There are situations where patients are transferred from several regions of the State of Rio de Janeiro [1];

2. The ambulances can only transport one patient at a time. There are several classes of accidents that originate the calls and demand different actions by the rescue crew according to the injuries caused [2];

3. Only a selection of accidents and injuries are considered in the study. The accident occurrence is seasonal, varies according to the day of the week and time of the day. The experience of the GSE command points out, for example, the peak of traffic accidents on Friday and Saturday nights [7];

4. The number of workers at the hospital reception is insufficient to cope with the increasing and variable demand [1]. Thus, all the time spent receiving the patients arriving exclusively through rescue group is processed without taking in consideration the waiting time. Being this work part of a subset of the hospital operation, the patterning of the reception at HMMC is considered separately.

2.3 The Observed System

Based upon the observation of the system, some characteristics stand out for evaluation of the operation alternatives to be simulated. It is evident that GSE does not have the necessary capacity to attend the present demand of calls. As observed, only 62% of the calls are effectively answered and 1% of the patients that arrive at HMMC come with rescue groups. Even if the GSE could answer all the calls, this percentage would be about 2%. It is clear that an adequate pre-hospital care is essential as it contributes to improve the quality of care and reduce the costs.

The delivery of the patient and the entrance to the hospital is the final stage of rescue operation, which started when the since the 'incident'. It is argued that all the waiting times involved in the process do not add value to the health of the patient. Thus, all the waiting periods that correspond to the rescue group operation such as primary care, transfer and delivery have to be carefully considered and synchronized hospital admission system. The whole process is liable to efforts aiming improvement. Reducing waiting times before hospital care is a key factor to improve the performance of the used of the material and human resources involved with any activity of the emergency care. Some of the hospital activities, however, could be easily managed.

3 Modeling the Rescue Operation

3.1 Purposes of the Model

The purposes of the simulation reflect the needs of the observed system. Besides keeping up with the simultaneous studies about the admission system of the HMMC and the focusing on the rescue service, the present study evaluates the impact of changes in the pattern of GSE services over the arrival of patients at the hospital. The supply level changes according to the increase or reduction of human and material resources required for a particular operation.

The impact of the changes is then evaluated in terms of the quality of care. It would be used basically to evaluate investments in ambulances, rescue crews and infra structure. The investment would lead to a progress in the welfare of the population. It is argued that the upgrading of the services leads to a reduction of the existing economical and social costs and also to a decline in the unnecessary waiting times. The existing figures show cases of sequels and even deaths caused by an inefficient pre-hospital care.

3.2 The Simulation Model

Because the problem studied here is complex, formulation is a very difficult task. The building of the logical model representing the formulation of the problem is, in many instances, the most difficult aspect of the modeling. In fact, understanding what the problem is may be the object of the whole exercise. One should be prepared to constantly undertake reformulation to obtain a common understanding of the problem as part of the modeling process. The function that the computer model serves, is to perform a medium of communication for the structuring of the problem for all participants in the decision making process [6].

A simulation is designed in order to identify the critical points, analyze alternative policies and investigate different ways of undertake the problem. Based on the observation of the system, one can then develop a model that responds to the proposed questions. The first step of this part of the work is to evaluate the model alternatives. As the available data are not sufficient to embrace all the steps of the GSE operation, only the most important aspects of the system will be validated against real data. Acceptable random number generators are used to produce some of the parameters that are used in the case where data are not available. The model shown in the Figure 1 was developed in the software Arena – version 4.0 [8].

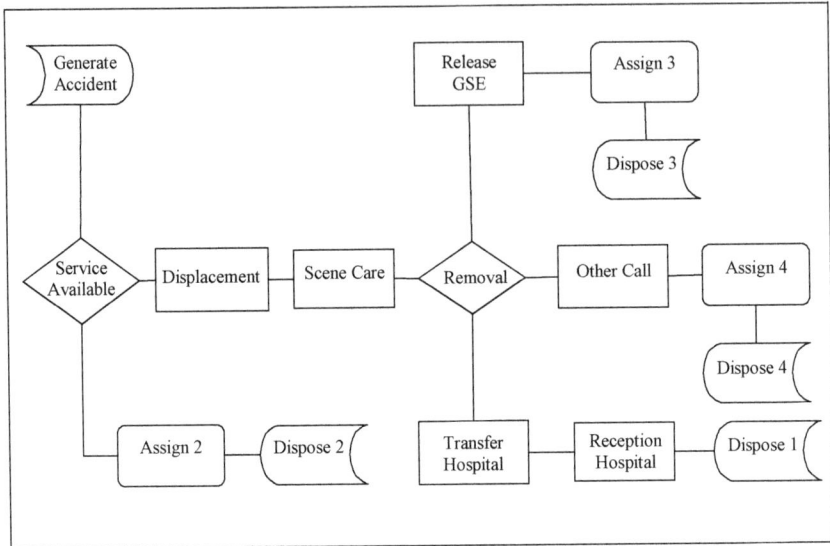

Figure 1: Model developed in the Arena software

The pre-hospital care service is modeled as a sequence of activity flows that reflects the functioning of the operation. The occurrence of an incident generates a call. The arrival pattern comes from random variable; its distribution represents the frequency of calls in the HMMC area. The real data reveals that only 62% of the calls are answered by the GSE. The others are refused and leave the system, mainly because of the limitations imposed by the existing facilities.

The decision-making process in the simulation model is made trough objects that determine the course of action that follows each decision [9]. The flow represents activities that takes simulation time and requires a number of entities to be performed. If any condition is not fulfilled, the simulator generates a waiting period. For example, if any of the essential entities required for the rescue operation is been used or is unavailable, the victim should wait. The hypothesis considered includes estimated time for each of the activities to be performed.

Simulation would be useful to:
- Evaluation of the existing system;
- Reduction of the reception time at the hospital;
- Increasing the number of rescue vehicles;
- Reduction of the reception time and increasing the number of vehicles;
- The above, plus a reduction of the displacement time.

4 The Simulation

To obtain the necessary background information, one must take into consideration a number of factors, which are directly or indirectly related to the real system, such as the normal patterns of seeking and receiving medical care and the factors affecting the urgency of need for such care [10]. The model developed is used to evaluate several alternatives, divided into two groups. The first group evaluates the system performance considering both the demand and supply constant. The experiment attempts to improve the attendance index and the efficiency of the process. The second group evaluates the performance of the system as the demand and supply of services change.

4.1 The Experiment

Six experiments are made in order to evaluate the two groups of alternatives:

1. Use the observed parameters of operation, resources and duration of time;

2. Evaluate the system's performance if all calls are effectively answered;

3. Assess the value of the reduction of 50% of the hospital reception time;

4. Besides improving the reception service, consider an 50% increase on the demand, keeping the present supply and 4 ambulances;

5. Besides improving the reception service and the present demand, increase 80% of the supply and increase the number of ambulances to 5;

6. Finally, besides maintaining the above alternative, increase the supply in 100% and increase the number of ambulances to 6.

4.2 The Results Obtained

The results of each of the alternatives and additional statistics are produced for a period of 30 days. The data is then compiled on an Excel worksheet and comparative graphs are made. The graphs show the results of the alternatives for each group separately, allowing a comparison between the impact of the operational improvement and the suggested upgrade of the services.

The simulation model allows one to explore a number of other hypotheses of interest to all parties involved in the emergency admission system. A preliminary evaluation revealed some interesting ways of tackling this very complex problem. Table 1 shows, for example, a progressive reduction in the patient's waiting time under the second alternative.

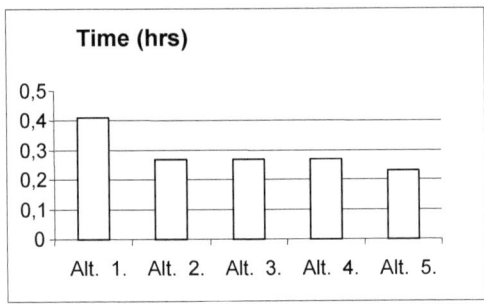

Table 1: Patient waiting times

The results showed that:
- It is necessary to increase the number of rescue units;
- The time wasted at the reception affects the whole operation;
- The patient waiting times are reduced under the second alternative;
- The waiting time starts to be 'acceptable' under the fourth alternative;
- The total reduction of waiting time is significant under the fifth alternative and
- The resources are used completely in both the first and second alternatives.

The evaluation of the alternatives of the first group reveals:
- There is a slight reduction in the value added to the health of the patients, when the reception time is reduced;
- The operation is not feasible when the supply increases 100%. The waiting times are unacceptable;
- There is a reduction on the waiting time and on the size of the queue, but these figures are still higher than the current case;
- The overall attendance time reacts well as the reception becomes faster.

The evaluation of the alternatives of the second group reveals:
- The increase of the demand should be synchronized with the supply;
- It is advantageous to invest in the improvement of the rescue services;
- The reduction in the overall attendance time is highly dependent on the waiting times of the intermediate activities. In the most favorable hypothesis studied the activities times are constant and the demand and supply are harmonized.

Many other reports and graphs can be obtained from the simulation of the six operation alternatives tested. It is clear that the increasing the demand and the supply will affect the whole operation. Other improvements on the performance of the activities could be proposed, like a reduction on transportation time, use of different vehicles during the rush hours and so on.

5 Discussion

The simulation model is very useful to answer some of the questions concerning the arrival of the patients through the GSE. The model considers the accident occurrence at random and does not evaluate factors that can improve or reduce the accident rate. It is clear that in cities like Rio de Janeiro there is more to do is this direction that meets the eye for the traffic accidents, violence and lack of information are still a major problem to be solved.

Reliable data and more accurate information are necessary to a further and realistic cost-benefit analysis of the proposed alternatives, in order to provide an adequate information support system to the pre-hospital system. Improvements of these services will be beneficial to all hospitals and consequently to the public health system.

5.1 The Demand for Services

As we have seen, only a low percentage of the emergency arrivals at the HMMC come through the GSE. It is noticeable that an increase in the level of services of the rescue group does not imply in a substantial increase in the demand upon the hospital admission system. Preliminary calculation reveals that 10% of the calls are effectively taken to this hospital [5]. The actual demand caused by the GSE represents less than 2% of the hospital emergencies. This discussion, however, requires a more detailed reflection, which is beyond the scope of this paper.

It is of fundamental importance, for the health authorities, offering a quality care. The pre-hospital care offered by the GSE is of good quality. The actual emergency service provided by the hospital is also of good quality. It is argued that the main problem resides at the hospital admission system. There are. There are already some initiatives in this direction [3,4]. It would be very beneficial for Health System standardize and integrate the services in order to offer a quality care larger number of users. A communication system about the accidents, allowing the hospital to be prepared for the delivery of the patients is essential. However, implementing the new ideas is not as easy task.

5.2 The Randomness of the Demand

The definition of an emergency patient rests on medical criteria and can be given as - one who has medical condition requiring immediate hospital attention and prompt treatment. This 'emergency patient', however defined, is viewed subjectively during the admission process by the patient, the doctor and the administrator accordingly to their particular role in the process. The number of requests for emergency admissions can vary widely from hospital to hospital and fluctuate considerably from day to day within one hospital [5,6]. A large increase of some kinds of accidents on the weekends is an evidence of that.

The occurrence of incidents that result in a hospital emergency usually considered as a random phenomenon. However it is possible to interfere and reduce the occurrence of certain events (traffic accidents, shot gun, violence, etc.). Some factors are well known as prevention programs, legislation, alcohol consumption control, economical status and social topics among others. Identifying those factors and evaluate their influence over the occurrence of accidents would be highly beneficial to evaluate the impact of external measures, controllable or not, would have over the hospital demand.

Controllable measures are those that can be determined either by the government or by the society, as well as awareness programs, laws, etc. Non-controllable measures would be growth variants of economical growth and sociable difference that cannot be simply determined by a government or even by the society. Once again, the simulation does not answer this question properly. Actually, the approach has efficient resources to evaluate the impact of variants in the occurrence of accidents over the demand of HMMC, but it does not seem to be efficient to study the influence of those external agents.

6 Conclusion

The experiments with the simulation model leads one to conclude by the adequacy of improving the supply of the GSE service and seek for reduction of the time to execute the activities, which do not add value to the health of the patient. It seems more important the evaluation of the benefits that can be obtained by the advances aiming to improve systems of a similar nature. The achievement of a standard and integrated admission system care in all levels of service would be very beneficial. It is clear that the modeling and the simulation of the system beyond the organization limits promote a better understand of the system in an embracing way and allows a reduction in the randomness that depend on external factors.

The learning of the functioning the system is of great value. The simulation approach gives a good idea about system operation although it does not provide support for strategic decisions that dependent on qualitative and untouchable factors. Thus it seems very interesting to use a combination of complementary approaches to further evaluate the dynamics of system studied. Some strategic questions and features of the system eligible for improvement are not properly studied yet.

Most changes will, of course, create new demands on the admission systems and affect the operation of all hospitals. The proposed initiatives however, contribute to the understanding of the essential part of a number of current social problems. Some of these problems affect people's quality of life. The actions of increasing the number of ambulances and reducing the duration of operations are difficult, but not impossible. For example, eight new ambulances will be enough to enable the GSE to cope with all calls. It is clear that the GSE contributes only a low percentage of the emergency cases of the HMC.

Finally it's necessary to point that when we studied systems beyond the organization limits, the cost-benefit analysis of the proposed alternatives should consider the impact on the chain for a posterior negotiation of assumption of the reached results. At the patient arrival system at HMMC through GSE the investment in the offer of rescue services benefits the hospitals and the society as a whole. On the same way the improvement of the hospital reception service increases the availability of its resources, for the society and for the health system.

Acknowledgements

We are grateful to the GSE for their interest and practical support, which provided the basic data used in this study. To our Prof. Mario J. F. De Oliveira for his patience, continuous encouragement and help.

References

[1] E. Paixão et al, *Projeto novo perfil*, Hospital Miguel Couto, Rio de Janeiro, RJ, Brazil, (2000).

[2] S.R.T.D. Barros, *Análise ergonômica da mitigação de acidentes em via pública: um estudo de caso no GSE do Corpo de Bombeiros Militar do Estado do Rio de Janeiro*, M.Sc Thesis, COPPE/UFRJ, Rio de Janeiro, RJ, Brasil, (1998).

[3] L.N.P. Toscano, *Uma ferramenta integrada de suporte a decisões em casos de emergências médicas hospitalares*, Dsc Thesis, Federal University of Rio de Janeiro, (2001).

[4] N. Achão Filho, *A simulação como método de avaliação da qualidade de atendimento hospitalar: o caso na emergência de um hospital municipal*, M.Sc Thesis, COPPE/UFRJ, Rio de Janeiro, RJ, Brasil, (2002).

[5] M.J.F. De Oliveira and L.N.P. Toscano, Emergency information support system for Brazilian public hospital, In: Rauner, M.S., Heidenberger, K. (Eds), *Quantitative Approaches in Health Care Management*, Peter Lang, (2003), 235-251.

[6] M.J.F. De Oliveira, 3D Visual simulation platform for the project of a new hospital facility, in: V de Angelis, N.Ricciardi & G. Storchi (Eds.), *Monitoring, Evaluating, Planning Health Services*, World Scientific Publishing Co. Pte. Ltd., (1998) 39-52.

[7] M.B. Carneiro, Normalização dos serviços de emergência no Estado do Rio De Janeiro: Reorganização do subsistema de emergência no Estado do Rio de Janeiro. *CREMERJ*, (1995).

[8] D. Prado, *Usando o Arena em simulação*, Editora Desenvolvimento Gerencial, Belo Horizonte, MG, Brazil, (1999).

[9] M. Pidd, *Modelagem empresarial: Ferramentas para tomada de decisão*, Ed. Bookman, Porto Alegre, RS, Brazil, (1998).

[10] D.C. Lane, C. Monefield and J.V. Rosenhead, Looking in the wrong place for health care improvements: a system dynamics study of an accident and emergency department, *Journal of the Operational Research Society*, 51 (2000) 518-531.

EVALUATION OF HEALTH CARE

INVESTMENT POLICY IN THE HEALTH SYSTEM OF THE CZECH REPUBLIC FROM THE INTERNATIONAL PERSPECTIVE

MARTIN DLOUHY

University of Economics, Prague

Abstract

Investment policies in the health systems of developed countries are analyzed with special interest in the Czech health system. The data used in the study come from the OECD Health Data 2000. The relations between the level of investments, economic development and health status of population are studied. The concept of supplier-induced investment is introduced. It is shown that the measurement of health investments is inadequate and the efficiency of investment policies cannot be properly evaluated at the current level of knowledge.

Key words: investment policy, health system, supplier-induced investment

1 Introduction

Investment policy is an important tool the Czech ministry of health has for the health system regulation. In real life, the health sector is being accused of constructing new hospital pavilions and acquiring modern health technology without a concept of appropriate geographical standards and without ensuring their rational use [5]. The expensive technology is under-utilized or is utilized redundantly to be profitable.

From the communist regime, the Czech health sector inherited several megalomaniac hospital projects, which were not stopped after the fall of communism and which now induce big financial expenses. The ministry of health began, together with health insurance funds, to regulate hospital construction and the supply of health technology. The system is still far from being perfect. A comparative analysis of the Czech Republic with other OECD countries may reveal some new findings, which can help to formulate a more rational health policy.

2 Theoretical Background

The health system requires a combination of a large number of different inputs. There are three principal health system inputs: human resources (physicians, nurses and other personnel), physical capital (buildings and equipment) and consumables (pharmaceuticals, energy, services). Figure 1 shows their roles in the health system [11]. Physical capital (buildings and equipment) deteriorates and becomes obsolete. Investment is the addition to the stock of capital. The formulation of investment policy is a critical decision about the future of a national health system. Investment decisions usually cannot be cancelled, generate future recurrent costs and even needs further investments. Many major hospitals in all countries serve as examples of that process. Once built, a hospital becomes an issue of local politics. The current physical infrastructure is a product of long-term historical evolution, which gives a limited space for the present government decisions. In this paper, the investment policy in the Czech health system is analyzed from the international perspective.

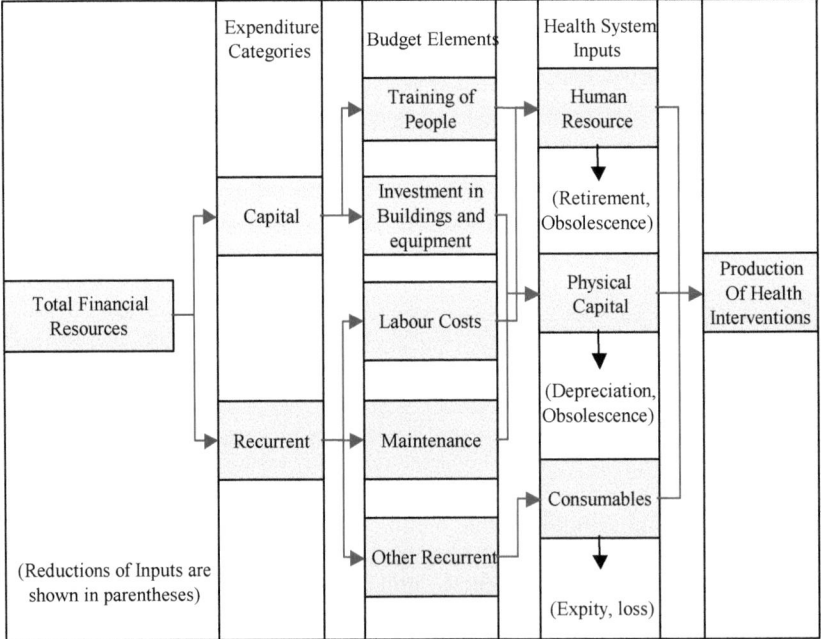

Figure 1: Health system inputs: from financial resources to health intervention

According to the economic theory [10], firms invest to earn profits. The major economic forces that determine investment are, therefore, the revenues produced by investment, the cost of investment, and by state of expectations about the future. An important relationship connects investment spending and the interest rate. It is complicated to apply these economic findings to the health sector, where the criteria have to be broader, rather than strictly commercial. For such circumstances, alternative methods of capital investment appraisal are proposed [6].

It is also interesting that investment decisions are usually made outside the organization (especially if it is a public one) and involve a variety of stakeholders with political power. Thus, the investment is a result of a mixture of competing political, economic and medical aspects. It is argued [7] that those who work in hospitals are in the best position to know what they need to do their jobs properly, but, conversely, they are less well placed to take a whole-system perspective. For the reasons mentioned above, we incline to take a pragmatic and empirical approach.

3 Data Availability

The records come from OECD Health Data, which is a comprehensive database released annually on CD-ROM. The 2000 edition contains available data from 29 member countries. It potentially represents 29 observations, but, in reality, some observations are missing. We have to go back to data from 1996 to get a relatively sufficient number of observations. One must be very careful regarding cross-country comparisons. The basic definitions may have different meanings from country to country; hence, the power of our analysis is limited and must be treated with caution. The list of indicators that we use is:

- Gross domestic product in USD in purchasing power parity per capita (GPD);
- Total current health expenditures in USD in PPP per capita (CUR_HE);
- Total investments on medical facilities in USD in PPP per capita (INV);
- Infant mortality per 1000 live births (INFANT);
- Total number of in-patient beds per 1000 inhabitants (BEDS);
- Total number of computed tomography scanners per million inhabitants (CT);
- Total number of magnetic resonance imaging units per million inhabitants (MRI).

4 Empirical Analysis

Based on the 1996 observations, the total investments on medical facilities range from 28 to 127 USD in purchasing power parity per capita. It represents 1.45 - 9.71% of total health expenditures and 0.16 - 0.68% of gross domestic product. In this section, three hypotheses are investigated.

Are health expenditures related to the economic level of the country? A close association between health expenditures and income is known [3, 9]. The output of regression (1) indicates a moderately strong linear relationship between the current health expenditures and gross domestic product (Figure 2). The white point represents the position of the Czech republic. The level of health expenditures corresponds to the economic level of the Czech republic. There is a statistically significant relationship between the investments and gross domestic product (2), but this association is much lower than it is in the case of current expenditures (Figure 3). The Czech republic spends relatively more than expected at the given level of GDP. The Czech data are, however, unreliable, not satisfying the basic identity of national health accounts implying that the total health expenditures are the sum of current expenditures and investments (see Table 1).

$$\text{CUR\_HE} = -774.5 + 0.121908 \text{ GDP} \qquad \text{R-squared} = 0.7913 \qquad (1)$$
$$\text{SE} \qquad (295.993) \ (0.01475) \qquad \text{Df} = 18$$

$$\text{INV} = 24.9293 + 0.00221953 \text{ GDP} \qquad \text{R-squared} = 0.1286 \qquad (2)$$
$$\text{SE} \quad (28.2577) \ (0.00136166) \qquad \text{Df} = 18$$

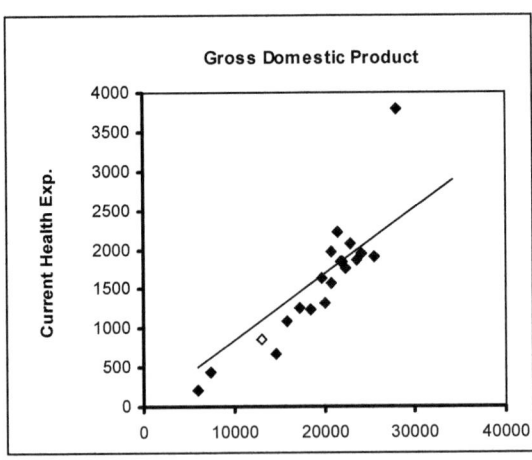

Figure 2: Current health expenditures and GDP, 1996

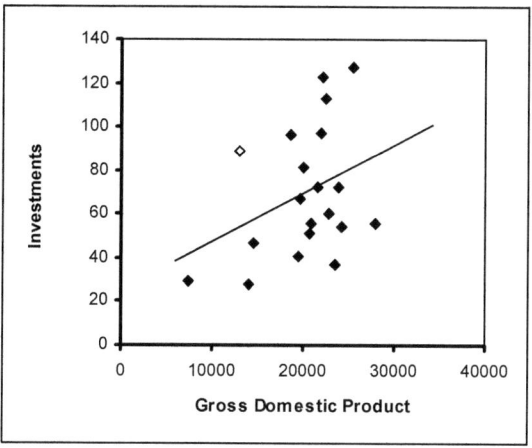

Figure 3: Investments on medical facilities and
GDP, USD in PPP per capita, 1996

Year	Current Expenditures	Investments	Total Health Expenditures	Difference
1995	827	105	902	30
1996	865	89	917	37
1997	886	81	930	37
1998	882	83	930	35

Table 1: Health expenditures in the Czech republic 1995 - 1998,
purchasing power parity per capita

Does money produce more health? Infant mortality is often cited as a useful
indicator of the health level in a community. It is the number of deaths of people
aged less than one year that occurred during a year per 1000 live births during the
same year expressed as a rate. There are statistically weak associations between
infant mortality and all independent variables (3-6).

The results suggest that the socio-economic level of the country (measured by
GDP) is a more significant determinant of health than the health service indicators
(the current expenditures, investments, and the numbers of CTs and MRIs). We
get similar findings when using the life expectancy at birth as a measure of health
status. For the Czech Republic, it is important to consider that the high level of
investments on medical facilities is not likely to be the best strategy to reduce the
East-West health gap.

INFANT = 15.8167 − 0.00508329 CUR_HE   R-squared = 0.2256   (3)
SE   (3.91321) (0.00223915)   Df = 18

INFANT = 7.33089 − 0.0222906 INV   R-squared = 0.1185   (4)
SE   (1.08293) (0.0143271)   Df = 18

INFANT = 11.76 + 0.030 CT -0.788 MRI   R-squared = 0.1168   (5)
SE   (3.298)   (0.391)   (1.378)   Df = 13

INFANT = 20.4946 − 0.000672429 GDP   R-squared = 0.3705   (6)
SE   (3.40318) (0.000168666)   Df = 27

Do health care providers induce more investments? The concept of supplier-induced demand [8] says that the provider aims to maximize its income or other arguments in its utility function. The asymmetry of information between the doctor and patient (and the insurance fund) is the key to manipulate a patient to an increased level of consumption. This concept may be reformulated to a supplier-induced investment. We assume that a greater number of providers produce more services and, also, induce a greater need for investments on facilities and equipment. There are at least three arguments for this:

1. The existing high level of fixed assets needs to be maintained;

2. In the public health system, public subsidies mean getting investment at zero or low cost (capital as a free good), which is surely a strong incentive to start lobbying and over-investing in capital;

3. If my neighbor has this machine, then I need it, too. It is usually justified on the basis of equity between two groups of people and it usually leads to the doubling of high-tech services on the supply side;

4. New technology increases the professional prestige of doctors and improves the competitive position of the provider;

5. High investments are a way of defense in the bed length of stay reduction policy. Only supernatural power would be able to close a newly built and excellently equipped hospital.

In our small analysis, we use the number of beds as a proxy for the inpatient sector size. If the idea of supplier-induced investment is right, high levels of beds will be related with high levels of investments.

Regression (7) may support this idea, since the model is significant at the 95% level. The visual presentation of data is, however, less convincing (Figure 4). The group of different processes and low quality of data may lead to high variability and hide existing relationships.

There is no statistically significant relationship between beds and current health expenditures (8). There is also a low support for the idea that richer countries will have more beds at the disposal (9). This is no surprise, since we witness the opposite trend of bed reduction policies. Technical progress and lower costs in outpatient care caused a decline in the number of beds and reduction in the average length of stay.

Health systems are likely to invest relatively more in modern medical technologies and drugs than in buildings and beds. It is, however, impossible to support this idea by data, since the associations between the numbers of CT scanners and MRI units (as proxies for all technologies) with investments are also low.

$$INV = 42.73 + 3.81541 \text{ BEDS} \qquad R\text{-squared} = 0.2301 \qquad (7)$$
$$SE \quad (14.163)\,(1.6926) \qquad\qquad Df = 17$$

$$CUR\_HE = 1203.57 + 53.9491 \text{ BEDS} \quad R\text{-squared} = 0.0479 \qquad (8)$$
$$SE \qquad (428.377)\,(58.3203) \qquad\qquad Df = 17$$

$$BEDS = 2.685 + 0.000225474 \text{ GDP} \quad R\text{-squared} = 0.1792 \qquad (9)$$
$$SE \qquad (1.936)\,(0.0000976) \qquad\qquad Df = 25$$

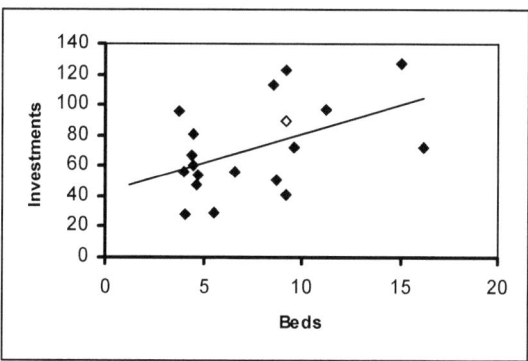

Figure 4: Number of beds per 1000 inhabitants and investments (USD, PPP per capita, 1996)

5 Conclusion

Investment policy should be and important tool of national health policy. Nevertheless, there is great lack of reliable information on health investments at international level. The measurement of health investments is clearly inadequate. The Czech data (at least in OECD Database) are unreliable, not satisfying the identities of national health accounts. The efficiency of national investment policies, at international level, cannot be evaluated at the current level of knowledge.

There is little systematic evidence on the impact of investment decisions on the performance of health systems [1]. Undoubtedly, decisions on capital investments require more public attention, even if the international health databases cannot help to formulate more rational health policies. In the paper, the concept of supplier-induced investment is introduced, however it needs more theoretical work and empirical verification. There is only weak statistical relationship between beds and CT/MRI (as proxies for physical capital) and investment or current health expenditures.

Acknowledgements

The author appreciates the support from the Grant Agency of the Czech republic, project numbers: 402/01/0161 and 402/01/0133.

References

[1]   O. Adams, et al., Human, physical and intellectual resource generation: Proposals for monitoring, *World Health Organization (WHO)*, (2002), (http://www3.who.int/whois/discussion_papers/discussion_papers.cfm).

[2]   Credes, Comparative analysis of 29 countries, *OECD Health Data 2000*, Paris, (2000).

[3]   A.J. Culyer, Cost containment in Europe, *Health Care Financing Review*, Annual Supplement, (1989) 21-35.

[4]   M. Dlouhy, Investment policy in the health system of OECD countries, In: *Mathematical Methods in Economics*, Technical University of Ostrava, (2002).

[5] J. Jaros and K. Kalina (Eds), Czech health care system: Delivery and financing, Prague, *Czech Association for Health Services Research*, (1998).

[6] T. Keenan, Capital investment appraisal in the NHS, In: C. Cropper, P. Forte, (Eds.), Enhancing Health Services Management, Buckingham, Open University Press, (1997).

[7] M. McKee and J. Healy, (Eds.), Hospitals in a changing Europe, *Open University Press*, Buckingham (2002).

[8] A. McGuire, J. Henderson and G. Mooney, *The economics of health care*, Routledge, (1994).

[9] C.J.L. Murray and A.D. Lopez (Eds.), *Global comparative assessments in the health sector*, WHO, Geneva, (1994).

[10] P.A. Samuelson and W.D. Nordhaus, *Economics,* Fifteenth Edition, McGraw-Hill, (1995).

[11] WHO, The World health report 2000 - *Health Systems: Improving Performance*, Geneva. (2000).

COST-EFFECTIVENESS EVALUATION OF SANITATION PROJECTS USING THE DALY INDEX

MARIA H. BRACHOWICZ, JAIME G. BELLIDO, CESAR DAS NEVES
Federal University of Rio de Janeiro, Rio de Janeiro, Brazil

Abstract

The cost-effectiveness analysis is applied to study the impact of sanitation programs in morbidity due to fecal-oral diseases such as: cholera, dysentery, typhoid and paratyphoid fever, poliomyelitis, viral hepatitis and intestinal infections. The target population is the inpatient children, between 0-4 years of age, living in Volta Redonda that is a municipality of the Rio de Janeiro State. Disability Adjusted Life Years (DALY) is the chosen effectiveness indicator. The results of the study show a decrease in the indicator's values and progress in population health, subsequent to improvements in the services of the local sanitation company, which had enhanced their services, specially drain, collection and treatment of sewage.

Key words: cost-effectiveness analysis, disability adjusted life years, fecal-oral diseases

1 Introduction

The use of Cost–Effectiveness Analysis (CEA) is on the rise to evaluate the efficiency of specific interventions in public sectors. The analysis usually looks at the ratio of financial expenditure and effectiveness, such us: dollars per life-year gained, dollars per case prevented, dollars per quality-adjusted life-years gained and dollars per disability–adjusted life-years [1]. This study applies this technique to the assessment of projects in the field of health and sanitation. The chosen effectiveness indicator is DALY that measures the burden of the diseases. The health damage considered here is rather more physical than mental [2].

The municipality of Volta Redonda is located into one of the most polluted areas of the state of Rio de Janeiro. The main river of the region, called the Paraiba do Sul, serves this and another 52 municipalities of the state. The water is impure and contaminated by domestic and industrial waste. One of the most serious health problems is the occurrence of diseases caused by the ingestion of contaminated water. There is an increase in the incidence of fecal-oral diseases among children with less than four years old. The situation of the mortality due to fecal–oral diseases among children between 0 to 4 years old during the period 1991 to 1996 is shown in the Table 1.

Municipality	Years					
	1991	1992	1993	1994	1995	1996
Volta Redonda	5	1	6	4	6	4

Table 1: Deaths due to intestinal infectious diseases during the period: 1991 to 1996, in Volta Redonda. Source: DATASUS/SIM

Figure 1 shows the graph of the morbidity due to fecal–oral diseases, from 1992 to 1997, among children between 0 to 4 years old. According to the Information and Notification System (SINAN) and the Health State Secretary (HSC), it was found between children of the same age, 330 cases of diarrhea in 1998 and 220 cases in 1999. The total population of Volta Redonda was, in 1999, of 239,571 inhabitants.

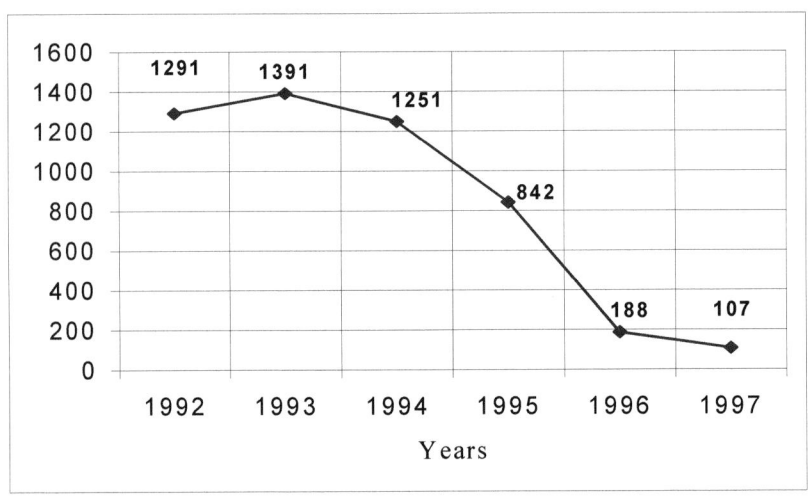

Figure 1: In-patient children, 0-4 years old, with intestinal infectious diseases, in the Municipality of Volta Redonda, (1992-1997)

The cost–effectiveness estimation model presented in this paper uses DALY as the chosen effectiveness indicator. The data contemplates the year of 1997 in the municipality of Volta Redonda. A sample of 0 to 4 years old children cases that show fecal–oral diseases followed by a complete recovery is chosen for the study.

2 Methods

Taking into account that each health problem results in four possible outcomes (death, disability before death, permanent disability, or full recovery), (see Figure 2), we will calculate the number of DALY lost for each one of these four scenarios [3].

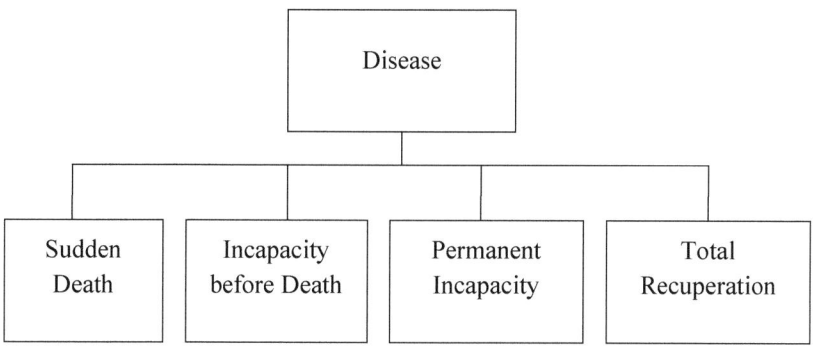

Figure 2: Four possible outcomes for each health problem

The following aspects have to be considered in the construction of the DALY indicator:
- The life years lost due to premature death;
- The comparison of different conditions of the disability or pain;
- The age influence;
- The comparison between the current and future health condition;
- The patients' choice to be treated.

The number of years lost due to premature death or the number of life years saved when death was avoided are measured according to the age. The world largest life average is equal to 82 years for the Japanese women. Supposing that the standard years of life belongs to the higher probability of life, the numbers of 80 years old for men and 82.5 years old for women is chosen [2].

The degree or weight of the disability or pain allows one to compare different conditions. In that way, weights in the range from 0 to 1 are considered:

- "0" = healthily and
- "1" = death

As far as weight of ages are concerned, the younger the people are, healthier they are expected to be. The top age for healthy person considered here is 25 years old. It is assumed that after this age the health condition decrease slowly [4]. According to the World Health Organization [3], the formula to assess those weights is:

$$\text{Weight function of age:} = Cxe^{-\beta x}, \text{where:}$$

C = Constant equivalent to 0,16243
β = Constant equivalent to 0,04
x = age
e = Constant equivalent to 2,71

The time preference is the comparison between the current and the additional health values obtained in the future. The discount rate is estimated in the calculations of the future benefits. This procedure is recommended when comparing the costs and benefits in the Cost–effectiveness model, especially in health programs. The discount rate used in the DALY construction is 3% a year, and the formula to assess the time preferences is:

$$\text{Discount function} = e^{-r(x-a)},$$

where:

r = discount rate = 0,03 (fixed value)
x = age
e = constant equivalent to 2,71
a = year (initial)

Choosing the person, who will receive the health treatment, is given priority to few individuals that are suffering pain or incapacity through considerable period, instead to choose people who are suffering in short periods. The reduction of the physical capacity, due to some disease is measured using the weights assessed for the resulting incapacity and the exponential formula. The DALY formula due to incapacity in the "x" age, is:

$$DALY(x) = (D)(Cxe^{-\beta X})(e^{-r(x-a)})$$

2.1 DALY Equation

The construction of DALY due to morbidity by fecal–oral diseases followed by total recovery includes the above recommendations and checks if the individual in consideration, with pain or incapacity, is at the top of his expected life. It is also necessary to add the total number of DALY lost since the year when the incapacity happened (a), until the year of his death (L+a). Then, the formula is:

$$\int_{x=a}^{L+a} DALY(x) \ dx = DC \int_{x=a}^{L+a} xe^{-\beta x - rx + ra} dx$$

For the estimation of DALY among children between 0 to 4 years old, it is used the formula:

$DALY =$

$$-\left[\frac{(D)(0,16243)(2,71^{-(0,04)(a)})}{(0,04+0,03)^2}\right]\left[(2,71^{-(0,04+0,03)(L)}(1+(0,04+0,03)(L+a))-(1+(0,03+0,04)a)\right]$$

where:

L = Years of life left to age "a"
D = weight of the incapacity

3 Results

Table 3 shows the DALY missing by incapacity and total recuperation during the period 1992-1998. The weight of the incapacity D=0.5, was considered. It can be seen a slight increase in the number of cases, in the period 1992-1993, from both gender. The number of cases, for both 0-4 years old boys and girls start to decrease, from 1994

The estimated DALY for boys, in 1993, is about 289. The estimate for girls, over the same period of one year, is about 280. This figure goes down to about 20 in four year's period. The estimate for boys follows basically the same fashion, going down about 24, in 1977.

Year	Boys of 0 – 4 years old	Girls of 0 – 4 years old	DALY estimated for boys	DALY estimated for girls	DALY both sex
1992	695	596	284.48	243.95	528.43
1993	707	684	289.39	279.97	569.36
1994	634	617	259.51	252.55	512.06
1995	436	406	178.46	166.18	344.65
1996	112	76	45.84	31.11	76.95
1997	58	49	23.74	20.06	43.80
1998	65	58	26.61	23.74	50.35

Table 3: DALY missing by incapacity due fecal – oral diseases

Table 4 shows DALY estimated for sewage collection and water supply in the Municipality of Volta Redonda, during the period 1992 to 1998.

Year	DALY	% Population with drained sewage	% Population with piped water
1992	562.4493	87	99
1993	739.6989	89	99
1994	614.4763	91	99
1995	515.1034	94	99
1996	315.5680	96	99
1997	111.9559	99	99
1998	118.5050	99	99

Table 4: DALY and % population served with sewage and piped water
Source: Estimated DALY and (SAAE/VR)

Figure 2 shows the DALY assessed among children between 0 and 4 years old with fecal-oral diseases in the Volta Redonda Municipality, 1992 -1998.

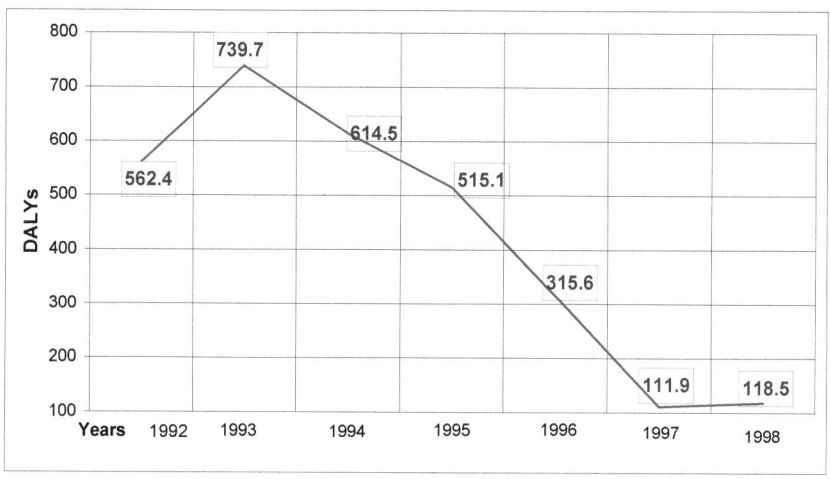

Figure 2: DALY assessed. Period: 1992 to 1998

Table 5 shows DALY missing and cost by DALY avoid with investments in potable water, collection and treatment of sewage (Incapacity considered of two years). The data source is from SAAE/VR and the DALY estimated. According to the results obtained in Table 5, the population health had improved when the local company of water and sewage has increased the sanitation services occurred specially in water and sewage's drain and treatments.

Year	DALY	DALY avoided	Investment Water	Investment Sewage	Cost Water	Cost Sewage
1992	562.449	–				
1993	739.699	-177.250				
1994	614.476	125.223				
1995	515.103	99.373				
1996	315.568	199.535				
1997	111.956	203.612	R$ 176,73	R$ 296,215	R$ 868	R$ 1,455
1998	118.505	-6.549				

Table 5: DALY missing and cost by DALY avoid with investments in potable water and of Sewage treatment

4 Conclusion

A cost-effectiveness analysis has been successfully made to evaluate the sanitation program and situation of the morbidity by fecal–oral diseases in one of the largest and important municipalities of the Estate of Rio de Janeiro. The most important result is the social one, because children between 0 and 4 years old compose the target population. The approach is appropriate, because one is dealing with projects in which the benefits and/or costs are not easily measured and are difficult to be expressed in monetary units.

Then CEA analysis is applied to measure the impact of sanitation services versus the morbidity by fecal–oral diseases and focus the year of 1997. The effectiveness indicator chosen, DALY and the results of the experiment, during the period 1992-1998, have shown a decrease in the DALY assessed among children between 0 and 4 years old with fecal–oral diseases in this municipality.

The cost-effectiveness evaluation of sanitation projects with impacts in health and sanitation area using the DALY index is a simple and valuable method to show decision makers the importance of increasing the investments in social projects. Water and sewage systems for the population are basic examples of areas for potential application of the method. Other sectors should also be evaluated. Because of the reduction in the incidence of the morbidity among children with fecal–oral diseases, continued investments in this area are necessary. This would bring a significant contribution for further social advances.

Acknowledgements

This work was supported by OPS/OMS. (Project: Economical Evaluation of Projects with Impacts on Health Area – Case Study: Hydro Pollution in the Municipalities of Rio de Janeiro State, Brazil, Reference: HDP/HDR/RG-T/BRA/1483).

References

[1] R.M. Gold, J.E. Siegel, B.L. Russell and C.M. Weinstein, Cost effectiveness in health and medicine, *Oxford University Press*, New York, USA, (1996).

[2] J.L. Murray, D.A. Lopez, The global burden of disease – A comprehensive assessment of mortality and disability from diseases, injuries, and risk factors in 1990 and projected to 2020, *Library of Congress*, Washington DC, USA, (1996).

[3] N. Homedes, The disability adjusted life year (DALY) definition, measurement and potential use, *Human Capital Development and Operations Policy*, Washington DC, USA, (1999), (http://www.worldbank.org/html/extdr/hnp/hddflash/workp/wp_00068.html).

[4] M. Brachowicz, *Economic evaluation of projects with impacts in health field: Hydro pollution in Rio de Janeiro State*, Ph.D. Thesis, Federal University of Rio de Janeiro, (2001).

[5] R. Beaglehole, R. Bonita and T. Kjellstrom, Basic epidemiology, *World Health Organization,* Geneva, Switzerland, (1993).

[6] M. Brachowicz, J.G. Bellido and C.D. Neves, Daly-disability adjusted life years as an effectiveness indicator in health and sanitation, *International conference on emerging infectious diseases*, CDC - Atlanta, Georgia, USA, (2002).

[7] M. Brachowicz, C.D. Neves and C.A.N. Cosenza, Cost-benefit versus cost-effectiveness: Application in public health and environmental studies, *4th Latin-American Meeting of Mathematics and Ecology*, National University of Cuyo, Mendoza, Argentina, (1998) 24 - 28.

PERFORMANCE EVALUATION

PERFORMANCE ASSESSMENT OF DENTAL CLINICS THROUGH PC-ORIENTED DATA ENVELOPMENT ANALYSIS

MARCOS P.E. LINS, ANTONIO C. GONÇALVES,
ELIANE G. GOMES, ANGELA C.M. SILVA
Federal University of Rio de Janeiro, Brazil

Abstract

In this work, we assess the performance of the dental care program, which has been carried out by the Rio de Janeiro municipality, with regard to coverage of basic procedures in dentistry. The main drawback of classical Data Envelopment Analysis (DEA) models is that they impose radial projections onto the efficient frontier, leading to Pareto inefficient regions. Non-radial models can contribute to overcoming this problem. We present here a new non-radial method to project inefficient units, according to a least variance direction provided by the Principal Component Analysis (PCA) method. One interesting result is to allow distinction between inefficiency due to operational and assignment aspects. We hope that this work will contribute to helping the municipality in improving the efficiency of its clinics. As we suggest here, this could be accomplished either through redistribution of resources or improved coverage.

Key words: data envelopment analysis, dental clinic, principal components

1 Introduction

The Unified Health System (SUS) is the Brazilian governmental system for public healthcare, covering the whole country. Undertaking SUS activities is a responsibility shared among the federal government, state and city managers, and counts on important participation of the local society, through the health councils. Since the beginning of the 80's, the SUS has expanded the national coverage of healthcare assistance and its programs, developing the final decentralized structure for healthcare assistance, as a consequence of the public health network unification. During the 90's, the SUS structure was detailed by the basic operational norms established by the health ministry. The management levels then became the "full management" or "advanced system". The municipal district of Rio de Janeiro took over the "full management" of the municipal health system in 1999 and assumed, among other obligations, the responsibility for managing the operating units network, including those already operated by municipal authorities.

With the decentralization of SUS, each municipal district has a guaranteed minimum amount of resources for primary care, according to its population, unlike the others resources that are based on fees for services provided. This procedure not only minimizes the disparity in the resources distribution, but also allows the local manager to assume his real responsibilities.

Primary care is defined as the group of actions intended to promote health, prevention and rehabilitation. The primary care budget implanted due to the decentralization process of SUS provides each city with a minimum source of revenue that is calculated based on its population, unlike the other resources transfer.

Consolidation of this restructuring process requires training, dissemination of techniques and evaluation of impacts. Execution of the planned actions is continuously followed up by the local managers and occasionally by the health councils, based on systemized information, allowing qualitative and quantitative evaluation.

The most important activities developed by the oral care program in the municipal district of Rio de Janeiro are:
- Control of the primary causes of tooth decay through educational actions for promoting oral hygiene and fluoride application;
- Periodontal disease treatment;
- Support for dental emergencies (unscheduled appointments);
- Support for specialized treatments through specific forwarding (dental assistance for those who have physical or mental disabilities, endodontics, orthodontics and oral prosthesis.

Considering these activities, the procedures related to primary care in dentistry are classified into four categories:

1. Group procedures;

2. Preventive individual procedures;

3. Basic dentistry;

4. Basic surgical dentistry.

Groups of categories (1)-(2) and (3)-(4) constitute the preventive and conclusive procedures, respectively. Official assessment and control is based mainly on coverage index, defined by the ratio between the number of annual procedures and the target population. The latter is composed of pregnant women, and children under fourteen. Municipal public units in Rio de Janeiro performed 1,860,413 basic dental procedures in 2000, considering both preventive and conclusive. This corresponds to 1.3 actions/inhabitant/year, lower than the previous goal of 3.0 actions/inhabitant/year established by the health ministry.

2 Units and Variables

This work is concerned with performance assessment of state-owned dental clinics in the Rio de Janeiro municipality, with regard to coverage of basic dental procedures. We focused this study on 106 municipal health units, which provide basic dentistry services, distributed among 26 Administrative Regions (ARs). These regions constitute homogeneous Decision Making Units (DMUs) in the sense that they accomplish the same tasks with the same objectives according to the oral hygiene program. The map in Figure 1 shows some of these Administrative Regions for the Rio de Janeiro municipal district.

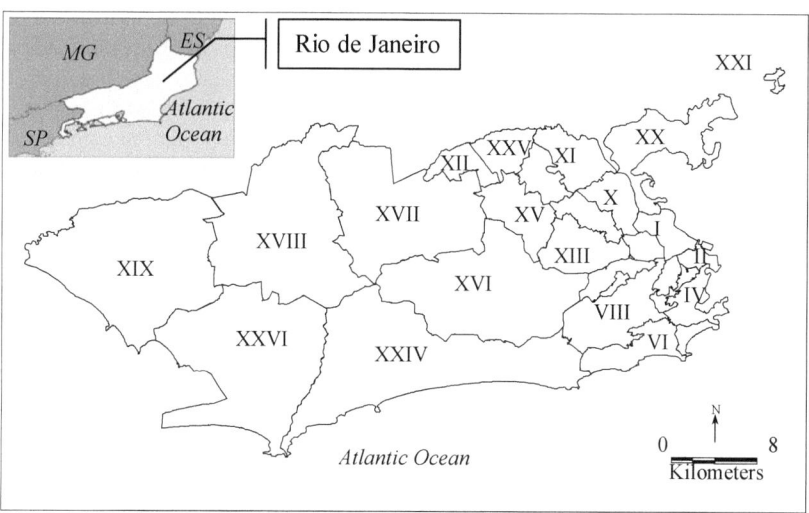

Figure 1: Rio de Janeiro municipal district and administrative regions

The choice of the variables should result from causal relationship, trying to explain the production of basic actions in the system, comprising both preventive (individual and collective) and conclusive procedures. The variables selected a priori, which may be endogenous (variables directly linked to the basic actions production) or exogenous (environmental variables), are shown in Table 1.

Kind	Variable
Endogenous Inputs	• Number of dentists • Number of working hours • Total number of clinics
Exogenous Inputs	• Average revenue of family head • Percentile of family heads with revenue up to 2 minimum salaries • Target population (children under 14 and pregnant women)
Output	• Number of preventive procedures • Number of conclusive procedures

Table 1: Variables selected a priori for evaluation of the oral hygiene program

The number of actions depends on the dentistry staff, weekly hours worked, and number of clinics. Besides, regions with lower income present greater demands for this free service. The variables that represent the average salary (based on the minimum) of the family head and the proportion of family heads with income up to 2 minimum salaries reflect this situation. Finally, it is important to consider that the population covered by the program is composed of children under 14 and pregnant women.

The data source for the endogenous variables and basic production in dentistry is the Information System of the Unified Health System (SIA/SUS), containing information about planning, control and evaluation of the actions and services in health clinics. Data regarding the administrative regions (exogenous variables) were computed from the Rio de Janeiro statistical annual (1996-1997). The number of pregnant women was based on the birth rate of 2.5%, applied to the total population in each region, as established by the ministry of health.

3 Data Envelopment Analysis (DEA)

The DEA approach was developed by Charnes et al. [2] to determine the efficiency of productive units, where it is not predominant or one does not want to consider the financial aspect. In the present case, DEA allows one to evaluate the relative efficiency of each administrative region as the assessed Decision Making Unit (DMU), taking into account the resources at its disposal (inputs) and the results achieved (outputs).

The objective of DEA consists of comparing a certain number of DMUs that accomplish similar tasks and differ in the amounts of inputs they consume and outputs they produce. There are two classic DEA models: Constant Returns to Scale (CRS or CCR) [2], which considers constant returns to scale, and Variable Returns to Scale (VRS or BCC) [7], which considers variable returns to scale and does not assume proportionality between inputs and outputs.

Besides identifying efficient DMUs, the DEA models allow one to measure and locate the inefficiency, based on a linear piecewise frontier production function that identifies the benchmarks for inefficient DMUs. This benchmark is determined by the projection of inefficient DMUs onto the efficiency frontier. There are two basic orientations for projections according to basic DEA models: input (when one wants to minimize the resources, keeping the outputs constant) and output orientation (when one wants to maximize the outputs without reducing the inputs).

In this article, the BCC model with output orientation is used, since one intends to increase the actions in dentistry. The linear programming problem for each DMU is presented below.

$$\text{Max } h_o = \sum_{i=1}^{m} v_i x_{io} - v_*$$

Subject to

$$\sum_{j=1}^{s} u_j y_{jo} = 1$$

$$\sum_{j=1}^{s} u_j y_{jk} - \sum_{i=1}^{n} v_i x_{ik} + v_* \leq 0 , \quad k = 1,...,n$$

$$u_j, v_i \geq 0 \quad \forall x, y$$

$$v_* \in \Re$$

In this model, for the DMU under analysis, the efficiency is given by h_o^{-1}, the inverse of the objective function; x_{ik} represents the input i of DMU k; y_{jk} represents the output j of DMU k; v_i and u_j represent the weights given to the inputs i and the outputs j, respectively; v_* is a scale factor (when positive, it indicates that DMU operates in a region of increasing returns to scale; if negative, decreasing returns to scale) [4]. If h_o^{-1} is equal to 1, the DMU under analysis is considered efficient. The decision variables of the LPP (I) are v_i, u_j and v_*.

The choice of the BCC model arises from the fact that an efficient region does not need to have the maximum relationship between outputs and inputs. This characteristic allows regions of different sizes, for instance, Campo Grande and Centro, to be analyzed using the same model.

4 Selection of Variables

The canonical correlation analysis calculates common weights wr and zi for all of the units, in such a way as to maximize the correlation among linear combinations of the two groups (inputs and outputs) [6]. Coefficients of canonical correlation are calculated for alternative pairs of groups of independent variables, yielding measures of correlation that were used for selecting the variables that will be used in the DEA analysis. In this case study, the variables that will constitute the DEA model are:

- Inputs: number of dentists (DENT) and the target population (TAR);
- Output: total actions (preventive + conclusive) (ACT).

The data set is presented in Table 2, where the DMUs are considered to be the municipalities in Rio de Janeiro. The variable Targeted Population is an indicator of the number of people that would demand basic attention services. It is an estimate for the number of children and pregnant women living in families whose head earns less than two minimum salaries.

The DMUs are basically decision-making units, represented here by 26 of the municipalities of the city of Rio de Janeiro. The inputs are the number of dentists and the targeted population. The outputs are the number of actions performed. The largest aimed population lives is Bangú and the number of selected dentists is 44. The target population is of 81,238 inhabitants and 170,336 actions were performed in the region. The smallest group lives in the island of Paquetá. The targeted population is of 205. The number of selected dentists is 5 and 3,507 actions were performed.

| DMUs | Inputs | | Output |
(Municipality)	Number of Dentists	Targeted Population	Number of Actions
I Portuária	6	5,720	22,105
II Centro	21	2,053	26,884
III Rio Comprido	17	7,529	66,836
IV Botafogo	25	5,667	83,629
V Copacabana	7	2,612	22,477
VI Lagoa	31	8,892	44,985
VII São Cristóvão	12	8,604	42,101
VIII Tijuca	13	5,705	35,818
IX Vila Isabel	38	7,023	91,465
X Ramos	22	50,726	34,340
XI Penha	19	34,172	58,424
XII Inhaúma	21	13,320	63,294
XIII Méier	50	25,721	103,245
XIV Irajá	20	16,652	71,818
XV Madureira	25	35,332	92,136
XVI Jacarepaguá	46	42,185	101,144
XVII Bangú	44	81,238	170,336
XVIII Campo Grande	39	56,396	146,758
XIX Santa Cruz	46	49,542	253,913
XX Ilha do Governador	32	13,973	122,375
XXI Paquetá	5	205	3,507
XXII Anchieta	10	19,521	47,231
XXIII Santa Tereza	6	3,493	23,416
XXIV Barra da Tijuca	21	6,293	30,488
XXV Pavuna	8	30,258	42,655
XXVI Guaratiba	11	15,181	59,033

Table 2: DMUs, Inputs and Output

Figures 2 and 3 show partial productivity, considering one input at a time. The former reveals that regions of Santa Cruz, Ilha do Governador, Vila Isabel, Botafogo and Paquetá present 100% efficiencies due to the high relationship between number of actions and the target population. Figure 3 reveals that regions of Santa Cruz, Guaratiba, Pavuna, Santa Teresa and Paquetá show 100% efficiencies due to the higher relationships between actions and number of dentists.

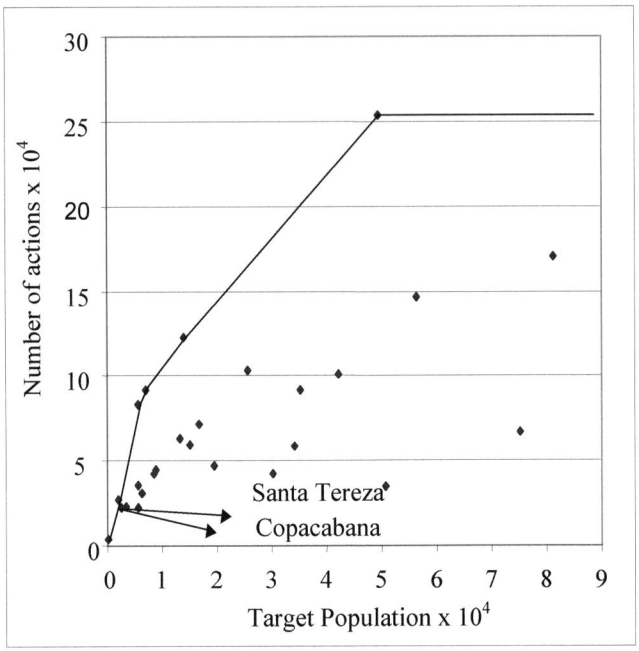

Figure 2: Relationship among TAR and ACT

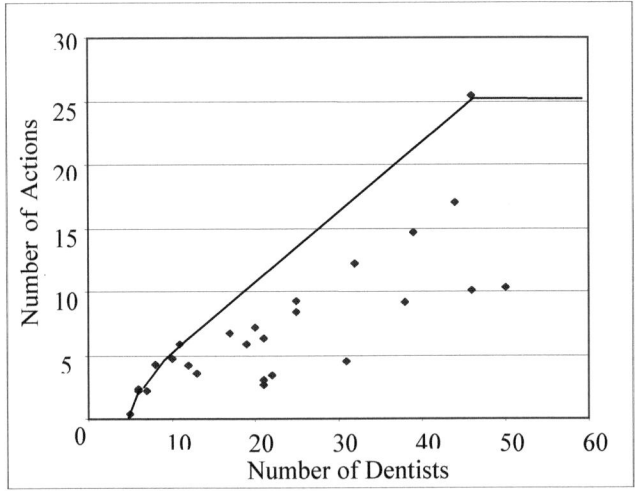

Figure 3: Relationship among the variables DENT and ACT

We remind that Paquetá presents 100% efficiency because it presents the smallest population among the municipalities. We can stress three different analyses:

1. The comparison between Ramos and Barra da Tijuca is interesting because both present similar values for the variables number of actions and dentists (Figure 3), with low productivity (actions per dentist). However, Barra da Tijuca presents a very reduced target population, about 1/8 that of Ramos (Figure 2). This suggests that the low productivity in Barra da Tijuca arose from the lack of demand, unlike in Ramos. Similar analysis can be accomplished comparing Jacarepaguá and Lagoa;

2. Ramos and Santa Cruz possess the same target population. However, the number of actions in Santa Cruz is about 7 times larger than that in Ramos;

3. The ARs of Jacarepaguá and Santa Cruz present 46 dentists and with a similar target population, but the number of actions in Santa Cruz is 2.5 times larger.

5 PC-Oriented Data Envelopment Analysis

The classical radial, input oriented, envelope DEA model, with Variable Returns to Scale (VRS) can be written:

$$\text{Min} \quad h$$
Subject to
$$hx \geq \sum \lambda_j x_j$$
$$y \leq \sum \lambda_j y_j$$
$$\lambda_j \geq 0, \quad \forall \ j$$
$$\sum_{j=1}^{n} \lambda_j = 1$$

A more generalized non-radial model based on Value Efficiency Analysis [7] was adopted here, allowing non-oriented projections.

$$\text{Max} \quad k + \xi . S^- + \xi . S^+$$

Subject to

$$X \lambda + S^- = X_o - kdx$$

$$Y \lambda - S^+ = Y_o + kdy$$

$$\lambda \geq 0$$

$$S^-, S^+ \geq 0$$

$$1\lambda = 1, \text{ where } \mathbf{1} \text{ is a unitary vector}$$

Where [dx, dy] is the vector that specifies the direction of projection. The central idea is to search for the direction of minimum variance, in order to project inefficient DMUs. This should point out projections that are, on average, closer to the observed DMU. The Principal Component Analysis (PCA) can accomplish this task, as it yields eigenvectors ranked according to the variance they add to the data set. So, the last eigenvector can be taken as the direction of projection in the non-oriented model [5,8].

Both PC-oriented and output-oriented DEA models were implemented, resulting 10 efficient and 16 inefficient regions. From now on, we are going to study the inefficient units. Table 3 shows three rows for each municipality (DMU). With regard to inputs and outputs, the first row presents observed data, the second, projections according to PC-oriented DEA and the third, projections resulting from output-oriented DEA model. We can also see, in the middle of the Table, the slacks-based measurement efficiencies - SBM [3], split into input and output (inverse) efficiencies. On the right, the Table displays the peer groups.

We notice that PC-DEA resulted in larger peer groups, indicating a lesser degree of Pareto-inefficiency. Lower efficiencies were found in the regions of Lagoa, Jacarepaguá, Ramos and Barra, that should more than double their production of actions, in order to achieve efficiency, according to output-oriented model.

We can devise 2 groups of Pareto-inefficient DMUs: the first composed of units that present Pareto efficient projections: Lagoa, Inhaúma and Meier, according to PC-DEA (Table 3), the second composed of those that present Pareto-inefficient projections.

Among the DMUs of this second group, some presented slacks with respect to target population (Ramos, Bangú, Campo Grande, Penha, Jacarepaguá, Portuária). Results for three of them (Ramos, Bangú and Campo Grande) presented slacks in both models: PC-DEA and Output oriented DEA, meaning that they have a large target population when compared to their number of dentists and actions.

On the other hand, among all the DMUs, only three: Centro, Méier and Jacarepaguá, resulted in a decrease in the number of dentists in both PC-DEA and Output oriented DEA models. This means that they present a large number of dentists, compared to their target population and number of actions.

Considering the above analysis, we can suggest relocation of dentists from Centro, Méier and Jacarepaguá to Ramos, Bangú and Campo Grande, involved by dotted line in Figures 5 and 6.

DMUs, Observed and Orientation		Dentists	Population	Actions	Efficiency of Inputs	Efficiency of Outputs	Peer Group
I - Portuária		6	5720	22105			
P.C.	Oriented	6	3312	22322	0,99	1,01	XXI ; XXIII
Output	projections	6	3493	23416	1,00	1,06	XXIII
II - Centro		21	2053	26884			
P.C.	Oriented	12	2053	30615	0,56	1,14	IV ; XXI
Output	projections	12	2053	30615	0,56	1,14	IV ; XXI
VI - Lagoa		31	8892	44985			
P.C.	Oriented	21	8892	82511	0,69	1,83	III ; IV ; XIX
Output	projections	31	8892	99091	1,00	2,20	IX ; XX
VII - São Cristóvão		12	8604	42101			
P.C.	Oriented	10	8604	48609	0,86	1,15	XIX ; XXIII ; XXVI
Output	projections	12	8604	53833	1,00	1,28	III ; XIX ; XXIII
VIII - Tijuca		13	5705	35818			
P.C.	Oriented	11	5705	43889	0,84	1,23	III ; XIX ; XXIII
Output	projections	13	5705	494	1,00	1,39	III ; IV ; XXIII
X - Ramos		22	50726	34340			
P.C.	Oriented	13	32765	70116	0,59	2,04	XIX ; XXV
Output	projections	22	37363	120487	1,00	3,51	XIX ; XXV
XI - Penha		19	34172	58424			
P.C.	Oriented	14	33418	77272	0,75	1,32	XIX ; XXV
Output	projections	19	34172	103778	1,00	1,78	XIX ; XXV ; XXVI

DMUs, Observed and Orientation		Dentists	Population	Actions	Efficiency of Inputs	Efficiency of Outputs	Peer Group
XII - Inhaúma		21	13320	63294			
P.C.	Oriented	17	13320	79733	0,80	1,26	III ; XIX ; XXIII
Output	projections	21	13320	92630	1,00	1,46	III ; XIX
XIII - Méier		50	25721	103245			
P.C.	Oriented	35	25721	162378	0,70	1,57	IV ; XIX ; XX
Output	projections	37	25721	165820	0,73	1,61	XIX ; XX
XIV - Irajá		20	16652	71818			
P.C.	Oriented	17	16652	85409	0,83	1,19	XIX ; XXIII ; XXVI
Output	projections	20	16652	97244	1,00	1,35	III ; XIX ; XXVI
XV - Madureira		25	35332	92136			
P.C.	Oriented	20	35332	110828	0,81	1,20	XIX ; XXV
Output	projections	25	35332	137101	1,00	1,49	XIX ; XXV
XVI - Jacarepaguá		46	42185	101144			
P.C.	Oriented	30	41388	164588	0,65	1,63	XIX ; XXV
Output	projections	43	42185	226706	0,94	2,24	XIX ; XX
XVII - Bangu		44	81238	170336			
P.C.	Oriented	37	44660	200428	0,84	1,18	XIX ; XXV
Output	projections	44	48527	242794	1,00	1,43	XIX ; XXV
XVIII – C. Grande		39	56396	146758			
P.C.	Oriented	32	42348	175097	0,82	1,19	XIX ; XXV
Output	projections	39	45990	214997	1,23	1,46	XIX ; XXV
XXII Anchieta		10	19521	47231			
P.C.	Oriented	9	19521	49548	0,94	1,05	XXIII ;XXV ; XXVI
Output	projections	10	19521	53419	1,00	1,13	XXIII ;XXV ; XXVI
XXI – B. da Tijuca		21	6293	30488			
P.C.	Oriented	15	6293	56056	0,69	1,84	III ; IV ; XXIII
Output	projections	21	6293	74292	1,00	2,44	III ; IV ; XXIII

Table 3: Results from PC-Oriented DEA

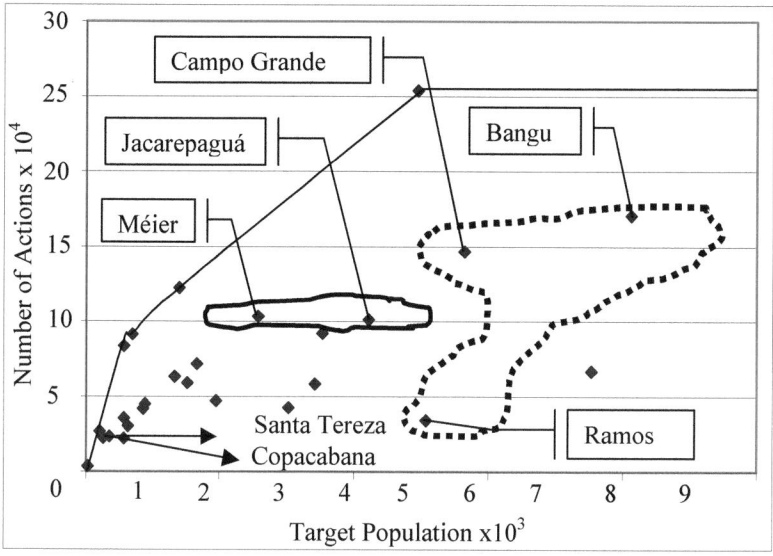

Figure 4: Regions presenting excessive target population

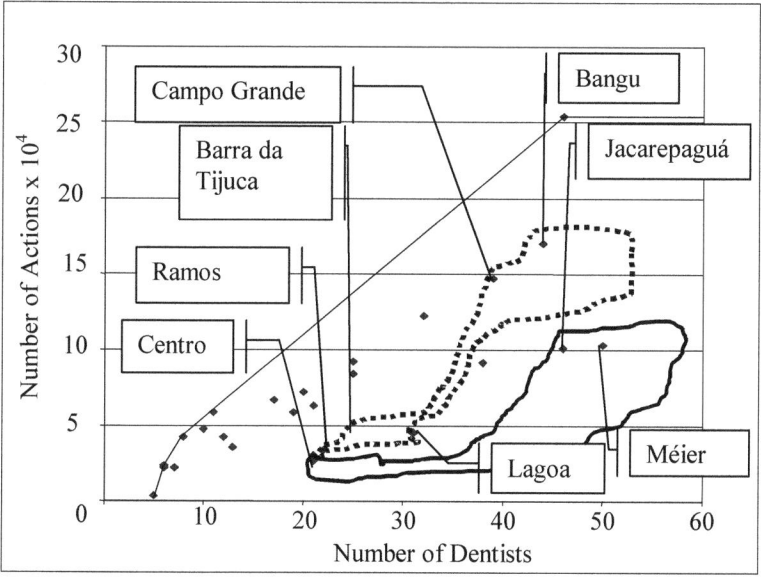

Figure 5: Regions presenting excessive number of dentists

6 Conclusions

This work introduces a new concept of target population, taking income into account, which allows a better capture of the demand for public health services. Two indicators used separately by the ministry of health and the municipal secretary of health: coverage of target population and productivity of dentists, were integrated. The methodology used for this purpose was the data envelopment analysis, which is characterized by establishing relationships among the productive units, considering the management of resources for the production of results. The analyses allowed to assess positive and negative aspects of the regions and to identify benchmarks and targets. We believe that the results of this work can support the managers of the Program of Dental Health of the Municipality Rio de Janeiro, as assistance in making decisions regarding economizing resources, labor transfer and coverage of the target population considering the demand patterns.

Comparison between output-oriented and PC-oriented DEA models shows that:
- Substantial increase in production required by the former model can be counterbalanced by some additional decrease in resources in the latter;
- Both models suffer from projections onto Pareto-inefficient portions of the frontier: 7 in the PC-oriented and 9 in output-oriented model.

The structure of the frontier could be more easily understood, allowing recommendations like relocation of resources (dentists).

References

[1] R. D. Banker, A. Charnes and W.W. Cooper, Some models for estimating technical scale inefficiencies in data envelopment analysis, *Management Science*, Vol: 30 (9), (1984) 1078-1092.

[2] A. Charnes, W.W. Cooper and E. Rhodes, Measuring the efficiency of decision-making units, *European Journal of Operational Research*, Vol: 2, (1978) 429-444.

[3] W.W. Cooper, L.M. Seiford and K. Tone, Data envelopment analysis: A comprehensive text with models, applications, References and DEA-Solver Software, *Kluwer Academic publishers*, USA, (2000).

[5] B. Fleury and H. Riedwyl, Multivariate statistics a practical approach, *Chapman and Hall*, USA, (1988).

109

[6] A.C. Gonçalves, *Um estudo de eficiência e cobertura das ações básicas do programa de saúde bucal da prefeitura da cidade do Rio de Janeiro*, Msc Thesis, Federal University of Rio de Janeiro, (2001).

[7] M. Halme and P. Korhonen, Restricting weights in value efficiency analysis, *European Journal of Operations Research*, Vol: 126, (2000) 175-188.

[8] I.T. Jolliffe, *Principal component analysis*, Mathematical Institute University of Kent Canterbury, England, (1986).

MULTIVARIATE ANALYSIS OF FECAL-ORAL DISEASES IN RIO DE JANEIRO

SANTIAGO S.R. CARVAJAL, JAIME G. BELLIDO,
MARIA BRACHOWICZ, CESAR DAS NEVES
Federal University of Rio de Janeiro, Brazil

Abstract

One of the most serious health harms in the state of Rio de Janeiro is the incidence of diseases associated with contamination, due to the pollution of the most important rivers that are used for water consumption. The ingestion of polluted water causes fecal-oral diseases. Several municipalities have shown that their sanitation systems are precarious and there is a lack of adequate treatment of water and sewage. This paper focuses in the infant population with less than four years of age and applies the Principal Components technique to the analysis of the reduction of sanitation variables. The analysis raise concerns about a number of environmental factors and their effects on the population studied. It identifies the municipalities with best health conditions, and those municipalities that present larger probability of fecal-oral diseases.

Key words: principal components, sanitation, fecal-oral diseases

1 Introduction

The state of Rio de Janeiro shows many problems associated with the environmental care. There is a lack of water and sewage treatment in some municipalities. One of the most serious health problems is the occurrence of diseases caused by the ingestion of contaminated water [1]. There is an increase in the incidence of fecal-oral diseases among children with less than four years of age. The effect on the population must be taken in serious consideration. Fifty-five children between 0 to 4 years old died in 1997, caused by diseases such as cholera, dysentery, typhoid fever, poliomyelitis and (A or E) hepatitis. Three thousand and ninety six cases showing diarrhea and other intestinal infections were treated in hospital [2].

This study was conducted, from 1992 to 1997, in the basin of the Paraiba do Sul River. This river supplies almost 90 % of the piped water, consumed by the population of Rio de Janeiro. The mortality rate of the inpatient children in the

Middle Paraiba region has increased 4,28 % during the period. This region embraces 12 municipalities and is located in the northwest of the basin. The data used here is collected from 42 municipalities during the year 1991.

2 The Data

Table 1 shows the municipalities of each micro-regions of the Paraiba do Sul River basin. The data, related at municipality - base level, in1991, according to the Brazilian demographic census. The data collection is made in three different places:

- The Center of Information and Data of Rio de Janeiro (CIDE), [3], [4], [5];
- The Unified Health Data System (DATASUS) [6] and [7];
- The Brazilian Institute of Geography and Statistics (IBGE) [8].

The following variables, expressed in percentage of people, are obtained:

- Do have piped water at home (ACI);
- Do not have piped water at home (ASC);
- Do have sanitary installation at home (ISD);
- Shares sanitary outdoor facilities (ISC);
- Do not have sanitary indoor facilities (NIS);
- Uses trash collection service (LCD);
- Burns the trash (LXE);
- Throws the trash in the river, pond, lake or floor (LJX).

The other variables, expressed in percentage, are the numbers of:

- Illiterate people (NAL);
- Hospital beds available (LEH);
- Children, between 0 and 4 years old, with fecal-oral diseases (DIM);
- Children population from 0 to 4 years old (PIM).

MICRO-REGION	MUNICIPALITIES
ITAPERUNA	01. Italva
	02. Itaperuna
	03. Laje do Muriaé
	04. Natividade
	05. Porciúncula
SANTO ANTÔNIO DE PÁDUA	06. Cambuci
	07. Itaocara
	08. Miracema
	09. S. Antônio de Pádua
CAMPOS DOS GOYTACAZES	10. Campos dos Goytacazes
	11. São Fidelis
	12. São João da Barra
TRÊS RIOS	13. Paraíba do Sul
	14. Sapucaia
	15. Três Rios
CANTAGALO/CORDEIRO	16. Cantagalo
	17. Carmo
	18. Cordeiro
NOVA FRIBURGO	19. Bom Jardim
	20. Duas Barras
	21. Nova Friburgo
	22. Sumidouro
SANTA MARIA MADALENA	23. Santa Maria Madalena
	24. São Sebastião do Alto
	25. Trajano de Morais
VALE DO PARAIBA RJ	26. Barra Mansa
	27. Itatiaia
	28. Piraí
	29. Resende
	30. Rio Claro
	31. Volta Redonda
BARRA DO PIRAÍ	32. Barra do Piraí
	33. Rio das Flores
	34. Valença
VASSOURAS	35. Engenheiro Paulo de Frontin
	36. Mendes
	37. Miguel Pereira
	38. Paty do Alferes
	39. Vassouras
SERRANA	40. Petrópolis
	41. São José do Vale do Rio Preto
	42. Teresópolis

Table 1: Micro-Region and Municipalities of the Paraiba do Sul
RiverBasin

3 Methods

In order to assess both, the associated risk factors of morbidity by fecal-oral diseases in between 0-4 years old children and the status of the sanitation conditions in the municipalities of Rio de Janeiro State, we used the principal components technique of the statistical multivariate analysis. This technique transforms a set of p correlated observed variables X_1, X_2, ..., Xp into another set of p uncorrelated indices Y_1, Y_2, ... ,Y_p using the algebraic properties of the eigenvalues (characteristic values) and the eigenvectors (characteristic vectors) of the variance-covariance matrix of the X-variables. The indices are ordered so that Y_1 displays the largest amount of variation, Y_2 displays the second largest amount of variation and so on. In other words, if Var (Y_i) denotes a variance of Y_i, it will result in Var (Y_1) $\geq$ Var (Y_2) $\geq$ ... $\geq$ Var (Y_p). The Y_is are nominated the principal components.

Usually, the values of most variances on the principal components are so low that they can be considered negligible. Therefore, only few components with not negligible variances take account by the total variation in the data set. The variation is explained in the p original X variables using a smaller number of Y variables [9], [10].

3.1 Procedure for the Principal Components Analysis

Let us consider a set of data on p variables, X_1, X_2, ... , X_p, for n individuals, (see Table 2), where x_{ij} denotes the observation or the sample value of the X_j variable for the ith individual.

Individual	X_1	X_2	X_3	...	X_p
1	x_{11}	x_{12}	x_{13}	...	x_{1p}
2	x_{21}	x_{22}	x_{23}	...	x_{2p}
Λ	Λ	Λ	Λ		Λ
n	x_{n1}	x_{n2}	x_{n3}	...	x_{np}

Table 2: Data for Principal Components Analysis

Let s_{ii} and s_{ij} be, respectively, the sample variance of X_i and the sample covariance of X_i and X_j (i , j = 1, 2, ... , p);

Let S = (s_{ij}) be the sample variance-covariance matrix of X variables and let λ_1, λ_2, ... , λ_p the eigenvalues of this matrix ordered so that $\lambda_1 \geq \lambda_2 \geq ... \geq \lambda_p$.

For $j = 1, 2, ..., p$, let $a_j = [a_{1j}, a_{2j}, ..., a_{pj}]^T$ be the eigenvector associated with the jth eigenvalue of matrix S, with the constraint $a_j^T a_j = 1$.

Consequently, the first principal component of the complex of sample values of the variables $X_1, X_2, ..., X_p$ is the linear combination $Y_1 = a_1^T X$, where $X = [X_1, X_2, ..., X_p]^T$.

That is to say,

$$Y_1 = a_{11}X_1 + a_{21} X_2 + ... + a_{p1} X_p$$

The coefficients are the elements of the eigenvector associated with the greatest eigenvalue λ_1 of the sample variance-covariance matrix of the observations. The a_{i1} are unique up to multiplication by a scale factor, and if there scaled so that $a_1^T a_1 = 1$, the eigenvalue λ_1 is interpreted as the sample variance of Y_1.

The second principal component is the linear combination:

$$Y_2 = a_{12}X_1 + a_{22} X_2 + ... + a_{p2} X_p$$

The coefficients are the elements of the eigenvector of the variance-covariance matrix and corresponding to the second largest eigenvalue λ_2. With the constraint $a_2^T a_2 = 1$, the sample variance of the second component is λ_2.

In general, the jth principal component of the sample of p-variate observations is the linear combination:

$$Y_j = a_j^T X \quad \text{or} \quad Y_j = a_{1j}X_1 + a_{2j} X_2 + ... + a_{pj} X_p$$

The coefficients are the elements of the eigenvector of the sample variance-covariance matrix S corresponding to the jth largest eigenvalue. With the constraint $a_j^T a_j = 1$, the sample variance of the jth component is λ_j.

Therefore, the total system variance is:

$$\lambda_1 + \lambda_2 + ... + \lambda_p = \text{trS},$$

Where trS denotes trace of S. The proportion of the total variation explained by the jth principal component is, then,

$$\lambda_j / \text{trS} .$$

Usually, few principal components are needed to explain a major proportion of the total variance. In many applications, some variables have an undue influence on the principal components. In order to avoid this fact, it is usual to consider the variables X_1, X_2, ... , X_p to start having zero mean and variance one at the beginning of the analysis. This signifies to work with the sample correlation matrix R, instead of the sample variance-covariance matrix S. All elements of the R diagonal are one, that is to say, $trR = n$. In this case, the proportion of total variance explained by the principal component Y_j is λ_j/n.

Table 3 displays the mean and variance values for each one of the variables studied. In the present work, some of the variables have their mean and variance lower than the corresponding values of the other variables (see Table 3). For that reason the sample correlation R matrix is chosen. Table 4 shows the sample correlation R matrix.

Variables	Mean	Variance
ACI	838.294	9899.879
ASC	155.165	10196.311
ISD	893.403	4162.784
ISC	32.156	731.158
NIS	67.900	3778.819
NAL	299.334	3616.763
LEH	5.404	39.304
LCD	443.658	48579.219
LXE	426.376	33419.392
LXJ	123.425	6880.948
PIM	97.070	56.546
DIM	2.539	6.512

Table 3: Mean and Variance of the Variables

	ACI	ASC	ISD	ISC	NIS	NAL	LEH	LCD	LXE	LXJ	PIM	DIM
ACI	1.00	-.998	.815	-.002	-.876	-.801	.128	.549	-.449	-.485	-.310	-.080
ASC	-.998	1.00	-.812	.002	.878	.794	-.160	-.538	.439	.481	.314	.077
ISD	.815	-.812	1.00	-.360	-.905	-.570	.024	.498	-.450	-.341	.077	-.312
ISC	-.002	.002	-.360	1.00	-.061	-.173	.121	-.064	.152	-.165	-.198	.390
NIS	-.876	.878	-.905	-.061	1.00	.681	-.134	-.490	.401	.434	.020	.152
NAL	-.801	.794	-.570	-.173	.681	1.00	-.209	-.703	.545	.673	.580	-.082
LEH	.128	-.160	.024	.121	-.134	-.209	1.00	-.024	.094	-.183	-.307	.304
LCD	.549	-.538	.498	-.064	-.490	-.703	-.024	1.00	-.932	-.599	-.226	.086
LXE	-.449	.439	-.450	.152	.401	.545	.094	-.932	1.00	.270	.100	.024
LXJ	-.485	.481	-.341	-.165	.434	.673	-.183	-.599	.270	1.00	.391	-.283
PIM	-.310	.314	.077	-.198	.020	.580	-.307	-.226	.100	.391	1.00	-.296
DIM	-.080	.077	-.312	.390	.152	-.082	.304	.086	.024	-.283	-.296	1.00

Table 4: Correlation Matrix

4 Results

The SAS statistical software enterprise guide is used for the multivariate analysis of the data. The analysis of the variance induces one to take until the fifth component, for it gives 90% of data variability. (See Table 5 and Figure 1).

Component Number	Percentage of Variance	Cumulative Percentage
1	46.25320	46.25320
2	18.46142	64.71462
3	11.03836	75.75298
4	7.55810	83.31108
5	6.40179	89.71286
6	4.82827	94.54113
7	3.78542	98.32655
8	1.01455	99.34110
9	0.63814	99.97925
10	0.02075	100.00000
11	0.00000	100.00000
12	0.00000	100.00000

Table 5: Percentage of Variance and Cumulative Variance

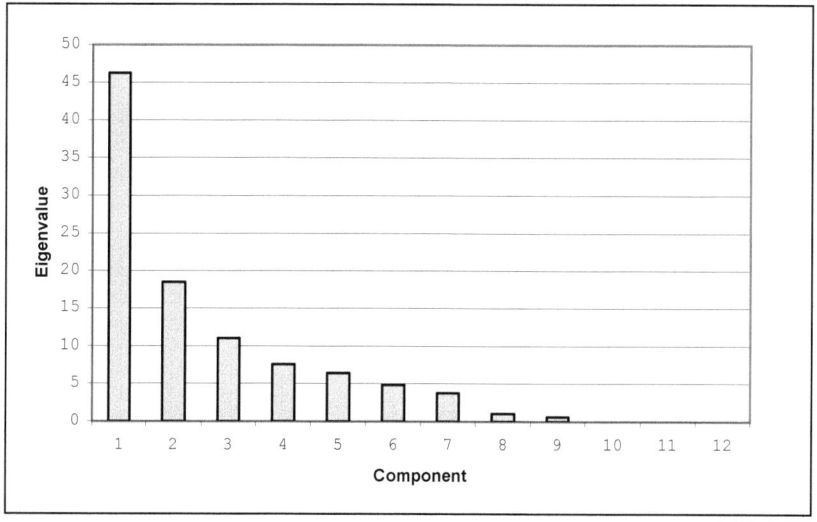

Figure 1: Screen Plot of the eigenvalues of the principal components

Table 6 displays the eigenvectors associated with the five first eigenvalues, whose coefficients can be used to describe the relationship between the municipalities and the different variables considered in this study.

Variable	Prin 1	Prin 2	Prin 3	Prin 4	Prin 5
ACI	-.39514	-.05100	0.21781	0.06071	0.04270
ASC	0.39366	0.04494	-.23515	-.04133	0.08325
ISD	-.34485	-.32471	0.18609	-.05218	0.15679
ISC	0.00431	0.43299	0.11958	0.71972	-.00248
NIS	0.36711	0.14163	-.28163	-.23145	-.18743
NAL	0.38328	-.17904	0.02823	0.00537	0.22553
LEH	-.06846	0.32880	0.37196	-.53918	0.47469
LCD	-.33045	0.01290	-.52375	-.02343	0.13881
LXE	0.27547	0.10491	0.57147	0.05525	-.15970
LXJ	0.27616	-.27193	0.10722	-.03699	-.034622
PIM	0.14901	-.43924	0.00733	0.34954	0.62661
DIM	0.00655	0.51400	-.13201	0.04938	0.45682

Table 6: Eigenvectors associated to the five larger characteristic roots

In particular, one looks at the bi-plot: "principal component 1 versus principal component 2". Figure 2 shows the results of the 42 municipalities versus the 12 variables of the model considering the first two main components. It can be seen that among ten of the most important municipalities the municipalities, (Petrópolis, Nova Friburgo, Volta Redonda, Valença, Mendes, Itatiaia, Tres Rios, Cordeiro, Resende and Teresópolis), only three of them (Petrópolis, Volta Redonda and Valença) have appropriate sanitation at home facilities. Their population is more literate than the others municipalities that show acceptable sanitation conditions: such as piped water, drain sewage and trash collection service.

The municipality of São Sebastião do Alto presents the worst conditions of sanitation and quality of life, followed by the municipalities of Sumidouro, São João da Barra, Trajano de Morais, Santa Maria Madalena, Cambucí, Lage do Muriaé, Italva, Natividade.

The municipality with the largest population (Porciúncula) shows a considerable number of 'illiterate' residents not served with piped water, drain sewage, sanitary facilities at home and also without trash collection service. Unlike Sumidouro, where the trash is thrown 'outside the houses' (in the river, pond, lakes, floor, etc), the municipalities of Cambuci, Natividade and Italva, show a higher amount of trash being buried.

Itaocara and Santo Antônio de Padua, present more '0 to 4 years old children' with fecal-oral diseases, caused by intestinal infectious diseases due to the ingestion of polluted water from human and animals waste. Those two and other six municipalities (Miracema, Itaperuna, São Fidélis, Carmo, Barra do Piraí, and Miguel Pereira), present a larger number of common sanitary facilities, as they are also located close to the variable 'number of hospital beds available'.

A large number of '0 to 4 years old children' is also observed in six of the municipalities (Duas Barras, Rio das Flores, Bom Jardim, Paty do Alferes, Sapucaia and São José do Vale do Rio Preto).

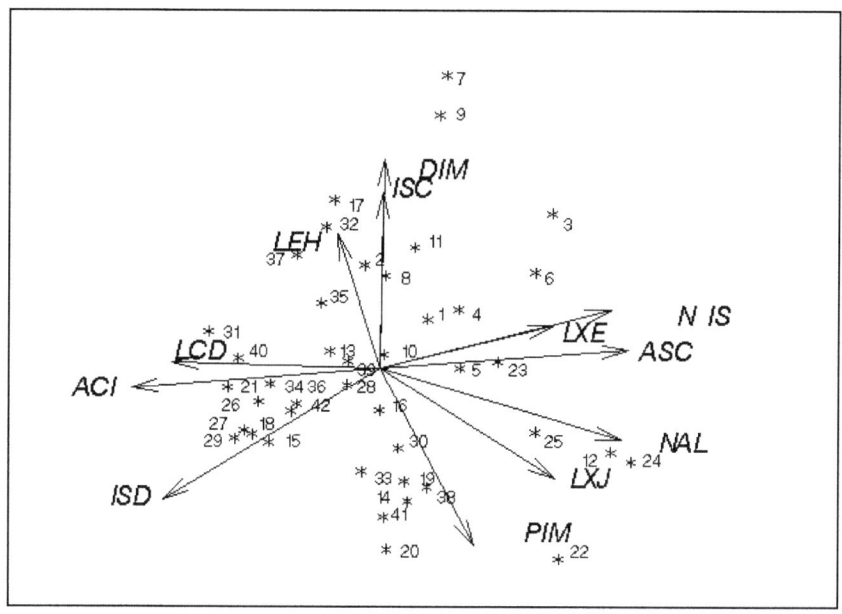

Figure 2: Bi-plot of the 42 municipalities Vs the 12 variables of the model considering the first two main components

5 Conclusion

The technique of the principal components applied to the study of public sanitation and the others variables of this study, besides reducing in a considerable way the number of the inputs variables, also presents reliable results with regard to location of the variables and the municipalities. It identifies those municipalities with best health condition and those municipalities that present larger probability of fecal-oral diseases such as cholera, dysentery, typhoid and paratyphoid fever, poliomyelitis, viral hepatitis and intestinal infections for lack or precarious sanitation.

Many of the municipalities of Rio de Janeiro studied here have shown that their sanitation systems are precarious and there is a lack of adequate treatment of water and sewage. Those problems increase the incidence of children between 0 and 4 years old with fecal-oral diseases, also, other influences, such as poverty, raise concerns about a number of environmental factors and their effects on the population, must be taken in serious consideration.

Acknowledgments

This work was supported by OPS/OMS. (Project: Economical Evaluation of Projects with Impacts on Health Area – Case Study: Hydro Pollution in the Municipalities of Rio de Janeiro State, Brazil, Reference: HDP/HDR/RG-T/BRA/1483)

References

[1] F.E. McJunkin, Agua y salud humana, OPS/OMS, *Ed. Limusa*, México D.F., (1988).

[2] M. Brachowicz, *Economic evaluation of projects with impacts in health field, case study: Hydro pollution in Rio de Janeiro State*, Dsc Thesis, Federal University of Rio de Janeiro, (2001).

[3] CIDE - Center of Information and Data of Rio de Janeiro, População do Rio de Janeiro 1872 – 1996, CD-ROM, General Office of State of Planning and Control - *Government of the State of Rio de Janeiro*, (1998).

[4] CIDE - Center of Information Data. Rio de Janeiro, Anuário Estatístico do Estado do Rio de Janeiro 1997, CD-ROM, General Office of State of Planning and Control - *Government of the State of Rio de Janeiro*, (1998).

[5]   CIDE - Center of Information and Data of Rio de Janeiro, Guia Sócio - Econômico dos Municípios do Estado de Rio de Janeiro, General Office of State of Planning and Control - *Government of the State of Rio de Janeiro*, (1998).

[6]   DATASUS - System of Data of the Unique System of Health, Lista de Tabulação, (http://www.datasus.gov.br/cid-10/cid-10.htm), *Classificação Internacional de Doenças,* Rio de Janeiro, (1998).

[7]   L. Heller, Saneamento e saúde, *OPAS/OMS,* Brasília, (1997).

[8]   IBGE - Brazilian Institute of Geography and Statistics, *Sistema de Informações Municipais*, CD-ROM, Rio de Janeiro, (1999).

[9]   B.F.J. Manly, Multivariate statistical methods: A primer, *Chapman and Hall*, London, New York. (1986).

[10] D.F. Morrison, Multivariate statistical methods, Second Edition, *McGraw-Hill Book Company*, (1976).

DECISION SUPPORT SYSTEMS

MODELING THE DYNAMICS OF INTENSIVE CARE UNIT OF A PUBLIC HOSPITAL AS A RENEWAL PROCESS

MARCO A. S. LAVRADOR [1], FÁTIMA M. H. S. P. DA SILVA [1],
MARIO J. FERREIRA DE OLIVEIRA [2]
[1]Universidade de São Paulo,
[2]Universidade Federal do Rio de Janeiro, Brazil

Abstract

A review of the previous work on modeling Intensive Care Units (ICU) reveals that the fitting of probability distribution is the usual way to analyze data resulting from observation of the patient's Length Of Stay (LOS). It is noticeable that there are in the literature only few attempts of modeling the dynamics of the use of beds. In this work the dynamics of both the use of beds and of the whole ICU are modeled. The first is treated as an alternate renewal process and the former as a parallel renewal process. Under the assumption that times between renewals follow an exponential distribution, one deduces the Probability Density Function (PDF) for the time until the n-th renewal. Starting from this function, it is possible to generate parameters that can be useful as a basis for administrative and planning policies. The data used for the parameter estimates was collected at the Hospital Cardoso Fontes, which is a general public hospital in the city of Rio de Janeiro. The PDF of the time until the n-th discharge of the ICU patients are obtained under the assumption that the time between renewals follows an exponential distribution.

Key words: length of stay, renewal process, ICU

1 Introduction

An examination of the OR studies in the health services both in the United Kingdom and in the United States permits a classification of efforts roughly according to problem areas. There is a set of problems related to demand and supply of facilities, from which one can trace the theoretical background of the problem studied here. One is particularly concerned with the dynamics of intensive care unit, which is related with the type of illness and the length of stay in hospitals. Both phenomena of need and duration of services are largely probabilistic in nature, though these are sometimes dominated by systematic factors such as seasonal variation, schedules and so on. Such problems have attracted the attention of the earlier researchers [1], [2], [3], [4].

It is possible to trace by the 1960's the growing interest in the admission systems. According to previous reviews [5], [6], [7], a relevant number of published papers, that mention LOS studies, can be found in the literature. Due to a great expansion of the field, to review such a wealth of new material in a succinct manner and give the necessary credits to all researchers would be very difficult. An excellent source of references and review of applications made at meetings of the working group Operational Research Applied to Health Services [8] and more recent work can be found in the literature [9], [10].

The Hospital Cardoso Fontes is a 265 beds general hospital and serves, with other minor hospitals, a population of 450000 inhabitants of the Barra da Tijuca and Jacarepaguá districts. Several aspects of the current admission system have been analyzed: the physical lay-out, the flow of patients, the human and material resources, the availability of data, the forms to be filled in, the flow of information and other details of the current admission system. To obtain the necessary background information, one must take into consideration a series of factors, which are directly or indirectly related to the admission of the patients such as usual patterns of seeking and receiving medical care and factors affecting the urgency of need for such care.

The main difficulty associated with the ICU is the uncertainty attached to the admission and discharge because the short notice involved affords little planning flexibility. Thus, in periods of high demand one is frequently forced to refuse requests for admission. The administrative problem is two-fold and can be summarized as follows. While on the one hand, reasonable notice about the potential candidate to use the facility has to be given to the ICU, on the other hand, however the longer the notice the greater is the administrator uncertainty of the future bed composition and human and material resources available.

Thus, for sufficient information to be given to the administration and, at the same time, for efficient running of the facility to be achieved, an adequate method is required to support planning. In other words, one should model the dynamics of both the use of beds and of the whole ICU to generate parameters that could be used to guide policies. There is more to the task of the designing an adequate method than meets the eye however, for the admission is a continuous process in which patients arrived every day as serious emergency cases.

It is argued that information is a key point to help the hospital administration reorganize the services. M. Lavrador [7] has made a very important contribution to the use of the available information in the ICU of the same hospital. In his work the most of important data regarding the admission, stay and discharge by the ICU patients are organized in a data bank and an information support system provides means to help the staff of the ICU. The model presented here is based upon this particular system.

2 The Model

Renewal Process is a well-known theory in the field of system reliability. The main applications, in this field, falls in the planning and maintenance policies of system's components that change as time evolves. We say that a renewal occurs every time a system's component is replaced. The readers who want to deepen in the subject or need a more detailed explanation are referred elsewhere [7], [12], [13]. The foundation of this theory, in a glance, follows.

Consider a stochastic process $\{N(t); t \geq 0\}$. $\{N(t); t \geq 0\}$ is a counting process if:
1. $N(t) \in \{0,1,2,...\}$;

2. $s<t \Rightarrow N(s) \leq N(t)$;

3. $s<t \Rightarrow N(t)-N(s)$ is the number of events in (s, t].

In a counting process:

1. The state space is $\{0,1,2,...\}$

2. The only possible transition is: $i \rightarrow i+1$

If the random variables X_i denote the time between renewals and, the variables in the sequence $(X_1, X_2, X_3,)$ are independent and have the same distribution, this process is called an ordinary renewal process. From the distribution of X we can access the distribution of time S_n until the nth renewal, that is:

$$S_n = \sum_{i=1}^{n} X_i$$

The PDF of S_n is a n-folder convolution, so Laplace transforms is the key methodology to find this PDF.

Starting from the distribution of S_n, we can obtain parameters to aid politics of planning. For example, if N_t denotes the number of renewals until the time t, then the events are equivalent:

$N_t < n \Leftrightarrow S_n > t$

This implies that: $P(N_t < n) = P(S_n > t)$

Examples of parameters that can aid planning politics are: the mean number of renewals in a time interval, its variance, periodicity of events, etc. A review of the previous work on modeling ICU [7], reveals that the fitting of probability distribution is the usual way to analyze data resulting from observation of the patient's length of stay, but only few attempt of modeling the dynamics of the use of beds. In this paper the dynamics of both the use of beds and the whole ICU are modeled in the context of renewal process.

3 Objective

The main goal of this paper is to produce a model, which represents the dynamics of both the use of beds and the whole ICU of a public hospital using the renewal theory framework. The beds are treated as an alternate renewal process and the whole ICU as a parallel renewal process. Under the assumption that times between renewals follow an exponential distribution, one deduces the PDF for the time until the n-th renewal. The data, used for the parameter estimates, is composed of a sample of 925 cases from the ICU of a general public hospital.

4 A Single Bed as Renewal Process

One can imagine using a bed as an ordinary renewal process. In a simpler model, a renewal occurs every time a patient is discharged and a replacement follows immediately. That is, a new patient is allocated to the bed immediately after the vacancy of the bed. An example of a bed as an ordinary renewal process is shown in Figure1.

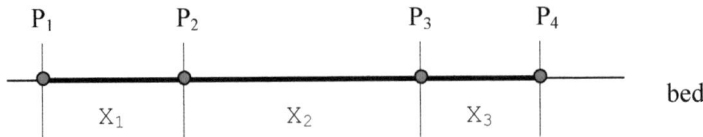

Figure 1: A bed as an ordinary renewal process

It can be seen in Figure 1 that, P_i attempts to represent the allocation of patient i to the bed. The variables X_i are the LOS, that is the time between discharges. In this case, the variable S_n is obtained as in section 1. After the discharge, the bed is vacant for a certain time, until the arrival of the next patient. It is clear that this is not a realistic model to modeling bed dynamics. Let:

- b denotes busy;
- v denotes vacant;
- X_i is time elapsed during the stay of patient i;
- Y_i is time that the bed remains vacant after the discharge of patient i;
- Z_i is time cycle of the bed between the arrivals of two patients.

Figure 2 shows a more realistic situation for the dynamics of the bed, and can be modeled as an alternate renewal process.

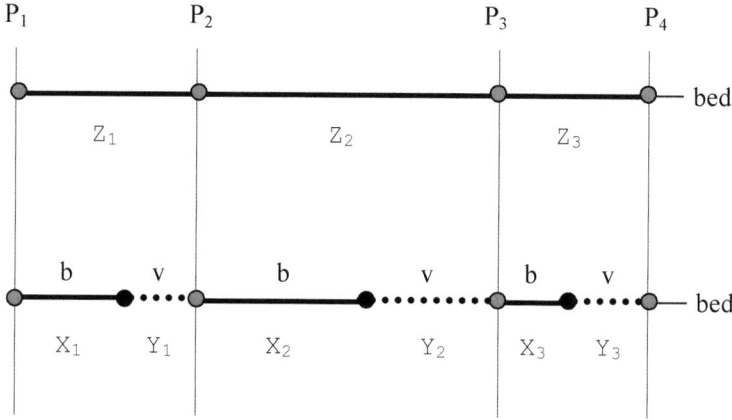

Figure 2: A bed as an alternate renewal process

As a function of the variables X_i and Y_i, the variable Z_i, the time of the ith cycle is given by: $Z_i = X_i + Y_i$. In this case, two processes exist: one formed by busy and other by vague: $(X_1, X_2, X_3,)$ and $(Y_1, Y_2, Y_3,)$. In the first, each component has an fdp given by $f_1(x)$ and, in the second by $f_2(y)$.

For effect of analysis they can be thought as an ordinary renewal process $(X_1+Y_1, X_2+Y_2, X_3+Y_3,)$. Its fdp would be given by the convolution of f_1 and f_2, with Laplace transforms: f_1* and f_2*.

The mean number of renewals in $(0,t)$ satisfies:

$$m^*(s) = \frac{f_1^*(s) f_2^*(s)}{s(1 - f_1^*(s) f_2^*(s))}$$

If interest exists in some characteristic of a particular process, it can be worked directly with this original process. For instance, if W is the probability of the bed to be busy at the time t, it can be shown that:

$$W^*(s) = \frac{1 - f_1^*(s)}{s(1 - f_1^*(s) f_2^*(s))} = m^*_2(s) - m^*_1(s) + 1$$

In particular, if the times among renewals are given by an exponential distribution, with parameters λ_v for vacancy and λ_b for busy, Lavrador [7] obtained the fdp of time (z) until the nth cycle (busy + vacancy) is:

$$S_n(z) = \lambda_v^n \lambda_b^n \frac{z^n (\lambda_b - \lambda_v)^{-n+1} e^{-\frac{1}{2}(\lambda_b + \lambda_v)z} A_{n-\frac{1}{2}}(\frac{\lambda_b - \lambda_v}{2} z)}{\Gamma(n)}$$

where:

$$A_{n-\frac{1}{2}}(w) = \gamma_{n-1}(w) \sinh(w) + \gamma_{-n}(w) \cosh(w)$$

The formula below extracted from [11] allows us to solve S_n for every n:

$$\gamma_{n-1}(w) - \gamma_{n+1}(w) = (2n+1) w^{-1} \gamma_n(w)$$

$$\gamma_0(w) = w^{-1} \quad and \quad \gamma_1(w) = -w^{-2}$$

5 A Whole Infirmary as Renewal Process

Despite the fact that a bed dynamics can be modeled in the context of renewal process, this is only a single element of a system, in this case a whole infirmary or a whole ICU. In general the main interest for the hospital manager falls in the management of whole system (infirmary or ICU). The management of a single, isolated bed cannot be very helpful to the manager.

The study of dynamics of whole infirmary (or ICU) should take into account the relationship among all the beds. But, in this case, the fact of the beds to be empty or busy loses the sense. In order to model the dynamics of the infirmary as a whole, based on the dynamics of each of the beds, we shall use the simplest renewal model to each bed: as an ordinary renewal process. Thus, the dynamics of the infirmary as a whole will be a composition of the individual bed dynamics, originating a new parallel renewal process.

Figure 3 illustrates this situation in an infirmary with p beds.

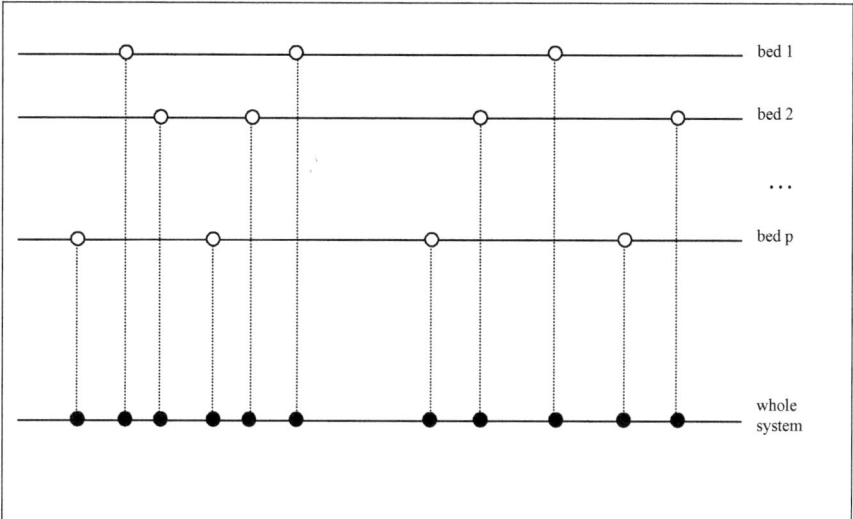

Figure 3: A whole infirmary as a parallel renewal process

The old process creates a new process. The renewals in the new process are projections of the other processes renewals. It can be shown that if the distribution of the time between renewals each bed is given by an exponential distribution with parameter λ', the resulting distribution for the time among renewals in the new process will also be exponential, with parameter $\lambda = p\lambda'$.

For the case above, Lavrador [7] obtained the fdp of time until the nth renewal:

$$S_n(y) = \frac{\lambda^n y^{n-1} e^{-\lambda y}}{\Gamma(n)}$$

6 Applying the Models to ICU Data

We use data from an ICU to apply these models.

The data used for the parameter estimates was gathered during the period of two years eight beds ICU and resulting in a total of 925 cases during this period.1981 to 1983, at the ICU of the General Hospital of Jacarepaguá, located in the city of

Rio de Janeiro, Brazil. In order to reduce the amount of algebra involved in the determination of the fdp of the times until the nth renewal, some few aberrant cases of LOS data was truncated. This allowed a goodness of fit for exponential distributions to the times among renewals, simplifying the determination of the PDF for S_n.

6.1 Applying the Model of Alternate Renewal Process to a Single Bed

Once we didn't know the original allocation of the patients to the beds, only for illustration effect a routine developed by Lavrador [7] was used to allocate patient randomly to the eight beds.

After we make the allocations, we selected the bed number 5 for application of the proposed methodology. The recomposition of this bed took to 120 patients and 119 vacancies.

The parameter λ for the exponential distributions resulting in $\lambda_b = 0.1739$ for busy and in $\lambda_v = 0.2924$ for vacancy.

According to theory presented the fdp for the whole cycle was:

$$f(z) = -0.4287(e^{-0.1739z} - e^{-0.2924z})$$

Now, using the formula for S_n presented in section 3, we can access the fdp for every n. For instance, the fdp for the time until the second and third cycles are:

$$S_2(z) = -0.0218z^2 e^{-0.2332z}\left(-\frac{\sinh(-0.0593z)}{0.0035z^2} - \frac{\cosh(-0.0593z)}{0.0593z}\right)$$

$$S_3(z) = 0.0046813z^3 e^{-0.23315z}(A+B)$$

$$where: A = -(\frac{1}{0.05925z} + \frac{3}{0.000208z^3})\sinh(-0.05925z)$$

$$B = -\frac{3}{0.003511z^2}\cosh(-0.05925z)$$

Figure 4 illustrates the graphics of the fdp.

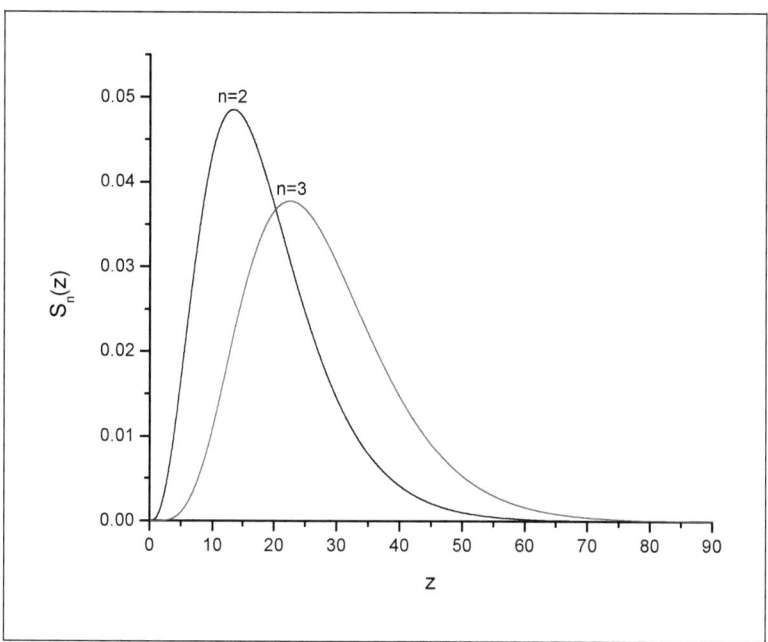

Figure 4: Probability density function for the time until the second and third renewals in an ICU bed

6.2 Applying the Model of Parallel Renewal Process to the Whole ICU

As in the case above if we fit a Weibull distribution for the time among renewals in the resulting parallel process, the hypothesis that the data follow this distribution will not be rejected. But, cutting a few cases (outliers), the hypothesis that the data follow an exponential distribution, is not rejected too. For the same reason we preferred to work with an exponential distribution. The parameter for the exponential distribution resulted in $\lambda=0.8368$.

Applying the formula for S_n, presented in section 4, we obtain:

$$S_n(y) = \frac{0.8368^n \, y^{n-1} e^{-0.8368y}}{\Gamma(n)}$$

For instance, the fdp for the time until the third, fifth and tenth renewals in the whole ICU are:

$$S_3(y) = \frac{0.8368^3 y^2 e^{-0.8368 y}}{2}$$

$$S_5(y) = \frac{0.8368^5 y^4 e^{-0.8368 y}}{24}$$

$$S_{10}(y) = \frac{0.8368^{10} y^9 e^{-0.8368 y}}{362880}$$

Figure 5 illustrates the graphics of these fdp.

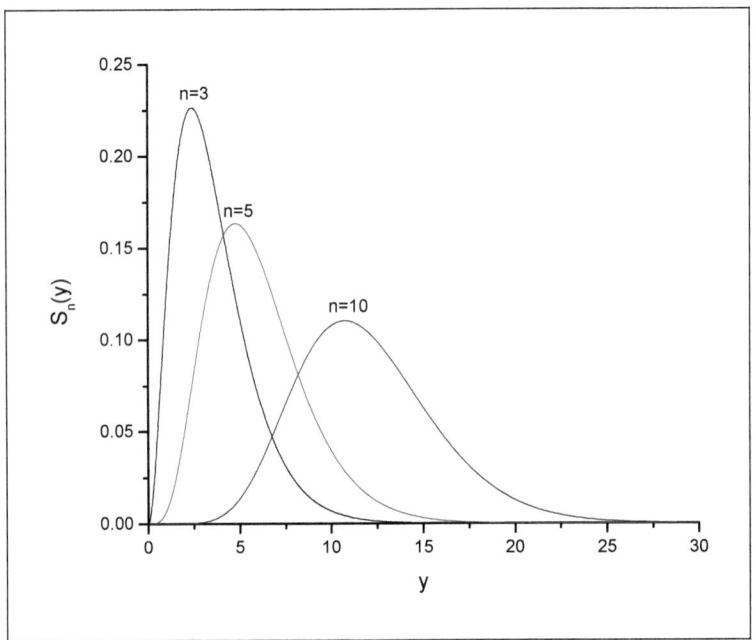

Figure 5: Probability densities functions for the times until the third, fifth and tenth renewals in a whole ICU

7 Conclusions

We have adapted a methodology of renewal process to modeling the dynamics of beds and the dynamics of an infirmary as whole. While this modeling, using alternate renewal process was very realistic for the bed dynamics it is of little usefulness in the sense that this is applied only to a system component.

On the other hand when we model the whole infirmary (or ICU) as a parallel renewal process, the results are applied to a whole system, allowing the manager to base planning politics for the whole system (infirmary or ICU). This way, with exception of special cases, for planning politics is more useful to model the system as a whole.

The knowledge of the probability density function for the time until the nth renewal allows the generation of parameters that can base politics of medium and long period.

References

[1] N.T.J. Bailey, Queuing for medical care, *Applied Statistics*, 3, (1954) 137-145.

[2] J.L. Balintfy, A stochastic model for the analysis and prediction of admission and discharges in hospitals, *Manag. Sciences Models and Techniques*, 2, (1960) 288-299.

[3] J.F. Bithell and H.B. Delvin, Prediction of discharge of hospital inpatients, *Health Services Research*, 3, (1968) 174-186.

[4] P.A. Fuhs, J.B. Martin and W.M. Hancock, The use of length of stay distributions to predict hospital discharges, *Medical Care*, XVII, 4, (1979) 355-368.

[5] J.H. Milsum, E. Turban and I. Vertinsky, Hospital admission systems: Their evaluation and management, *Management Sciences*, B-APPL 19:6, (1973) 646-666.

[6] M.J.F. de Oliveira, 3D visual simulation of hospital admissions, In: J. Riley (editor), *Planning The Future: Health, Service Quality and Emergency Accessibility*, Proceedings from ORAHS 2000, Glasgow 31st, July- 4th august, (2000) 77-96.

[7] M.A.S. Lavrador, *An information system for intensive care units with emphasis in renewal process*, Doctoral Dissertation, Federal University of Rio de Janeiro, (1990).

[8] M. Lagergren, Modeling as a tool to assist in managing problems in health care, In: D. Boldy, J. Braithwaite and I. Forbes (Eds.), Evidence Based Management in Health Care: The Role of Decision Support Systems, *Australian Studies in Health Service Administration*, No. 92, (2002) 17-36.

[9] P. Van Gemmel and R. Van Dierdonk, Admission scheduling in acute hospitals: does the practice fit with the theory?; *International Journal of Operations & Production Management*, 19 (9 and 10), (1999).

[10] J.M. Vissers et al., Optimization of the patient mix for hospital admission planning, in: *E Mikitis (editor) Proceedings of the 21st meeting of the ORAHS, Maastrick*, The Netherlands, ISBN 9984-19-146-X, (2000) 27-44.

[11] M. Abramowitz and I.A. Stegun, Handbook of mathematical functions, 9th edition, *Dover Publications*, New York, (1972) 1056.

[12] N.T.J. Bailey, The elements of stochastic process, *John Wiley & Sons*, (1964).

[13] D.R. Cox, Renewal theory, *Methuen & CO*, London, (1962) 142.

LINEAR PROGRAMMING MODELS TO SUPPORT RESOURCE ALLOCATION – THE CASE OF BREAST CANCER CHEMOTHERAPY

R.M.GÊNOVA[1], R. T.ALMEIDA[1], M.I.P.GADELHA[2]

[1]Federal University of Rio de Janeiro
[2]National Cancer Institute (INCA), Brazil

Abstract

The availability of data on public health care makes possible the utilization of more systematic methods to support the resource allocation in local health care. In this context, two models, based on linear programming, are defined using a database on cancer outpatient therapy production of Belo Horizonte city in Minas Gerais state, Brazil. The first model aims at maximizing the number of procedures performed in breast cancer chemotherapy, taking into account limited financial resources, and the second one aims at minimizing the resources to meet the demand for procedures of a predetermined population. The models allow a saving of up to US$ 40 per procedure for an average price of US$ 329, and more equitable access of the population to the services, since the unit production profile after application of model shows a distribution more similar to the municipality.

Key words: linear programming, breast cancer chemotherapy, resource allocation

1 Introduction

The technological complexity in the health care sector is asking for the improvement of the decision process concerning resource allocation in the sector. Thus, information and methods to combine and synthesize the available information is more and more demanding by the decision-makers. Operational Research (OR) techniques might be of great interest in the field, since they aim at improving the performance of organizations, by means of mathematical model [1]. Linear programming is one of OR techniques that have usually been used in two different ways: resource allocation [2-3] and quality of care assessment [4-6].

The growing availability of administrative data in Brazil is allowing the implementation of mathematical models to support the decision process. Despite the limitations of this type of data, it has the advantages of huge amount of records, short time between the event and its recording into the system, patient following up, minimization of bias regarding volunteers, change of behavior or treatment and observation of different subgroups in the population [7].

The cancer outpatient care demands a large amount of resources of the public sector. In 2000, it cost approximately 223 million dollars. The two main procedures used chemotherapy and radiotherapy ranked the fifth and the sixteenth position, respectively, among the more costing outpatient procedures in the public health care system [8]. This fact has motivated the decision-makers in the sector to claim for tools to improve the managing of resources and the quality of the cancer care in the country.

Since 1993, the National Cancer Institute (INCA) and the Ministry of Health have been implementing different actions in order to reorganize the cancer care. One of these initiatives is the system to control the use of chemotherapy and radiotherapy, by means of a previous authorization given by a local committee [9]. This system is called Authorization to High Complexity Procedures in Oncology (APAC-ONCO). The municipality of Belo Horizonte, in Minas Gerais state, was the pioneer in the implementation of this idea and started this process in November 1996, two years before the implementation of the APAC-ONCO in the whole country.

Having in mind the necessity realized by the decision makers of INCA and the availability of Belo Horizonte's health council data, we started this study aiming at developing models to support the resource allocation in local cancer care. Since the main idea was the optimization of resources in the field, we chose linear programming to develop the models. Given the large spectrum of the problem, we decided to focus the models in a specific type of procedure and tumor. Breast cancer chemotherapy was chosen because it is the most frequent procedure used in the outpatient care. In addition, breast cancer is the most frequent tumor (68.14 per 100,000) and has the highest mortality rate (16.66 per 100,000) among women in the city [10].

2 Method

2.1 Database

The database used to develop the models had 94,711 records of chemotherapy and radiotherapy production of the Belo Horizonte city, during the period of November 1996 to February 1999. Out of these 39,078 records were concerned to breast cancer chemotherapy, corresponding to 41% of the total production.

The main variables used in the models are described below:

- Health care unit: from a total of nine units offering cancer care in the municipality, seven dealt with chemotherapy;
- Treatment goals: five categories are identified – adjuvant (additive or ablative), preview surgery, palliative, curable and missing;
- Tumor staging: according to the International Union Against Cancer (IUAC) the tumor extent is classified in four stages (I, II, III e IV) [9];
- Procedure category: gives the number of procedures per each combination of treatment goal with tumor stage. Considering the most frequent combinations, six categories (P1 to P6) were used – P1 - adjuvant treatment in stage II, P2 - adjuvant treatment in stage III, P3 - palliative care in stage II, P4 - palliative care in stage III, P5 - palliative care in stage IV and P6 - all the remaining combinations;
- Monthly production profile per procedure category: gives the percentage of procedures per month per category of procedures performed in each unit or in the municipality. This variable was created specially to develop the models.

2.2 Model General Structure

Based on linear programming, two models are proposed. The first one aims at maximizing the number of procedures given the amount of financial resources available. The second one aims at minimizing the expenses, but meeting the municipality demand of breast cancer chemotherapy. The software Linear, Interactive and Discrete Optimizer (LINDO), version 6.1 was applied to implement the models [11].

2.2.1 Model 1

- Objective Function

To maximize the total number of procedures in the municipality

$$\text{Maximize} \quad Z = \sum_{i=1}^{I} \sum_{j=1}^{J} x_{ij}$$

where:

x_{ij} is the decision variable and means the monthly number of procedures per procedure category "i" in unit "j".

- Restrictions

1. Available monthly financial resources:

This restriction guarantees that the total monthly expenses do not exceed the maximum available resources "L".

$$\sum_{i=1}^{I} P_{Pi} \sum_{j=1}^{J} x_{ij} < L$$

where:

P_{Pi} means the price per procedure category "i".

2. Monthly production profile per procedure category:

This restriction guarantees that the monthly demand of category of procedure is being fulfilled, considering the epidemiological needs of the local population. It represents the minimum and the maximum percentage of procedures category in the municipality during the observed period (Table 1). For instance:

$$\sum_{j=1}^{J} x_{1j} \geq \min PP_{p1} Q_t \quad AND \quad \sum_{j=1}^{J} x_{1j} \leq \max PP_{p1} Q_t$$

where:

PP_{p1} is the production profile (Table 1) for procedure category 1, Q_t is the total amount of procedure performed in the municipality.

3. Unit production coefficient (cp):

It is estimated as the average monthly unit production per procedure category, in order to guarantee a minimum production for the largest units. It was implemented only for Unit 1 ($cp_1 >= 0,25$) and Unit 2 ($cp_2 >= 0,25$).

4. Unit production capacity:

Defined as the minimum and the maximum unit production, during the observed period, in order to not over or underestimate the unit capacity considering its infrastructure.

$$\sum_{j=1}^{J} x_{1j} \geq \min PC_j \quad AND \quad \sum_{j=1}^{J} x_{1j} \leq \max PC_j$$

where:

PC_j is the Production capacity of unit "j" (Table 2).

2.2.2 Model 2

- Objective Function

To minimize the production expenses

$$Minimize \quad Z = \sum_{i=1}^{I} P_{Pi} \sum_{j=1}^{J} x_{ij}$$

- Restrictions

Monthly demand

These restriction guarantees to fulfill the municipality monthly procedure demand "D".

$$\sum_{i=1}^{I} \sum_{j=1}^{J} x_{ij} = D$$

The remaining restrictions are the same already described in Model 1.

3 Results

3.1 Application Scenario

During the 28 months of observed production, 39,078 procedures in breast cancer chemotherapy were offered to the population with an average monthly price of US\$ 329.33 (1 US dollar equal to 2.17 local currency, April 2001). The largest monthly production in the municipality was 1,673 procedures with a total cost of US\$541,188.94. These values were used in the model to represent the parameters "L" and "D".

Table 1 pictures some of the values used in the models. The procedure category price was obtained from the SUS Table of procedure price for reimbursement practiced at the observed time. The monthly production profile per procedure category is also showed regarding the minimum and maximum needed procedures by the local population. These values were used to represent the restriction 2.

Table 2 pictures the unit production capacity, which was estimated by the minimum and the maximum production in the observed period. These values were used in restriction 4.

Category	Price (P_{Pi})	Production Profile (PP_{pi})	
		Mín (%)	Max (%)
P1	184	30	45
P2	235	10	20
P3	557	6	10
P4	557	5	10
P5	557	15	25
P6	189	6	15

Table 1: Price and monthly production profile

	U1		U2		U3		U4		U5		U6		U7	
	Min	Max	Min	Max	Min	Max	Min	Max	Min	Max	Min	Max	Min	Max
P1	141	240	118	192	36	148	22	65	22	37	22	67	22	37
P2	50	85	41	68	12	52	8	23	8	13	8	13	8	13
P3	27	46	32	52	10	40	6	18	6	10	6	18	6	10
P4	76	130	22	36	7	28	4	12	4	7	4	13	4	7
P5	50	85	64	104	19	80	12	35	12	20	12	36	12	20
P6	141	240	41	68	12	52	8	13	8	13	8	13	8	13

Table 2: Unit production capacity PC_j (minimum and maximum observed in the 28 months studied)

3.1.1 Model 1

Considering the available resources, given by parameter "L", Model 1 managed to produce 1,818 procedures with and an average price (Pm) of US$ 297.56. The model results can be seen in Table 3.

Procedure Category	Units							QP_i
	U1	U2	U3	U4	U5	U6	U7	
P1	240	192	148	65	37	67	37	786
P2	85	68	52	23	13	23	13	277
P3	38	32	10	18	6	18	6	128
P4	27	36	7	12	4	4	4	94
P5	76	104	29	12	12	36	20	289
P6	72	68	52	13	13	13	13	244
QU_i	538	500	298	143	85	161	93	$Q_t = 1,818$
GU_j (x1000$)	156.50	160.14	75.00	43.30	24.61	52,54	29.10	$G_T = 541.19$
Pm (dollar)	297.56							

Table 3: Model 1 results

The following symbols are used in Table 3:
QP_i - Quantity of procedures per category;
QU_i - Quantity of procedures per unit;
GU_i - Expenses per unit;
Q_t - Total quantity of procedures and
G_t - Total expenses.

3.1.2 Model 2

To cover the municipality demand of 1,673 procedures per monthly, the model allocated US$484,635.48 (Table 4), with an average price of US$289.68.

Procedure	Units							QP$_i$
Category	U1	U2	U3	U4	U5	U6	U7	
P1	240	191	148	33	37	67	37	753
P2	78	41	52	23	13	8	13	228
P3	38	32	10	6	6	6	6	104
P4	31	22	7	12	4	4	4	84
P5	76	64	63	12	12	12	12	251
P6	81	68	52	13	13	13	13	253
QU$_j$	544	418	332	99	85	110	85	Q$_t$ = 1,673
GU$_j$ (x1000$)	158.66	123.43	93.90	30.66	24.59	28.94	24.59	G$_T$ = 484.77
Pm (dollar)	289.68							

Table 4: Model 2 results

The following symbols are used in Table 4:
QP$_i$ - Quantity of procedures per category;
QU$_i$ - Quantity of procedures per unit,
GU$_i$ - Expenses per unit;
Q$_t$ - Total quantity of procedures and
G$_t$ - Total expenses.

3.2 Comparing Expenses Before and After Model Application

Table 5 pictures a comparison of the procedure average price between reality in the observed period and the models. The saving for models 1 and 2 are of approximately 32 and 40 dollars per procedure.

	Procedure Average Price (dollar)	Saving (dollar)
Reality	329.33	-
Model 1	297.56	32
Model 2	289.68	40

Table 5: Obtained saving for procedure by models

Another way to observe the changes provoked by the model application is to compare the production profile between municipality (Figure 1a) and unit before (Figure 1b) and after models (Figure 1c). Unit 5 was chosen as an example because it presented the biggest distance from the municipality production profile. It is possible to realize the inversion of profile after the models, adjusting the unit profile to the municipality.

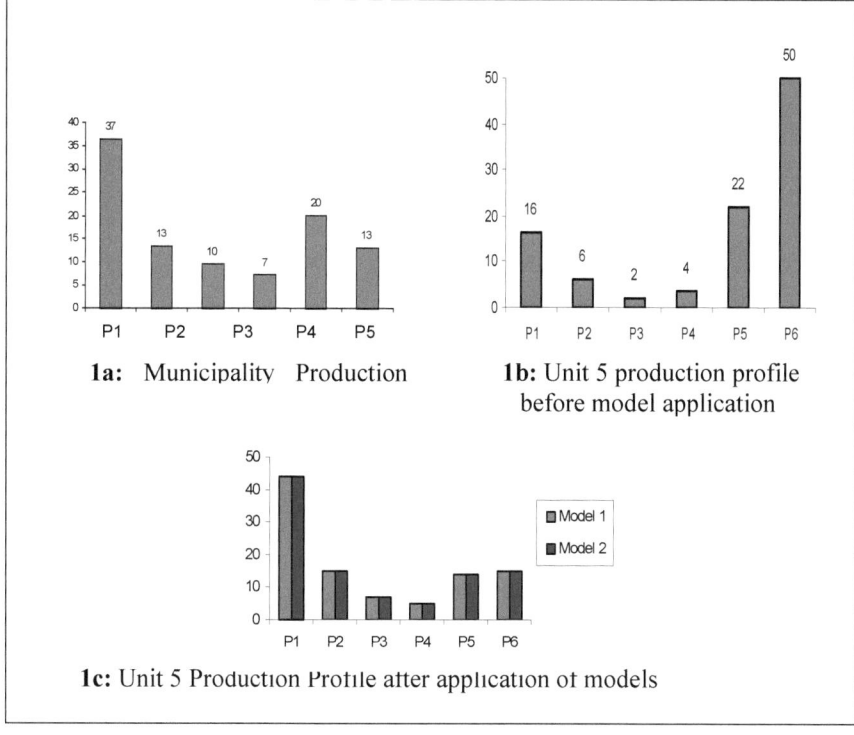

1a: Municipality Production

1b: Unit 5 production profile before model application

1c: Unit 5 Production Profile after application of models

Figure 1: Comparison of the production profiles

4 Discussion

The savings presented by the models if implemented in reality could represent a monthly economy of approximately 56 thousand dollars per month. In addition, the units procedure profile appears to be more similar to the municipality after the model application. This denotes a more consistent distribution of the patients among units, once there is no epidemiological or clinical reason to observe differences in the distribution of procedures offered by the units to the population for this type of tumor. The models can help the manager to control the behavior of units regarding the selection process of patients to treat.

Sensitivity analysis is done for the models and it shows that there is margin for tighter formulation of the models. This can be done considering a more realistic capacity of the units based on their infrastructure and human resources available, instead of estimating it by the maximum production of the units. At the time of the study this information is not available, however nowadays it is already possible to be obtained in the APAC-ONCO system.

The main contribution of the study is to show the potential that OR techniques have to improve the managing of health care system in Brazil. There are, nowadays, available huge databases on the production of the public health care services. The developed models are limited to one type of procedure and tumor. However it can be amplified to more procedures such as radiotherapy and image diagnostics also used to control and treat breast cancer, once data on the production of these procedures is also available in the APAC system. These models will allow the manager to have a general tool to understand what is going on in the municipality. In addition, the models could be used to simulate situations such as the exclusion of a unit, considered inefficient in the system or the inclusion of a new unit in order to increase the service supply to the population.

The applications are diverse and more data are going to be need as the complexity of the questions to be answered by the model increases. At the moment the biggest challenge is the low capacity of the local manager to deal with data analysis techniques and to structure the problem. Therefore, it is important to involve the managers in the model developing process and training them to use the models in daily life activities. The familiarity with the models could increase the interest and the willing to improve them, what is fundamental to the incorporation of the models in the routine of managers and increase the quality of the models to reflect the reality.

Acknowledgements

The authors would like to thanks Dr. Carlos Alberto Martins from Belo Horizonte's Health Council; Prof. Virgílio José Martins Ferreira Filho from Production Engineering Department of Federal University of Rio de Janeiro; and, the Council for the Improvement of Graduated Professional (CAPES).

References

[1] L. Delesie, Bridging the gap between clinicians and health managers, *European Journal of Operational Research*, 105, (1998) 248 – 256.

[2] M.C. Portela, *Modelo matemático de alocação de recursos em saúde perinatal*, Msc. Thesis, Federal University of Rio de Janeiro, Brazil, (1988).

[3] R. Shams and D.S. Smith, Use of location-allocation models in health service development planning in developing nations, *European Journal of Operational Research*, 123, (2000) 437-452.

[4] M. Linna, Health care financing reform and the productivity change in Finnish hospitals, *Journal of Health Care Finance*, 26 (3), (2000) 83-100.

[5] D.I. Giokas, Greek hospitals: How well their resources are used, *Omega*, 29(1), (1999) 73-83.

[6] S. Flessa, Where efficiency saves lives: a linear programme for the optimal allocation of health care resources in developing countries, *Health Care Management Science*, 3, (2000) 249-267.

[7] K.N. Lohr, Use of insurance claims data in measuring quality of care, *International Journal of Technology Assessment in Health Care*, 6, (1990) 263-71.

[8] DATASUS/Ministério da Saúde, Informações em saúde: Produção Ambulatorial. Departamento de Informática do Sistema Único de Saúde, (*DATASUS*), (Download from website http://www.datasus.gov.br), (2001).

[9] INCA/SAS/Ministério da Saúde, Bases Técnicas para Autorização de Procedimentos de Alta Complexidade, Instituto Nacional do Câncer (*INCA*), Rio de Janeiro, (1999).

[10] INCA/ Ministério da Saúde, Estimativa de incidência e mortalidade por câncer no Brasil. Instituto Nacional de Câncer (*INCA*), Ministério da Saúde, (http://www.inca.org.br/epidemiologia/estimativa2001/index.html), Rio de Janeiro, Brazil, (2001).

[11] LINDO, Linear, Interactive and Discrete Optimizer, (Download from website http://www.lindo.comT), (2000).

THE USE OF SIMULATION TO IMPROVE CANCER TREATMENT ACCESS

ANTÔNIO A. GONÇALVES[1], MARIO J.F. DE OLIVEIRA[2]

[1]Instituto Nacional do Cancer, [2]Federal University of Rio de Janeiro, Brazil

Abstract

The Brazilian National Health Services has been facing significant challenges in the last few years. The economic environment imposes serious budget restrictions and efficient control over the human and material resources. The demographic growth is generating an impact through the increase of the demand for health services. The hospital managers have to deal with complex systems whose components are strongly interconnected. Because of the recent changes in technology and in medical practice, it is difficult to foresee the best way to organize the disease treatment flow in cancer research centers. In this scenario there is a need for tools that enable the manager to accurately assess and quantify the impact of possible changes.

The objective of this article is to contribute for the reduction of the patient's waiting time to start cancer treatment. This corresponds to the time interval between the patient's registration and the execution of therapeutic procedures such as surgery, radiotherapy applications and chemotherapy. The adopted methodology is to analyze the patient's flow in a cancer reference hospital evaluating the access alternatives and the use of available equipment. A simulation model is used to identify the bottlenecks and evaluate alternatives for the allocation of resources improving the access and decreasing the time between the ordering cancer diagnosis exams and its effective accomplishment.

Key words: health care, cancer treatment, patient flow, simulation

1 Introduction

The Brazilian National Cancer Institute (INCA) is an agency under the direct administration of the ministry of health, associated with the health care secretariat. INCA has five specialized hospital units, in the state of Rio de Janeiro, providing medical and assistance services for cancer and related diseases. They offer services of diagnosis confirmation, evaluation of extension of the tumor, treatment, rehabilitation and palliative care. The Hospital of Cancer 1 (HC1) is the largest hospital of INCA and one of the best-equipped hospitals of the ministry of health. HC1 is a reference for cancer treatment and offers free treatment for patients with cancer in the state of Rio de Janeiro, since 1957. This hospital unit has 209 beds (including 16 beds of Intensive Care Unit- ICU) distributed in an eleven-floor building, that occupies an area of 33.000 m². Qualified multidisciplinary teams are responsible for the services of diagnosis confirmation, evaluation of the stage of the tumor, treatment and rehabilitation [10,11].

This work addresses the author's experience with a simulation model of a strategic service of HC1. The critical success factor in the fight against cancer is the execution agility of the diagnosis exams, which are necessary for identification of the morphology and the stage of disease. Agile diagnoses do contribute to the reduction of the waiting time in the beginning of the treatment. Patients and their records (physician's notes, laboratory test results, etc) often take different operational paths, but they are, in fact, always linked to each other. As such, one cannot complete a process without the other. When the laboratory result is delayed, the same occurs with the patient's treatment and so on.

HC1 managers have to deal with difficult challenges to recommend courses of action, among the various processes they need to study. This means they must recognize the types of processes found within the hospital, the performance of each process, the cause of delays and bottlenecks, the efficiency of actions and how the adoption of new policies, technologies or changes in the existing structure will affect that process. A discrete-event simulation model is developed here to assist managers devise potential procedures to reach the reduction of the patient's waiting time to start cancer treatment. In this application, simulation is used to identify the bottlenecks and evaluate alternatives for the allocation of resources to improve the access and to decrease the time between the ordering of the cancer diagnostic exams and its effective accomplishment.

Simulation models have been used in different areas of health care such as admission systems, scheduling appointments, patient flow, clinic staffing and facility sizing. Such models are powerful tools for analyzing a variety of applications over the past thirty years. R. Fetter and J. Thompson present one of the first simulation studies applied on the operations of a clinic [12]. G. Robinson, L. Wing and E. Davis [2] have already elaborated simulation models to solve problems related to the health and care system operation. The increased capacity of computers has made possible the design of much more complicated, detailed models. Also new graphical techniques have been developed that simplify the interpretation of results. In this direction, it is important to point out the work of M. De Oliveira [5], [6], [13] related to the capacity planning in projects of new hospitals using 3D visual simulation models.

Models concerned with applications that use simulation to study cancer health care services can also be found in several literatures. J. Sepulveda [1] addresses the experience with a simulation model of a full cancer treatment center. L. Baldwin, T. Elba and R. Paul [3] consider the adjuvant breast cancer trial, while M. Kattan [7] uses simulation of factors affecting machine-learning techniques.

2 Patient Treatment Flow

The whole patient treatment flow in a hospital of cancer is studied. Considering Figure1, an arriving patient checks in and waits for a triage, which is an examination to discover if a cancer diagnostic is positive. If the cancer diagnostic is negative the patient is directed to another kind of hospital. If the diagnostic is positive, the patient goes to the registration department and then is submitted to a series of exams to discover the type and the stage of cancer. The treatment only starts after these exams. The purpose of this work is to reduce the time interval between registration and the beginning of treatment, which, in some cases, can be over one month.

The whole patient treatment flow is studied but just the radiology facility, which is a strategic service of HC1, is modeled. Cancer diagnosis occurs in different steps. The focus of this work is related to the Computerized Tomography (CT) exams. There are three processes that take place at the radiology facility to perform a CT exam. All patients are scheduled and they arrive at the radiology facility by appointment. The first process is the receptionist attendance. Patients confirm their appointments and go to another room waiting for a nurse call. The second process occurs when patients are called by a nurse for the CT exam. Then, the patient goes back to the waiting room until an examining room is available. Finally, the patient accomplishes the CT exam. This exam requires a physician, a nurse and a radiology technician. Figure 2 shows the process flow to perform a CT exam.

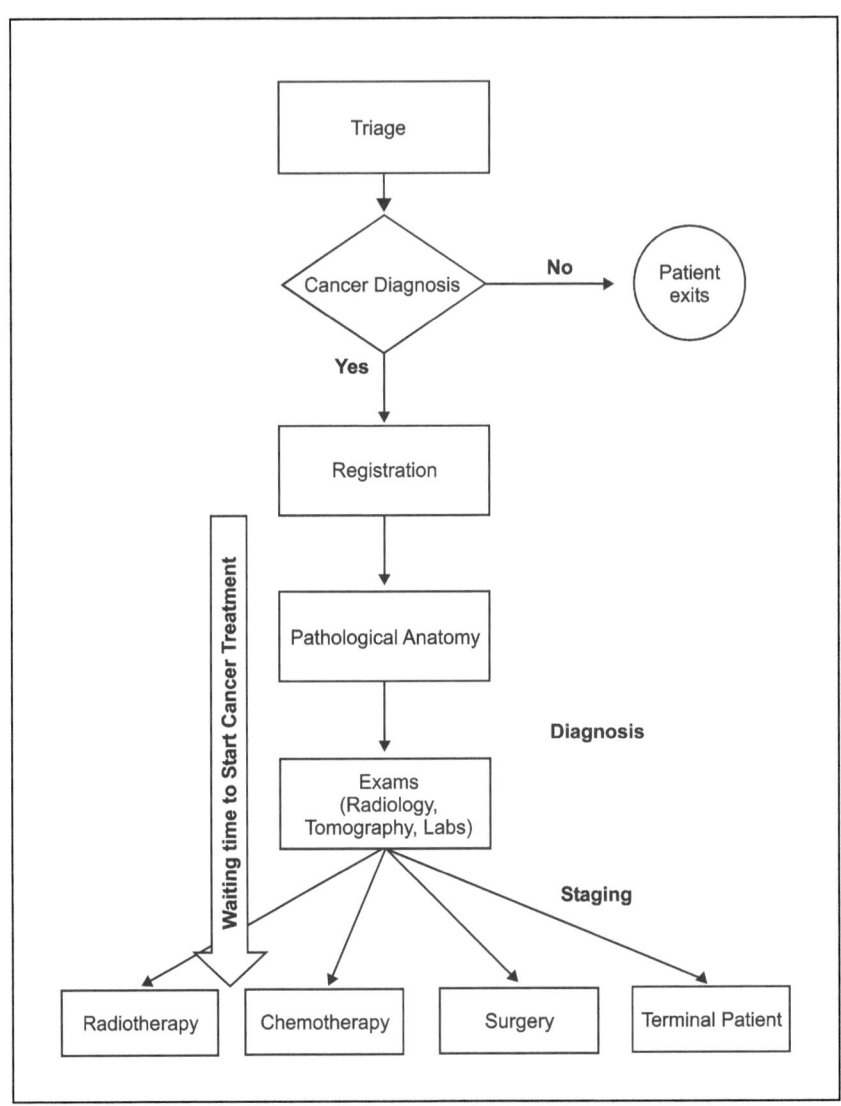

Figure1: Diagram of patient treatment flow

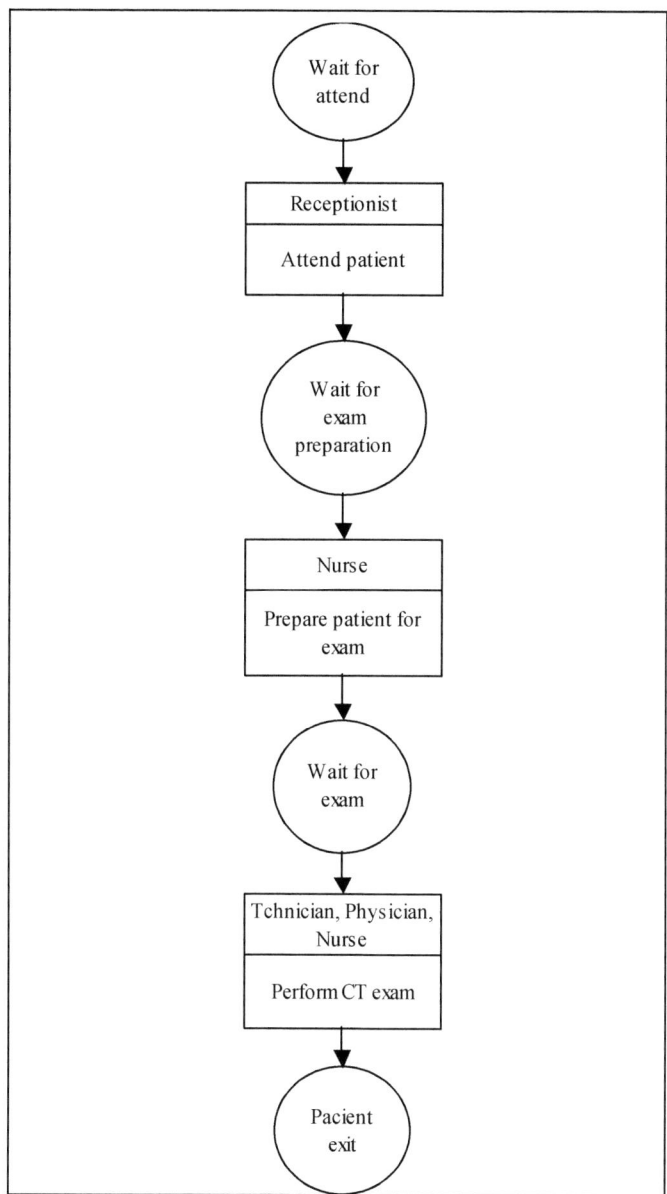

Figure 2: Flow paths at the radiology facility (CT exam)

3 Simulation Model

A simulation model for the cancer treatment center is created using the package Medmodel version 3.5. Medmodel is designed to be simple to use and tailored to the needs of health care managers, engineers and clinicians. As such, it provides a basis for the comprehensive evaluation of large, complex problems, which are representative of healthcare environment.

This model represents the patient's flow within the HC1's radiology facility as well as the human and material resources such as physicians, nurses, radiology technicians, receptionists, examining rooms and the CT scanners. The arrival of patients is generated from historical data gathered from the Hospital's Information System (HIS) and Radiology Information System (RIS). The computer model is able to emulate the scheduling patterns used by hospital personnel, as well as the typical variations (lateness, earliness) observed in real life. The model generates three different arrival schedules for radiology patients. Input analysis is also performed to determine the duration of the following activities:

- Radiology reception time;
- Patient preparation time;
- Medical radiology examination time;
- Computerized tomography examination time;
- Image scan time;
- Film production time.

Collecting patient's data is a difficult task considering the individual nature of the treatment and the necessity of privacy in relation to the medical history. During the data-collection process the daily activities of the personnel cannot be harmed. Thus, the data collecting must be carried through minimizing the required amount of aid of the health care staff.

Considering recent research [4], the most appropriate data collection instruments would be a tracking form and a survey. This work is conducted in three steps. Firstly, an observation is performed in order to understand the patient's flow at the radiology facility. Based upon the review of the clinical activities, the patient's flow could be broadly characterized as in Figure 2. The second step is a pilot study using a single-track form to record the patient's flow data. In this study, the procedures for improvement the tracking form delivery and design are reached. Radiology personnel help to identify the flow elements that either do not exist on the initial track form or cannot be adequately measured. The last step is to determine the duration of the patient's activities. A survey is carried out to collect data on the inter arrival time, and on time patients spend on the single queues and totally in the radiology facility. The survey took place in March 2002.

The simulation model is developed considering radiology personnel and facilities involved. Types and levels of resources are shown in Table 1.

Resource	Quantity
Doctors	3
Nurses	5
Receptionist	2
Radiology Technicians	3
Room for Patient Preparation	2
Examining Rooms	3
Computerized tomography	3

Table 1: Human and Physical Resources

The simulation model represents the patient's flow in the radiology facility to perform CT exam and its interaction with the human and material resources (Figure 4). HC1 opens at 07:00 a.m. and closes around 6:00 p.m. when all the patients, except the inpatients, leave the treatment center. The profile of the eligible patients to CT exam is classified into three types based on the sequence of the activities that they go in through the radiology facility. These patients are identified as inpatients, twin outpatients and picker outpatients. The treatment priorities are defined based on the profile of each patient type.

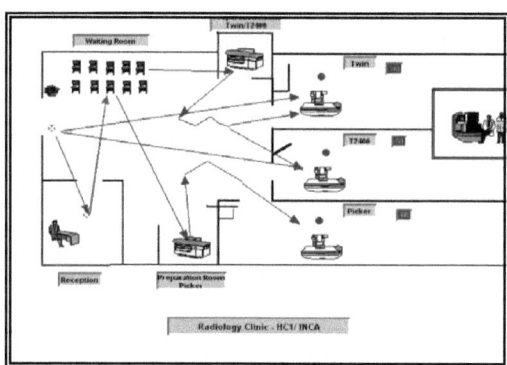

Figure 3: Simulation Model (Radiology Clinic - CT Exam)

Considering Figure 3, an arriving outpatient checks in at reception desk and then goes to the waiting room where he awaits to be called by a nurse. When both a nurse and a room are available, the patient goes to the room to be prepared for the CT exam. At this location, the nurse prepares and escorts the patient to an available examining room. In another situation, the inpatient goes straight to an available examination room based on the attendance priority. There are usually a nurse, a physician and a radiology technician in the examining room.

4 Model Validation

To validate the model, several techniques are employed in the radiology clinical model. This effort includes audit, review, walkthrough and production run. The physicians, radiology technicians and nurses validate the results. These are compared to the actual data capture of HIS.

The animation is an extraordinary tool to communicate and verify the model, since it allows tracking the patients as they move through the system. This strategy was applied by showing the simulation animation to the radiology personnel. The model is accepted as valid since it reflects the clinical environment.

5 Simulation Experiment

The focus of this study is the reduction of the patient's waiting time between the CT exam schedule and its accomplishment. Our target is to increase the capacity to accomplish CT exams. Simulation is used to investigate several "what- if" scenarios:

- Evaluate the existing system;
- Evaluate the number of the staff;
- Reduce the CT exam time;
- Increase the number of patients;
- Reduce the CT exam time and increase the number of Patients.

The simulation model allows one to investigate several scenarios of interest. As a whole, the experiments performed on the HC1's radiology clinic shows that the clinical environment is very sensitive to reductions in CT exam time. There are also improvements in the patient's scheduling rules. Experimentation with the system reveals that CT exam time reductions can be made, under certain conditions, with significant positive impacts on the patient's service time and clinic's capacity planning. The CT exam is composed by three sequential phases as shown in Figure 4. The rationale behind splitting the exam process into three phases is based upon a characterization of how the use of the CT scanner occurs during a patient exam.

The patient leaving the examining room when the CT scanner becomes available signals the end of patient's exam. The phase of film production does not require the presence of the patient.

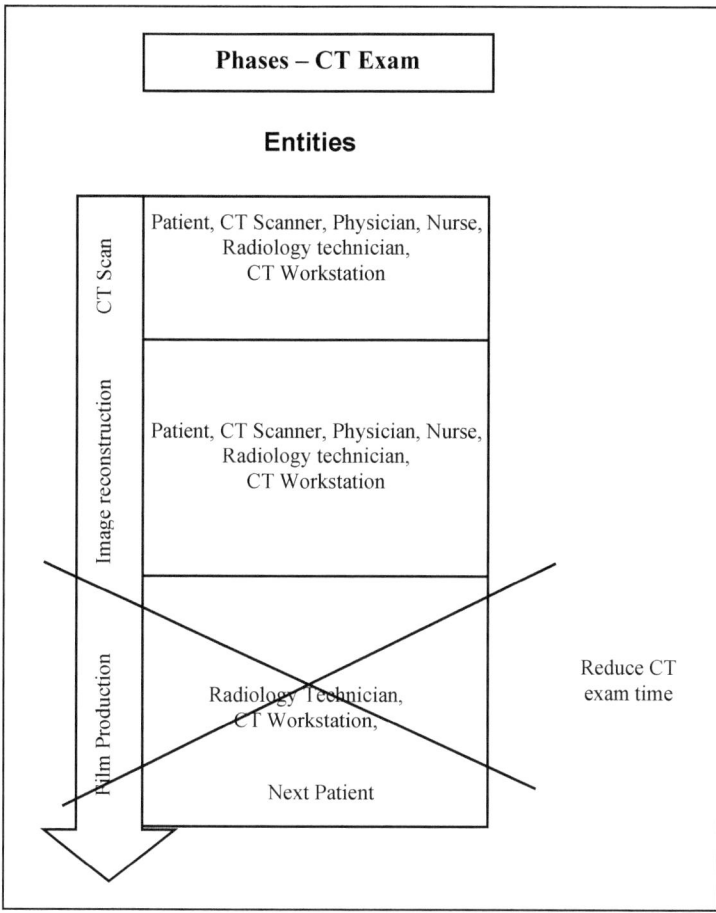

Figure 4: CT exam

Analyzing these three phases, one can find out a new scenario: reducing the CT exam time by removing the phase of film production in the patient's presence. A radiology technician using an extra workstation and therefore reducing the time of each CT exam could perform this phase. Model experimentation shows that this reduction can be made without sacrificing patient throughput or increasing staff overtime.

In Figure 5 and Figure 6, we present the simulation experiment results, which show that:

- The resources can be better used in the current system;
- The time wasted at the CT exam does affect the whole operation;
- There is a clear opportunity to increase the number of CT exams per day without the necessity to increase the number of CT scanners;
- There is a need to increase the number of workstations (cost of a CT workstation is only 10% of a CT Scanner's cost);
- The time wasted at the reception and at the preparation room does not affect significantly the total waiting time for the HC1´s patients.

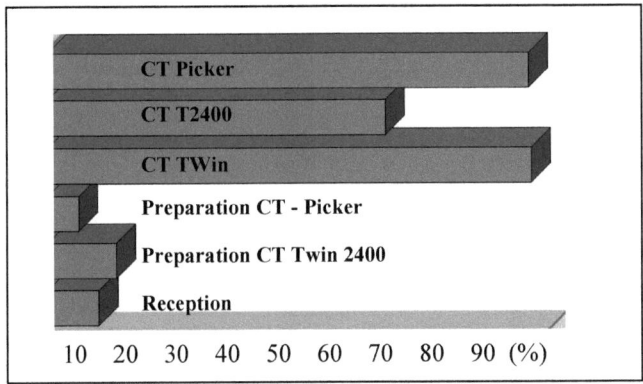

Figure 5: Location Utilization

The performance variable location utilization has showed that, under this utilization level, the time wasted at the reception and at the preparation rooms does not create queue of patients waiting to be attended. The high CT utilization rate illustrates the significant effects of this activity on patient flow time.

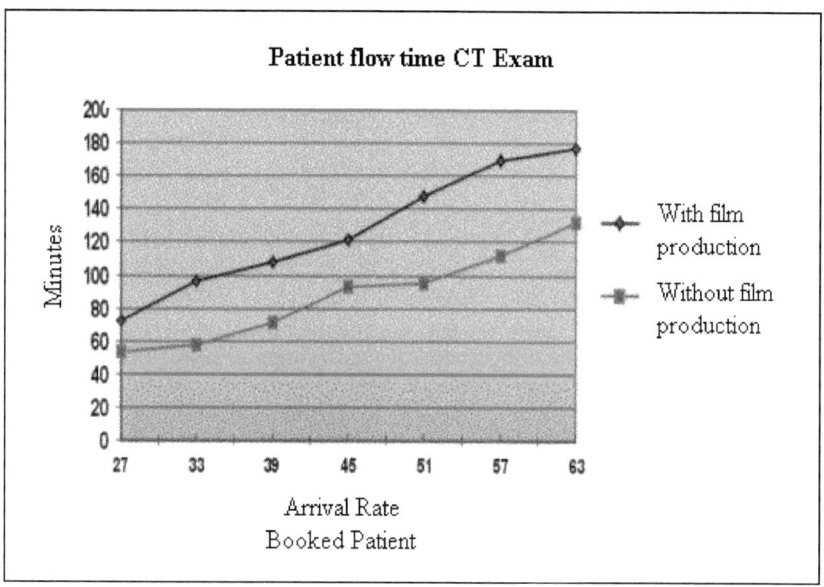

Figure 6: Patient Flow Time

The impact of the CT's exam time reduction on patient flow time is very significant as shown in Figure 6 when the average patients' flow time associated with the arrival rates are considered. The results given in both scenarios are representative of this improvement.

6 Conclusions and Propositions

This paper show how the simulation model allows health care managers perform risk-free what-if analyses to aid decision-making in a cancer treatment center or any health care facility. The simulation model demonstrates the power of this operational research method to identify bottlenecks and to evaluate alternatives for capacity planning and allocation of resources.

The study of strategic services of HC1 reveals several opportunities to improve cancer treatment access. There is a strong relationship between the number of CT exams and the time wasted at CT scanners. The simulation experiment reveals that it's possible to increase the number of exams without increasing the number of CT scanners. The results obtained from this analysis showed that important improvements in patients' flow time could be achieved.

The implementation of the suggested changes may cause significant improvements in the service of radiology of HC1. However this is only the beginning of a study that can be extended to all the services of the hospital according to a priority determined by the high management.

References

[1] J.A. Sepulveda, W. Thompson, F. Baesler and M. Alvarez, The use of simulation for process improvement in a cancer treatment center, *Proceedings of the Winter Simulation Conference*, (1999).

[2] G.H. Robinson, L.P. Wing and E. Davis, Computer simulation of hospital patient scheduling systems, *Health Services Research* 3, (1968) 130-141.

[3] L.P. Baldwin, T. Eldabi and R.J. Paul, Simulation modeling as an aid to decision-making in healthcare management: the adjuvant breast cancer trial, In: *Proceedings of the Winter Simulation Conference*, (1999).

[4] M.J. Côté, Patient flow and resource utilization in an outpatient clinic, *Socio Economic Planning Sciences* 33, (1999) 231-245.

[5] M.J.F. De Oliveira, 3D visual simulation platform for the project of a new hospital facility, In: V. de Angelis, N. Ricciardi and G. Storchi (Eds), Monitoring, evaluating, planning health services, *World Scientific publishing Co. Pte. Ltd.*, Singapore/New York/London/Hong Kong, (1998) 39-52.

[6] M.J.F. De Oliveira and L.N. P. Toscano, Emergency information support system for Brazilian public hospitals, In: M.S. Rauner and K. Heidenberger (Eds), Quantitative approaches in health care management, *Peter Lang*, Frankfurt am Main/Berlin/Bern/New York/Paris/Viena, Germany, (2003) 235-251.

[7] M. Kattan and R.B. Cooper, A simulation of factors affecting machine learning techniques: an examination of partitioning and class proportions, *Omega* 28, (2000) 501-512.

[8] M. Pidd, Computer simulation in management science, second edition, *John Willey & Sons*, (1988).

[9] National Cancer Institute - *INCA, Administrative norms*, Rio de Janeiro, (2002).

[10] National Cancer Institute - *INCA, Annual report 2002*, Rio de Janeiro, (2002).

[11] National Cancer Institute - *INCA, Rio de Janeiro*, Available in: http://www.inca.org.br / (2002).

[12] R.B. Fetter and J.D. Thompson, The simulation of hospital systems, *Operation Research*, September-October, (1965) 689-711.

[13] V. de Angelis, G. Felici and P. Impelluso, Simulation based DSS for the optimal planning of a transfusion center, In: M.S. Rauner and K. Heidenberger (Eds), Quantitative approaches in health care management, *Peter Lang*, Frankfurt am Main/Berlin/Bern/New York/Paris/Viena, Germany, (2003) 253-267.

ADMISSION SYSTEMS

A SIMULATION MODEL FOR SHORT-TERM FORECASTS OF THE SURGICAL WARD CENSUS

JAIME BELLIDO, MARIO J.F. DE OLIVEIRA

Federal University of Rio de Janeiro, Brazil

Abstract

One of the main difficulties associated with elective admissions to surgical wards is that patients have to be notified a number of days in advance of the day they should arrive at the hospital. It is not easy to state the exact number of beds that should be set free and hence the number of patients to be called up. This happens because of the variability associated with the date of discharge of current patients and the uncertainty caused by emergency requests. The objective of this paper is to describe a simple stochastic simulation model to evaluate the hospital census and make prognostics for the right utilization of resources. The tested model shows that it is more effective to be used for short-term forecasts.

Key words: hospital admission system, surgery simulation, census forecasts

1 Introduction

The organization of inpatients facilities is complex and varies from place to place. The admission is the entry door to health and care systems operation and it is one of the essential processes to establish the balance between the supply and the demand for services. The main concern of this paper is about the census variability and control in hospital wards that involve both elective and emergency patients. One of the main difficulties in the operation of this system is that the elective patients have to be notified in advance of the day they should arrive at the hospital. The variability associated with the discharge of current patients and the number of emergency requests makes it difficulty to state the exact number of beds that should be set free for use by the emergency and elective patients.

Several methods of estimating how many patients should be admitted on a given day can be found in the literature. The simplest method is to fix the number of admissions each day, independent of the daily count of the number of patients in the ward, that is the census [1]. Examination of the effect of the length stay (LOS) variability upon census can also be made [2]. Another easily managed system is admit elective patients until the census is raised to some target level [3].

Extensive bibliographical review points to earlier attempts to explore the stochastic feature of the census and how it can be applied to the problem studied here [4, 5, 6]. Policies that are more complex suggest an admission rule that is function of the census, which is determined by Markov process combined with linear programming [7]. A general review of the model is examined and an interactive program is designed to indicate the number of elective patients to be admitted in the following day for several levels of average census to minimize the overflow probabilities [4].

This paper sets out to develop an alternative approach to the admission system, which could afford greater flexibility than that offered by the methods described above. Since is extremely difficult to examine the system in all its complexity only by means of analytical methods, a stochastic simulation model is now developed. The aim is to analyze policies with a more flexible lead-time than one day alone. The simulator is fed with empirical data, and the census level and its variability measure the effectiveness of the admission system. The approach used here is simple and relatively easy to be used, if compared with other methods for the study of the hospital census operation. It does not require complicated mathematical formulas and provides a representation of the admission system that facilitates the understanding of its evolution.

2 The Hospital Census

It appears that the most suitable variable for developing OR models of the admission system is the hospital census, upon which models are based. The organization of inpatient facilities, however is complex, it varies from hospital to hospital and involves a series of factors and additional variables, which means that the admission problems of particular hospitals will often have features of their own. Thus approaches have many theoretical grounds in common, they often vary since the particular circumstances of the hospitals differ.

Most studies focus on, at least one of the three main features of the census upon which the admission policies rest, i.e. variability, prediction and control. The stochastic models have been used mostly to study census variability and prediction. Time series methods have been used to produce census forecasts for a general ward of a major hospital [8]. The performance of Box-Jenkins time series and automatic forecasting methods such as exponential smoothing, Holt, and Holt-Winters methods have been compared within a certain planning horizon [9]. Optimization models have been used chiefly for designing admission policies and exercising control over the census [8,10,11].

3 The Model

This section sets out to develop an alternative approach to the admission system, which could afford a greater flexibility than the previous models. Since is extremely difficult to examine the system by means of analytical methods alone, a simulation model is now developed. Complex problems that may not be treated analytically have been studied experimentally by simulation [12, 13]. The essence of simulation and modeling within the framework of practical and experimental applications is:

- The characterization of real-life objects by a set of abstract entities;
- The relationship between these entities;
- A set of unique mappings that give the abstract entities a real-world interpretation.

In this sense systems modeling is one of the basic knowledge-building processes and simulation is a knowledge-evaluation technique, which enables one to explore the possibility of knowledge and the limits of this possibility.

Simulation modeling is a process. There is a real world problem, which is formulated as a logical model that is converted into a computer model, which is then verified and tested to see if it is doing what one wants to do. The model is used as an operational model to produce some results, or some conclusions and is implemented after validation with the real world. The construction of the logical model representing the formulation of the problem is, in many instances, the most difficult aspect of the modeling. One should be prepared to constantly undertake reformulation to obtain a common understanding of the problem. In many instances, the function that the computer model service, is to perform a medium of communication for the structuring of the problem for all participants in the decision-making process [14].

3.1 Construction of the Model

The hospital admission can be seen as a multiple channel system [15], where the customers are the patients and the service stations are the beds [16]. In this paper, one considers a multiple-channel, single-phase admission system [14] that involves two types of arrivals: emergency that may not be controlled and elective that can be controlled by the system. The chosen approach is an event-based simulation model. Figure 1 shows a scheme of the system studied here. It represents the emergency and elective admissions from the arrival to the discharge. The service stations, which are the beds, are arranged in a parallel setting. A full discussion of the diagram can be fond elsewhere [16].

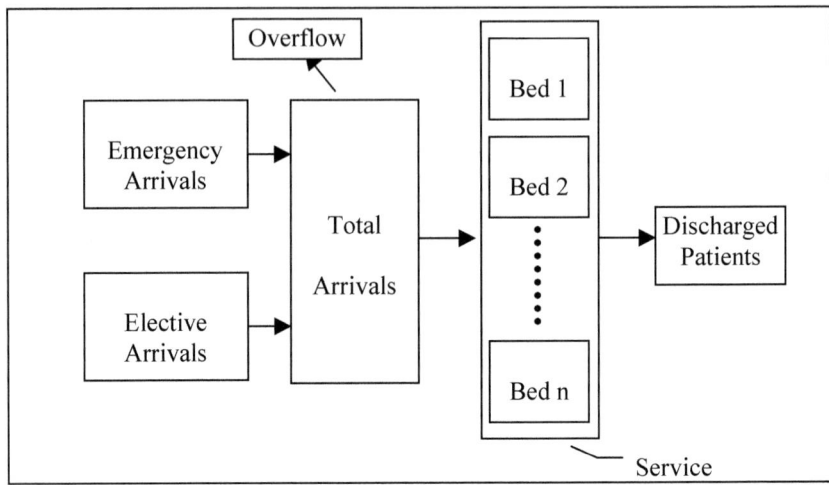

Figure 1: The ward admission system's scheme

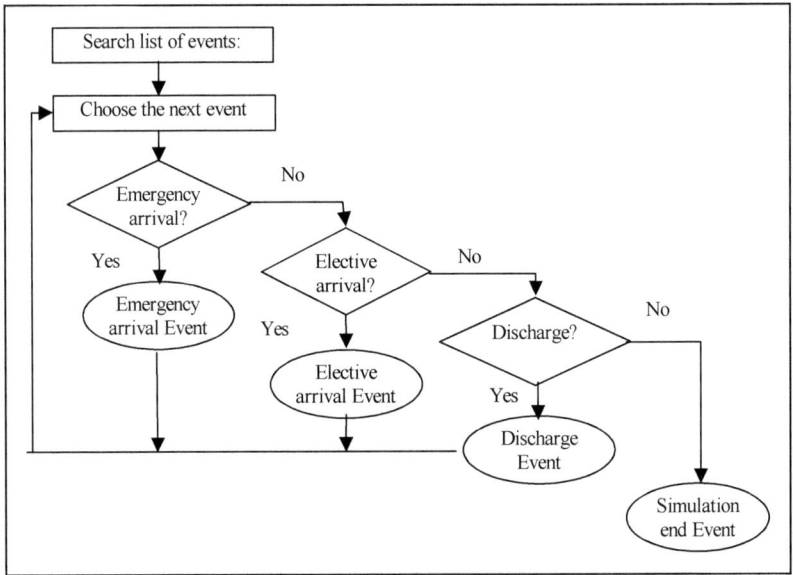

Figure 2: The simulation flow diagram

Figure 2 presents the flow diagram of the system's operation. Four subroutines are used for the following events:
- Emergency arrival;
- Elective arrival;
- Discharge;
- End of the simulation.

As a matter of example, the flow diagram of the emergency arrivals is shown in Figure 3, below:

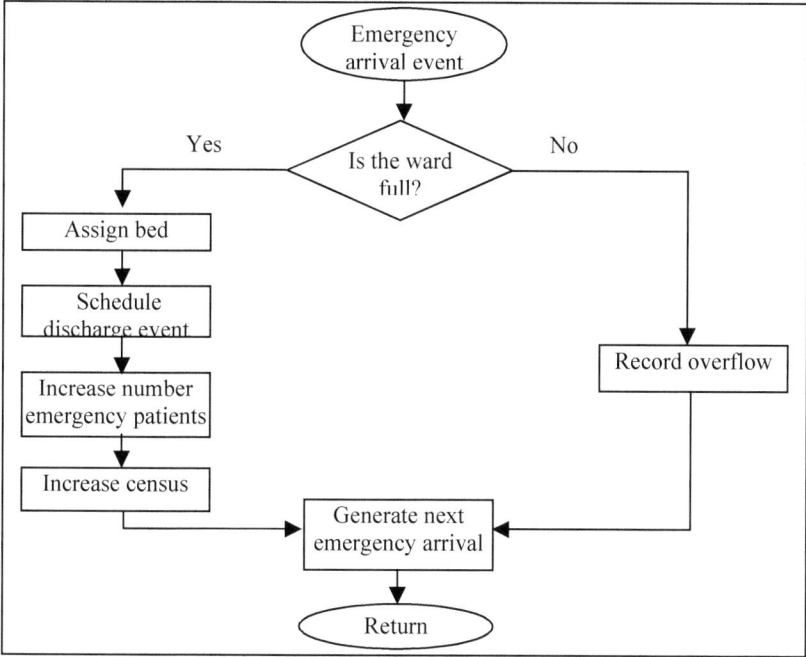

Figure 3: Flow diagram of the emergency arrivals

3.2 The Data

A 30 beds surgical ward that operates with elective and emergency patients is used as an example of the application of the model [9]. The daily census is observed for one-month period. Table 1 shows the daily number and the empirical distribution of emergency arrivals. It can be seen, for example, that in 63.3% of the days no emergency patients have arrived. In 20% of the days, there was one emergency case and in 96.7 % of the days, there were no more than two emergency cases.

Number of Arrivals per Day	Observed Frequency Distribution	Relative Frequency Distribution	Cumulative Frequency Distribution
0	19	0.633	0.633
1	6	0.200	0.833
2	4	0.133	0.967
3	1	0.033	1.000
Total	30		
Mean	0.567		

Table 1: Emergency arrivals distribution

Table 2 shows, for the same period, the daily number of elective arrivals and the observed, relative and cumulative frequency distributions. It can be seen that in 8 days there was no elective arrival. In 23.3% of the days, there was only one elective arrival and 3.3% of the days there was six arrivals. In 90% of the days no more than four elective arrivals have occurred.

Number of Arrivals per Day	Observed Frequency Distribution	Relative Frequency Distribution	Cumulative Frequency Distribution
0	8	0.267	0.267
1	7	0.233	0.500
2	8	0.267	0.767
3	2	0.067	0.833
4	2	0.067	0.900
5	2	0.067	0.967
6	1	0.033	1.000
Total	30		
Mean	1.767		

Table 2: Elective arrivals distribution

3.3 Parameters Verification

Based upon the relative frequency distribution from Table 1, the simulation model for the emergency arrivals is run and the randomness of the results that can be tested [15, 17]. It is possible to assess the 95% confidence interval for the average number of arrivals per day using the Student's t-distribution. The trust limits are calculated in a standard way as it proceeds:

95% Lower bound = $\overline{x}$ - $t_{0,05,n-1}$.se

95% Upper bound = $\overline{x}$ + $t_{0,05,n-1}$.se

where:
- n, is the size of the sample;
- $t_{0,05,n-1}$ is the value for the Student's t-distribution with probability 0.05 for n-1 degrees of freedom;
- se, is the standard error of the sample (being the standard deviation of the sample divided for the square root of the size of the sample).

The Student's t-distribution is used due to the size of the sample. The group of 20 values for the confidence interval of the average emergency arrivals is presented in the Figure 4. Four lines are shown in the Figure: the sample results, the arithmetic mean of each round and the upper and lower bound of trust. It can be assured, with 95% of confidence, that the true value of the average arrival (0.567) is located in the interval (0.095, 0.805). The limits of this interval converge as the sample increases. Similarly, it is assured with 95% of confidence, that the average number of the elective arrivals per day (1.767) is located in the interval (0.650, 2.050).

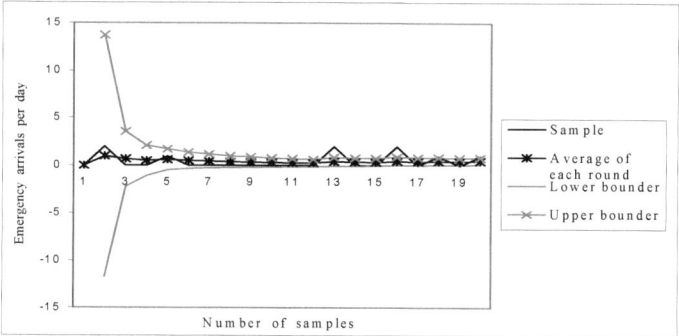

Figure 4: Interval of the stochastic simulation for the average

3.4 Validation of Model Results

According to the literature [17], without real data as comparison pattern, the only form of validating the model is a careful exam of the results in various situations. Although there is no base to verify if the data are reasonable for a certain situation, it is always possible to obtain some conclusions about how to change the relative performance of the system as some parameters are changed. It is especially important to convince the administrator of the credibility of the model so that he/she is willing to use it as a decision support tool. If the model is going to be used again in the future, the predictions should be registered carefully and the results make it possible to continue the validation process.

The simulation model is run for a 30 days period. Figure 5 shows that the bed of the simulation period and the average census level is 15.11.

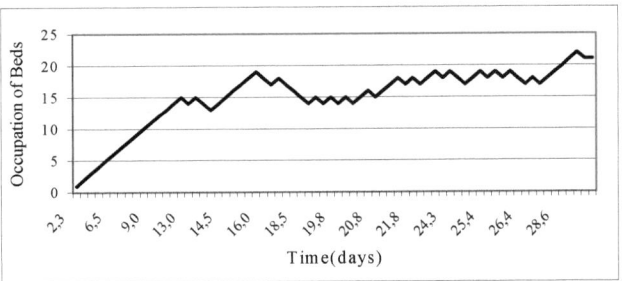

Figure 5: Simulation Results

The average length of stay is 10.754 days. Moreover, the model supplies the residual length of stay for the patients who are in bed at the end of the simulated time. This time, expressed in days, can be observed in the Figure 6.

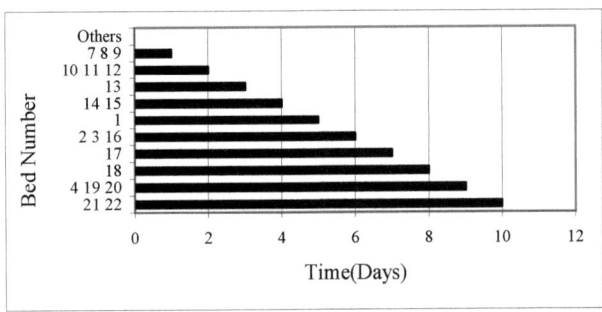

Figure 6: Residual time in the beds after 30 days

Now, the simulation is run to observe how the census behaves, under the hypothesis that the average LOS changes. Figure 7 shows that the average census is 7.55 when the LOS decreases from 10.754 days to 5 days, for example.

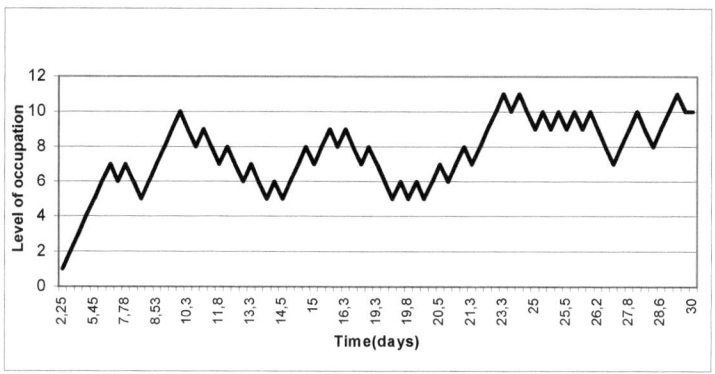

Figure 7: Census levels for average LOS equals 5 days

Figure 8 shows what happens when the LOS increases from 10.754 to 20 days, for example. It can be seen that, the average census level is 22, which is the maximum allowed value. After the total number of beds in the unit is reached, overload or rejection of patient starts.

The results shown in the illustrations 5, 6, and 7 prove that the model supplies a logical answer if LOS is elevated or reduced.

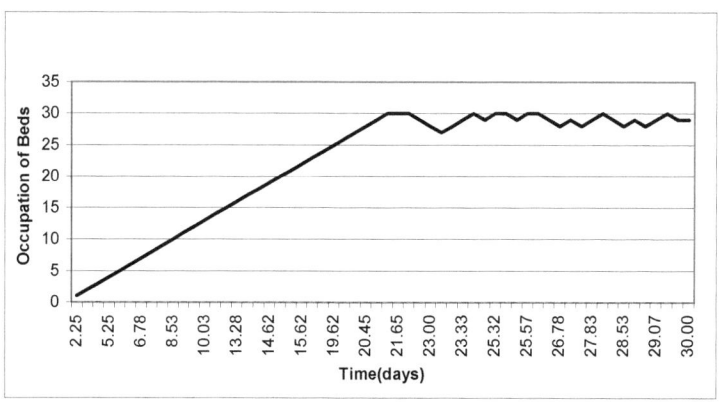

Figure 8: The census level when LOS increases 20 days

Figure 9 shows the census forecasts produced by the simulation model as compared. It can be observed that the model produces good predictions two days ahead, but the performance decreases as the lead-time increases. In the third day ahead there is a difference, which seems to increase in the following days.

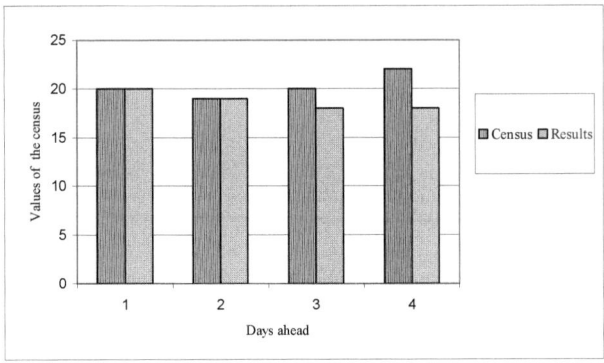

Figure 9: Comparison between model results and the census

The results let one to conclude that the model is a useful tool to study the census variability and to accomplish predictions of short period.

4 Conclusion

The simulation model proposed is easily understand and suitable for the complex problem studied here. The simulation of the admission system offers support to identify the major congestion points, overflows for example, analyze alternative policies, investigate different ways to undertake the problem and forecast the census.

The advantage of the approach is the flexibility to change the model in order to study many different cases that occur in practice. The model can be adapted, without many problems, just being necessary to change few parameters such as the number of beds and the arrival and the length of stay distributions.

The model shows the following results:
- The bed occupancy levels and its variation according to changes in the LOS behavior and the arrival parameters;
- The percentage of occupation of the beds for the simulated time;
- The number of the emergency patients rejected if they exist;

- The number of elective patients;
- The residual LOS times for each beds at the end of the simulation.

The model serves as a basis to plan new policies to schedule elective patients. The evaluation of the model shows its capacity to predict the behavior of the hospital census two days ahead. The prognostic capacity can only be extended when more information about the length of stay and arrival of patients becomes available. It is recommended the use of an information system attached to this model. This system could both continuously update the model and feed a census control mechanism.

Nowadays, the technological progress in computer hardware and software allows increased developments in the modeling area. The advances in computer graphics and on the computer languages enable the production of new graphical libraries, which can be used to produce complex models. 'Virtual' models can be made accurately and new possibilities of practical application in several areas arise.

References

[1]   J.P. Young, Administrative control of multiple channel queuing systems with parallel input streams, *Operations Research*, (1966) 14(1).

[2]   J.F. Bithel, *The rationalization and control of hospital admission systems*, Ph.D. Thesis, Oxford University, U.K., (1969).

[3]   J.P. Young, Stabilization of inpatient bed occupancy through control of admissions, *Hospitals*, 39, (1965) 41-48.

[4]   M.J.F. De Oliveira, *The use of information in planning hospital admissions with special reference to Glasgow western infirmary*, Ph.D. Thesis, Strathclyde University, U.K., (1982).

[5]   W. Shonick and J.R. Jackson, An improved stochastic model in occupancy related random variables in general acute hospitals, *Operations Research*, 21, (1973) 952-965.

[6]   J.J. Wiorkowsky and W.R. McLeod, Prediction and control of the size of an input-output system, *J.A.S.A.*, 66, (1971) 712-719.

[7]   P. Kolesar, A Markovian model for hospital admission scheduling, *Management Sciences*, 16, (1970) B384- B396.

[8] M.J.F. De Oliveira, Modelos de pesquisa operacional no planejamento de admissões hospitalares. *XX Simpósio Brasileiro de Pesquisa Operacional*, Rio de Janeiro, Brasil, (1987) 337-353.

[9] F.J.M. Pinto, *Comparação de métodos de previsão do censo hospitalar*, Msc Thesis, Federal University of Rio de Janeiro, (1988).

[10] J.H. Milsun, E. Turban and I. Vertinsk, Hospital admission systems- Theyr evaluation and management, *Management Sciences B-APPL* 19(6), (1973) 646-666.

[11] J.M.H. Vissers, Exploring new policies for hospital production control, In: J. Riley (editor), *Planing for the future: Health, Service Quality and Emergency Accessibility*, Proceedings ORAHS, Glasgow, (2000) 193-210.

[12] M.A. Badri and J. Hollingsworth, A simulation model for scheduling in the emergency room, *International Journal of Operations & Production Management*, 13, (1992) 13-24.

[13] M. Lagergren, Modeling as a tool to assist in managing problems in health care, In: D. Boldy (editor), *Evidence Based Management in Health Care: The Role of Decision Support Systems*, Australian Studies in Health Service Administration, 92, Sydney, (2002) 17-36.

[14] M.J.F. De Oliveira, 3D visual simulation platform for the project of a new hospital facility, In: V. de Angelis (Editor), Monitoring, Evaluating, Planning Health Services, *World Scientific Publishing*, (1999) 39 – 52.

[15] M.A. Law and D.W. Kelton, Simulation modeling & analysis, Second Edition, *McGraw Hill*, USA, (1991).

[16] J.G. Bellido, *Um modelo de simulação estocástica para o problema de admissão hospitalar*, Msc Thesis, Federal University of Rio de Janeiro, (1988).

[17] M. Pidd, Tools for thinking: modeling in management science, *Ed. John Wiley & Sons*, U.K., (1998).

POLICIES FOR EMERGENCY RESERVATION AND ELECTIVES SCHEDULING IN A HOSPITAL SETTING

JAN M.H. VISSERS

Utrecht and Eindhoven University of Technology, The Netherlands

Abstract

In-patient admissions can be classified – from the perspective of planning – as scheduled or non-scheduled. Scheduled in-patient admissions, also called elective patients, are selected from a waiting list or given an appointment for an admission date. Non-scheduled admissions, also called emergencies, need to be admitted immediately, as a consequence of a medical decision by a specialist at the outpatient department or at the emergency department. Within both flows different categories of patients can be distinguished on behalf of their requirement of resources. The type of resources required for an admission may involve beds, operating theatre capacity (in case of a surgical specialty), nursing capacity and intensive care (IC) beds.

To allow for admission of emergency patients capacity needs to be kept free. Therefore, a well-balanced policy to reserve an adequate amount of capacity for emergency admissions is an important support for managing the patient flow.

Setting the level of reservation too high will lead to less elective patients treated. If the level is too low, there will be difficulties with handling the emergency admissions. The leftover capacity needs to be scheduled as efficiently as possible with scheduled patients. Admission planning decides on the number of patients admitted for a specialty each day, but also on the mix of patients admitted. Therefore, a policy for admission scheduling can be an important support to manage the workload of in-patient admissions.

In this paper we discuss an approach that allows for defining a reservation policy for emergency patients and a scheduling policy for elective patients, while considering the combined effect of both policies on the handling of the total patient flow of the specialty. Previous approaches often concentrated on the best policy for handling one of the two types of patients – scheduled or non-scheduled. The paper describes the approach followed in this study and presents the results of a case study using this approach for general surgery.

Key words: patient flows, admission planning, emergency admissions

1 Introduction

The case-study hospital St. Maartensgasthuis in Venlo has, as all hospitals in the Netherlands, to deal with a growing demand, scarcity of resources and contracting purchasers that demand efficiency. Every year the hospital and purchaser make an agreement about the number of admissions the hospital is going to handle the next year. Based on this target number the hospital receives a budget fixed for that year. It is important for the hospital to reach the target number of admissions as near as possible. One way to achieve this is by a good admission policy. Another aspect that hospitals have to deal with is lack of availability of resources. The resources involved in this problem are: Operating Theatres (OT), Intensive Care beds (IC), normal beds, and nursing staff.

From a planning perspective, the hospital makes a distinction between two types of patients, emergency and elective. The emergency patients have to be admitted immediately, but the elective patients are placed on a waiting list. For both groups decisions have to be made by the hospital. For the elective patients the hospital has to decide which patients to admit every week. This decision directly influences the use of resources.

Emergency patients can never be rejected, so there should always be resources available to treat them. If necessary, elective patients are cancelled to provide enough capacity for the emergency patients. Because the hospital does not want to cancel elective patient often, the hospital reserves a percentage of all the resources available for emergency patients.

The size of this percentage is something the hospital should decide about. If they decrease this percentage, the use of resources will increase (because more elective patients are admitted), but more elective patients will have to be cancelled because of lack of resources. On the other hand, when they increase this percentage, more resources will stay unused (in case less emergency patients arrive) and the efficiency decreases.

The hospital wanted to know how policy decisions, made at an aggregate level, affect the use of resources such as beds and operating theatres. These decisions are as mentioned above: an in- or decrease of the reservation percentage and the number of elective patients that are admitted. The project's assignment was to develop a decision support tool based on a simulation model to improve the planning policy of the St. Maartensgasthuis Hospital. This tool should be able to:
- Evaluate the current situation in terms of use of resources and service to the elective patients measured in number of cancellations;
- Help in the determination of the percentage of reservation for emergencies that should be made;

- Show the effects of a change in the reservation percentage on the use of resources and the service to the elective patients;
- Determine the number of elective patients that have to be admitted every week to reach the annual target.

As mentioned above, the hospital has to deal with two kinds of patient inflow, the scheduled elective inflow and the random emergency inflow. In a previous project Myburg and De Kok [1, 6] modeled the elective inflow and developed a program, Optimix, which produces a schedule for admitting elective patients. The number of patients to be admitted each week is derived from the annual patient volume.

The patient flow of the specialty has been divided into several different groups of patients with more or less the same properties, such as length of stay, operation duration etc. The program Optimix produces a week schedule that gives for each day the number of patients that have to be admitted on that day. When this schedule is used, the target number of admissions is reached and the available resource capacities are used optimally. In this program the emergency patients are not considered.

The available resource capacity is the total capacity minus the resource capacity that is reserved for emergencies. The model Optimix, therefore, delivers per day a mix of elective patients given the resources constraints. The project undertaken had to extend the scope of approach to include also the emergency flow, and was a follow-up of a previous attempt [2].

2 Development of The Model

As mentioned earlier, the model should be able to handle three main things: the computation of the reservation percentages for emergencies, the scheduling of electives and the simulation of the entire system. In Figure 1, you can see how these three issues are related. In the following paragraphs the three parts of the model will be explained in more detail. Especially the input the model needs and the output the model will give will be discussed.

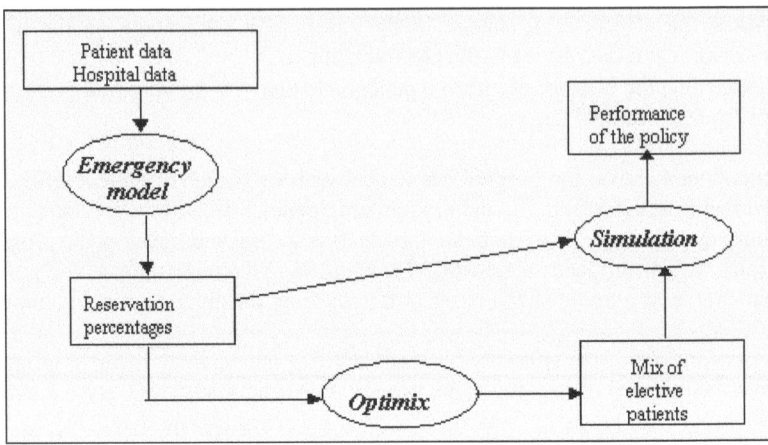

Figure 1: Problem structure

2.1 Model for Determining Level of Reservation for Emergencies

To get an approximation of the percentage of reservation, the formulas described in [3] have to be implemented. In order to compute the expected usage of all the resources by emergency patients the following data are needed:

- The number of patient groups;
- Expected arrival rate of patients of each group per day and per time of the day, in patients per hour;
- Expected service time and its standard deviation per group per phase, for operating theatres in hours and for the other phases in days;
- Number of nursing points used by a patient of each group per phase;
- Probability of using IC per group.

With these data the model can compute the expected usage by emergency patients. Using that, it computes the percentage of the resources that one expects to be used by emergencies and this is the percentage that can be reserved. So the output of this part is for each resource the percentage that is suggested to reserve for emergencies.

2.2 The Optimix Model for Scheduling Electives

In the first project [1] Optimix was developed and during a next project Optimix was implemented in Java [4]. This is the model that was used to compute an admission schedule for the elective patients. The model needs the following input:
- Number of patient groups;
- Number of days in the planning period;
- Target number of patients of each group that has to be admitted during the planning period;
- Total capacity available per resource per day;
- Percentage that is going to be reserved for emergencies per resource per day;
- Expected service time per group per phase.

The number of days in the planning period should not be too short because then patient groups with a low admission frequency cannot be included. On the other hand, the longer the period is taken, the longer the running time of the model will be. That is why we chose to fix this period to 28 days (4 weeks). The percentage of reservations can be either given as an input or computed by the first part of our model. The output of the model Optimix is an admission schedule that says how many patients of each group to admit at each day of the planning period. So in our case we receive an admission schedule for four weeks.

2.3 The Simulation Model for The Combined Patient Flow

The simulation part is the largest part of the model. It simulates the total system. In this section we describe the possible events and the way the stochastic processes are simulated. After that we discuss the input data that the model needs and finally the output that the model gives. In the simulation there are eight different kinds of events that can happen. Some of them are deterministic and some of them are stochastic. For an explanation of the phases distinguished in the stay of the patient, see also section 3.

1. Emergency Arrivals

When an emergency patient arrives in the hospital this patient immediately gets a bed. If there are no beds available an extra bed is created. This is counted as extra capacity. If there is at that moment an Operating Theatres (OT) available, the patient goes into that operating theatre and a new event, a service completion of phase 1, is generated. If there is no operating theatre available the patient is placed in a queue with highest priority. This means that as soon as an OT becomes available the emergency patient gets in. The time that the patient has to wait is recorded. This time should of course not become too long, because it is an emergency patient. After the event is handled, a new emergency arrival is generated randomly based on the Poisson distribution and the arrival rate of that group.

2. Elective Arrivals

In the model, this event takes place every morning at 9.00 a.m. All the electives, scheduled for that day by Optimix and not cancelled, are given a bed. If there are not enough beds available extra capacity is created. It is not possible to cancel these patients anymore. The patients that are scheduled for their operation on that day (that is the patients that have 0 length of stay in phase 0) are ordered according to their priority and placed in a queue for the OT. The operating theatres that are available at this moment and not reserved for emergencies are assigned to patients. For these patients a service completion event is generated. The patients, who are scheduled for their operation at a later stage, are put in phase 0 and their service completions are generated deterministically (because we assume that the length of stay in phase 0 is a fixed amount of days).

3. Service Completion Phase 0

In the model, this event always occurs at 9.00 a.m. of the day that the patient is scheduled for operation. The patient is released from phase 0 and put in the queue for the OT (phase 1). If an OT is available a patient is taken from the queue by priority and his service completion is generated.

4. Service Completion Phase 1

When an operation is finished the patient goes with a certain probability to phase 2, the IC. In that case he gets an IC-bed (if no IC-bed is available, extra capacity is created) and a service completion of phase 2 is generated. Otherwise the patient goes to phase 3 and a service completion in phase 3 is generated. The operating theatre is now available for a new patient. If there are patients in the queue the operating theatre is assigned to the patient with the highest priority. His service completion is generated. If there are no more patients in the queue the operating theatre remains idle until new patients arrive.

5. Service Completion Phase 2

When a patient is released from the intensive care he goes to phase 3 – recovery at a ward. Again a service completion for that phase is generated.

6. Service Completion Phase 3

After phase 3 the patient goes to phase 4. This gives a new service completion event for phase 4.

7. Service Completion Phase 4

When there is a service completion in phase 4, it means that the patient is discharged from the hospital. The patient is removed from the system.

8. Checking Event

Twenty-four hours before a patient should be admitted there is a check whether there is enough capacity available to admit. This happens at 9.00 a.m. every day after admitting the patients for that day. If it is necessary to cancel patients, patients with lowest priority are cancelled first. The patients that are not cancelled at this moment will all be admitted the next day, even if it turns out then that extra capacity is needed for them.

9. Start of Day

In the model, the day starts at 9.00 a.m. in the morning. All the resources are released and the administration is updated.

10. End of Day

This event is added because it is important to know whether it is day or night (for example for the arrival rates). The night in the hospital starts at 17.00 p.m.

11. Claim Event

After all the patients are admitted and transferred to the next phase all the resources (except for the OT) that these patients will use during this day are claimed. All the patients get a bed and the amount of nursing care that they need. Furthermore the patients in phase 2 get an IC-bed. This event also happens at 9.00 a.m. every day.

The generation of the stochastic service completion is done, based on the expected length of stay and its standard deviation. Following Adan, Eenige and Resing [5], we fit a distribution and based on this distribution we generate a random completion time.

Many events take place at 9.00 a.m. every morning. The order in which these events are handled is as follows: start of day; service completions in phase 0, 1, 2, 3 and 4; arrival electives; claim event; check event.

As an input for the simulation we need:
- The number of patient groups;
- Priority of each group;
- Expected arrival rate of patients of each group per day and per time of the day, in patients per hour;
- Expected service time and its standard deviation per group per phase, for OT in hours and for the other phases in days;
- Number of nursing points used by a patient of each group per phase;
- Probability of using IC per group;
- Fraction of the resource capacity available per day;
- Percentage that is going to be reserved for emergencies per resource per day;
- Admission schedule electives.

The analytical model can compute the reservation percentage or it can be given as an input. The admission schedule is the output from Optimix.

As output the model gives the performance measures of the system:
- Mean waiting time in the queue for the emergencies;
- Utilization per resource;
- Number of emergency arrivals during day and night for each day of the week;
- Number of elective admissions per day;
- Mean number of cancellations of elective patients per day of the week.

3 Data

In this section data will be provided on the specialty and case study setting. General surgery admits annually about 2800 patients, 40% emergencies and 60% electives. In 3.1 and 3.2 information is given on the patient groups and their characteristics. In 3.3 the available resources are shown.

3.1 Emergency Patients

For the emergency patients, nine groups are distinguished on behalf of their operating characteristics. Table 1 illustrates the number of patients for each group and the arrival rates.

For each patient group arrival rates are given in Table 1. It is possible to define in the model different arrival rates for each day of the week, and – for each day – for day-time and night-time, expressed in number of patients arriving per hour. As our analysis of arrival data in this hospital did only show significant difference between day and night, and working day versus weekend, our data do not distinguish between days of the week.

Patient Group		Annual	Working days		Weekend days		Arrival rate working day		Arrival rate weekend day	
No	Descript.	total	day	night	day	night	day	night	day	night
1	Abdom.	175	105	35	25	10	.050	.008	.030	.006
2	Append.	157	100	25	25	7	.048	.006	.030	.004
3	Vascul.	57	30	10	10	7	.014	.002	.012	.004
4	Hernia	43	20	10	10	3	.010	.002	.012	.002
5	Leg/foot	155	110	25	15	5	.053	.006	.018	.003
6	Femur/hip fracture	104	60	15	15	14	.029	.004	.018	.008
7	Arm/shoulder/hand	152	110	20	15	7	.053	.005	.018	.004
8	Rest (small)	54	30	10	10	4	.014	.002	.012	.002
9	Rest (big)	108	60	20	20	8	.029	.005	.024	.005
Total			625	170	145	65	.300	.041	.174	.039

Table 1: Emergency patient groups, volumes and arrival rates

Table 2 summarizes the operating characteristics for each group, and for each phase of the stay. Phase 1 refers to the phase of operation, and concerns the duration of the operation, expressed in the mean and standard deviation.

Phase 2 refers to the phase of stay in an Intensive Care bed. The probability indicates the proportion of patients in the group that will use an IC-bed. Duration refers to the number of days that the patient will stay in the IC ward. Nursing points refers to the nursing workload of the patient in this phase, expressed in number of nursing points per day.

Phase 3 refers to the post-operative phase, where the nursing workload might be higher than for the rest of the stay. Phase 4 refers to the recovery phase and rest of the stay until discharge.

Patient Group	Phase 1: Oper.		Phase 2: intensive care				Phase 3: post-operative			Phase 4: recovery			Total
	Durat. (hrs)		Prob	Durat. (days)		nurse	Durat. (days)		nurse	Durat. (days)		nurse	LOS
Descript.	μ	σ		μ	σ	pnts	μ	σ	pnts	μ	σ	pnts	days
1-Abdom.	2,2	.3	.6	1	.2	8	3	0,5	7	10	1	4	13,6
2-Append.	1	.2	0	0	0	0	2	0,3	5	1,6	0,2	3	3,6
3-Vasc.	3,3	.6	.7	1	.2	8	3	0,5	7	12,2	1,2	3	15,9
4-Hernia	1	.2	0	0	0	0	2	0,3	5	2,5	0,3	3	4,5
5-Leg/foot	1,5	.3	.1	1	.1	8	2	0,4	5	3,4	0,8	3	5,5
6-Femur/ hip facture	2	.3	.2	1	.1	8	3	0,5	7	10,8	0,6	4	14
7-Arm/ shoulder/ hand	1	.3	0	0	0	0	2	0,2	5	2,9	0,5	3	4,9
8-Rest (small)	0,8	.2	.1	1	.2	8	2	0,3	5	1,8	0,3	3	3,9
9-Rest (big)	2,4	.3	.5	1	.2	8	3	0,5	7	11,5	0,8	4	15

Table 2: Characteristics per phase for emergency patient groups

3.2 Elective Patients

Table 3 shows the 10 patient groups distinguished in the elective patient flow, and the volumes.

Patient Group		annual	week	4 weeks
no	description	total	average	average
1	abdominal	408	7,8	31
2	mamma	220	4,2	17
3	vascular	123	2,4	9
4	varicose veins	83	1,6	6
5	hernia	388	7,5	30
6	arm/shoulder/hand	73	1,4	6
7	leg	168	3,2	13
8	head/neck/skin	122	2,3	9
9	rest (small)	76	1,5	6
10	rest (big)	144	2,8	11
Total		1805	34,7	139

Table 3: Elective patient groups and volumes

The characteristics of the patient groups for electives are shown in Table 4. As some groups are admitted one day before the operation, also data for the pre-operative phase are shown. More-over, a priority order is given for the order in which cancellation takes place when the hospital is fully occupied, and elective patients need to be cancelled due to emergency arrivals (priority =10 is the lowest priority, so the first category eligible for cancellation).

		Patient Groups									
		Abdom.	Mamma	Vasc.	Varicos.	Heria	Arm/ shoulder/ hand	Leg	Head/ neck/s kin	Rest (small)	Rest (big)
Phases:	Priority ⟶	1	2	3	9	5	8	6	7	10	4
Phase 0:	Duration Aver.	1	0	1	0	0	0	0	0	0	0
Pre-op.	Nursing points	3	0	3	0	0	0	0	0	0	0
Phase 1:	Durat.(hrs) Aver.	1,4	1,1	3	1,3	0,7	1	1,8	0,8	0,8	2,4
Operation	Std	0,3	0,2	0,6	0,2	0,2	0,2	0,3	0,2	0,2	0,3
Phase 2:	Probability	0,5	0	0,4	0	0	0	0	0	0	0,1
Intensive	Durat.(day) Aver.	1	0	1	0	0	0	0	0	0	1
	Std	0,2	0	0,5	0	0	0	0	0	0	0,1
care	Nursing points	8	0	8	0	0	0	0	0	0	8
Phase 3:	Durat.(day) Aver.	3	2	3	2	2	2	2	1	1	3
post -	Std	0,5	0,2	0,5	0,2	0,2	0,2	0,2	0,3	0,4	0,4
oerative	Nursing points	7	5	7	5	5	5	7	5	5	7
Phase 4:	Durat.(day) Aver.	7,5	1,6	6,5	2,4	1,1	0,5	1,1	1	1	2,9
	Std	1,2	0,3	0,6	0	0,2	0,4	0,4	0,3	0,3	0,1
recovery	Nursing points	4	3	3	3	3	3	4	3	3	4
Total	LOS (day)	12	3,6	10,9	4,4	3,1	2,5	3,1	2	2	7

Table 4: Characteristics per phase for elective patient groups

3.3 Resources

Table 5 shows the resources that are available for general surgery. Each day general surgery has two operating theatres available, one IC-bed, 40 regular beds and 185 nursing points. During the weekend only one operating theatre is available. The operating theatre has an equivalent of 8 hours of operation time, during the day, and 16 hours for during the night. The IC-bed capacity is a proxy for the average number of beds available. The total number of beds in the IC unit is 6; these are shared between all specialties. The model also allows taking into account the phenomenon of bed borrowing. Table 6 illustrates this feature of the model. Borrowing of capacity can take place for IC-beds, regular beds and nursing staff. In this case there is one IC-bed available for general surgery in case an extra bed is required; this is borrowed from the total pool of IC-beds.

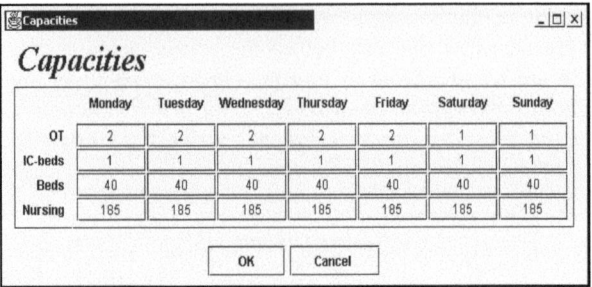

Table 5: Available resources for general surgery

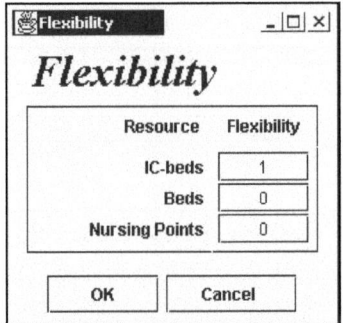

Table 6: Resource Availability

4 Results

4.1 Reservation for Emergency Patients

First, using the arrival rate data for emergency patient groups and the resource requirements of each patient group, the amount of capacity is determined to allow for admitting the emergency patients. These calculations are performed, using analytical formula. Table 7 shows the reservation proposals, expressed in percentages of the resources available.

	Monday	Tuesday	Wednesday	Thursday	Friday	Saturday	Sunday
OT	24	24	24	24	24	100	100
IC-beds	70	70	70	70	70	56	56
Beds	60	58	58	61	64	61	60
Nursing	61	57	56	60	63	59	59

OK   Cancel

Table 7: Percentage reservation for emergency patients

The percentages can differ for each resource type. During the week 24% of the operating theatre capacity needs to be reserved for emergency patients; in the weekend the reservation is 100% as there are no electives. For the IC 70% of its capacity needs to be reserved for emergencies during the week, while during the weekend 56% needs to be reserved. For regular beds the percentage reservation required for emergencies varies between 58% on Tuesday and Wednesday and 64% on Friday. For nursing staff the percentage reservation required varies between 56% on Wednesday and 63% on Friday.

4.2 Scheduling of Electives

When these reservation percentages are used, the leftover capacity is determined and this capacity needs to be filled with elective patients. Using the Optimix model performs this. The data used as input for the Optimix model are determined as follows:

- Planning period: 4 weeks;
- Number of patients scheduled: see Table 3;
- Available resources: see Table 5;
- Target utilization: defined by the reservation percentage;
- Cost function for weighing the importance of each resource type in the optimization process: Operating theatres and IC-beds are given a weight of 5 points, regular beds are given a weight of 4 points, and nursing staff is given a weight of 3 points.

For more information on Optimix, see the references [6, 7].

Then Optimix delivers a proposal for an admission schedule that will produce the best score of the objective function. The admission schedule proposed by Optimix is shown in Table 8. It shows for each day of the week in the 4-week planning period the number of patients of each patient group to be admitted.

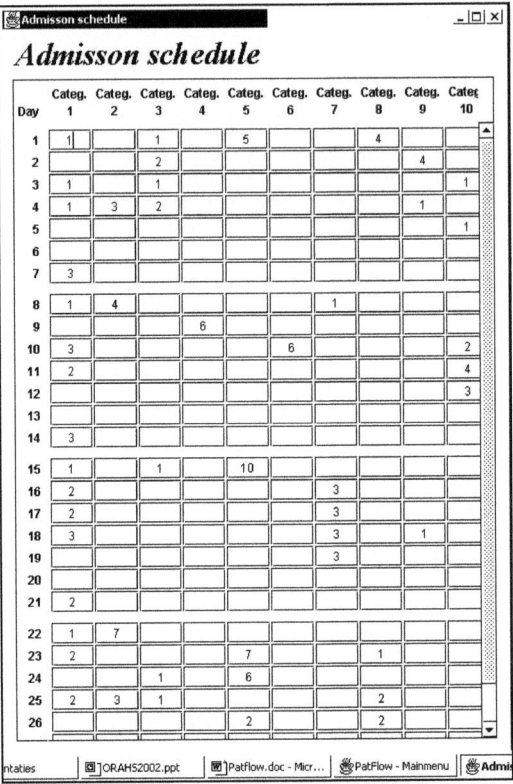

Admisson schedule

Day	Categ. 1	Categ. 2	Categ. 3	Categ. 4	Categ. 5	Categ. 6	Categ. 7	Categ. 8	Categ. 9	Categ. 10
1	1		1		5			4		
2		2							4	
3	1		1							1
4	1	3	2					1		
5										1
6										
7	3									
8	1	4					1			
9				6						
10	3					6				2
11	2									4
12										3
13										
14	3									
15	1		1		10					
16	2						3			
17	2						3			
18	3						3	1		
19							3			
20										
21	2									
22	1	7								
23	2				7		1			
24			1		6					
25	2	3	1					2		
26					2			2		

Table 8: Proposed admission schedule by Optimix

4.3 Simulation Results of The Combined Flow

The third step is to simulate the combined flow with the proposed reservation of capacity for the emergencies, and the admission schedule suggested by Optimix for the electives. Figure 2 and Table 9 show the results of the simulation. Shown are the numbers of OT hours, IC-beds, normal beds and nursing workload points required. The results shown are averages over 52 weeks.

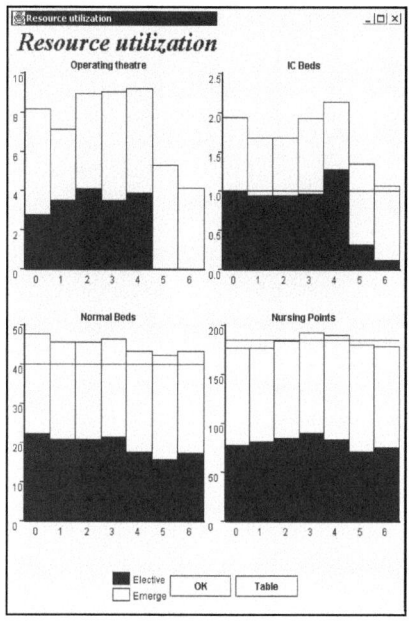

Figure 2: Simulation results

Table 9: Simulation results

Day	OT	IC	Beds	Nursing
		Electives		
1	2,7666	1	22,2308	77,4423
2	3,4852	0,9423	20,8462	80,4423
3	4,0727	0,9423	20,7308	85,0962
4	3,5095	0,9615	21,4815	90,2115
5	3,8732	1,2692	17,4808	83,1538
6	0	0,3077	15,5769	70,6154
7	0	0,1154	17,2885	75,25
Day	OT	IC	Beds	Nursing
		Emergencies		
1	5,4185	0,9423	25,4231	99,4038
2	3,6327	0,7308	24,75	96,4038
3	4,8811	0,7308	24,9038	98,8077
4	5,5186	0,9615	24,9615	102,1538
5	5,3405	0,8854	25,8289	106,7115
6	5,3004	1,0385	26,7308	109,5192
7	4,1325	0,9423	25,9423	103,0192
Day	OT	IC	Beds	Nursing
		Total		
1	8,1851	1,5385	40,3654	176,8462
2	7,1179	1,3462	40,2308	176,8462
3	8,9538	1,3269	39,5769	183,9038
4	9,0271	1,4038	40,1154	192,3654
5	9,2137	1,5385	38,9808	189,8654
6	5,3004	1,1154	38,6348	180,1346
7	4,1325	0,8846	39,0385	178,2692

ORAHS2002.ppt | Patflow.doc - Micr... | PatFlow - Mainmenu

The results show that IC-beds and beds are the bottlenecks, and that the OT has over-capacity. Elective patients can be cancelled in case no capacity is available. However, it is also possible to exceed the capacity allocated to general surgery because of capacity borrowing from other specialties in the hospital (see Table 6). Borrowing of capacity can take place for IC-beds, regular beds and nursing staff. If, for instance, 1 IC bed can be borrowed apart from the capacity of 1 bed allocated to general surgery, it implies that patients are cancelled when more than 2 patients require an IC-bed.

Table 10 shows the number of patients admitted over the simulation period. The total number admitted over the year is 2840 patients. The electives count 1758 patients (62%); the emergencies count 1082 patients (38%). From the emergencies 868 patients arrive during the day (80%) and 214 patients arrive during the night (20%). These data on the numbers of patients realized in a year of the simulation correspond fairly well with the numbers given in Tables 1 and 3.

Elective patients can be cancelled when too many emergency patients arrive. Another Table, which is not presented here for practical reason, provides information on the average number of cancelled patients per day of the week.

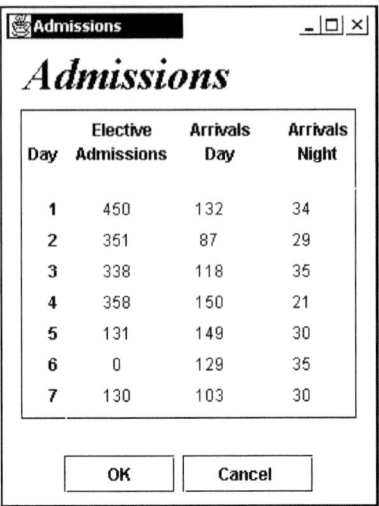

Table 10: Number of admitted patients
for simulation period

The results for the average cancellation show that on some days of the week the IC capacity is too small to allow for all admissions. On Wednesday on average 0.12 elective patients is cancelled, on Thursday about 0.23 and on Sunday about 0.65. Beds and nursing points are no bottleneck. The emergency patients sometimes have to wait for a free OT. The average waiting time for emergency patients to wait for an OT is slightly over one hour.

5 Concluding Remarks

In the introduction a number of issues were raised that have led to the development of the tool described before. This paper is a report on work in progress. The focus in this part of the project was on the development of a tool that is able to support the type of questions linked to the planning of admissions for general surgery. The quality of the data used needs to be improved to produce better information; now the data used are collected for the purpose of developing the model and to illustrate its working. Further work needs to be done to apply the model for decision making for the planning of general surgery on issues such as:

- Evaluation of the performance of the planning for general surgery;
- Determining the effect of different levels of reservation for emergencies;
- Determining the number of elective patients that can be admitted.

Acknowledgements

The author wishes to acknowledge Miriam Eijdems-Janssen, internal management consultant, from Ziekenhuizen Noord-Limburg and Talia Figarella and Lucie van der Logt, postgraduate students, from Eindhoven University for the collaboration in the project.

References

[1] R. De Kok and F. Myburg, Developing a decision support system for determining the optimal mix of patients for admission into a hospital, *Modeling project Mathematics for Industry*, Eindhoven University of Technology, (1999).

[2] A. Belitskaya and J.W. Weenink, Improving planning policy of patients and resources for the St. Maartens Gasthuis hospital in Venlo, *Modeling project mathematics for industry*, Eindhoven University of Technology, (2001).

[3] A. Deac and V. Voitishchuck, Developing a decision support system for the Thorax Centrum in Rotterdam, *Modeling project mathematics for industry*, Eindhoven University of Technology, (2001).

[4] T. Figarella and L. van der Logt, A decision support tool for the admission policy of Sint Maartensgasthuis Venlo, *Modeling project Mathematics for Industry*, Eindhoven University of Technology, (2002).

[5] I. Adan, M. van Eenige and J. Resing, Fitting distributions on the first two moments, *Probability in the Engineering and Informational Sciences* 9, (1995) 623-632.

[6] J.M.H. Vissers, M. Eijdems-Janssen, R. de Kok and F. Myburg, Optimisation of the patient mix for hospital admission planning. In: E. Mikitis, *Information, Management and Planning of Health Services*. Proceedings ORAHS99, (2000) 161-178.

[7] I.J.B.F. Adan and J.M.H. Vissers. Patient mix optimization in hospital admission planning: a case study. Special issue on "Operations Management in Health Care" of the *International Journal of Operations and Production Management,* vol: 22, number 4, (2002), 445-461.

3D VISUAL SIMULATION APPLIED TO A NEW THORAX DISEASE INSTITUTE

LUDMILA GABCAN, MARIO J.F. DE OLIVEIRA
Federal University of Rio de Janeiro, Brazil

Abstract

The objective of this paper is use a 3D visual simulation model to support the implementation of a modular and progressive project of new units of the Thorax Diseases Institute of the Federal University of Rio de Janeiro. The method enables one to produce the 3D visual simulation in order to observe the flow of patients, the attendance process and other important aspects of the new units operation. The analysis of the dynamics of the admission system reveals critical points in the studied module layout. The result is used to recommend changes in the original architecture project in order to improve the quality of the attendance process. It is argued that this methodology is easily applicable to other situations.

Key words: visual simulation, hospital admissions, flow of patients

1 Introduction

The Operational Research (OR) is a field that has produced a great amount of new tools to improve the way to structure and to think about existing problems that happens in several segments such as industry, education, environment and health. The OR methods are usually developed through formal and abstract models that seek a mathematical or logical description of some of the main characteristics of the real system being studied. Modeling is the art of building and uses such models as tools for the analysis of alternative policies and evaluation of operations. All models are basically tools for learning. They enable the study of systems that do not exist, so as to predict complicated consequences of actions and development, and also simulate experiments that are impossible or too costly to perform in reality.

The hospital as a supplier of services, for a long time has being recognized as an application field for the OR methods [1]. Models in the health and care systems operation area are proposed to evaluate how existing resources could be used in a more efficient way [2]. Traditionally this kind of application has been confined to issues such as appointment systems and waiting line management [3,4], staff scheduling and prediction of demand [5,6] and the planning of auxiliary services [7,8]. Such problems have early attracted the researchers' attention [9,10]. Nowadays, with the technological advances in hardware and software and the increased capacity of computers, new developments appear and progress in the modeling area is apparent. Models can be made more accurately and entirely new possibilities are open.

The visual simulation environment has been studied for over a decade. Guided by the fundamental requirements identified [11], incremental development and some prototyping approaches are used to develop a simulation model development environment. This technology has led to the creation of a 2D platform. 2D visual simulation models were used to study the efficiency of the operation of a surgical unit [12] and also the accident and emergency departments' [13].

A 3D visual simulation platform [14] is proven to be a powerful tool to ease the plan of new hospital facilities. This platform is used here to help managers understand complex internal interactions that happen in the implementation of the project of new units of a Thorax Diseases Institute [16]. A model of the admission system is used to evaluate the effect of changes and variations in the flow of patients and allocation of human and material resources. The 3D scenery was proposed, based upon the layout of one of the module [15].

2 The Problem

An old plan of the medical council of the Federal University of Rio de Janeiro is the reorganization of sectors of professional excellence in cardiology, pneumology, thorax and cardiovascular surgery, associated previously to the "Instituto de Tisiologia e Pneumologia". Located in the university campus, the Institute of Thorax Diseases (IDT) was created in 1996. There is a project to study the possibility to locate the new institute into an existing building, which remains empty for many years. The commission of implementation of the project adopts a strategy of progressive modules, planned so that the continuity of the construction the internal parts and the installation of the new units do not interfere with the working routine of the areas in operation. In this work only a specific module, the new building of IDT, is selected for study [16].

This health and care system operation problem is complex and its multidiscipline characteristic involves a close contact with a wide range of activities - other than medical - including pure and applied science, technology, and also political and economic organization. Medicine is a subject devoted exclusively to ministering to human needs. While clinical knowledge and ability are paramount there are many real and urgent problems in organizing the restricted resources available in hospitals so as to provide the community with the greatest possible benefit. Improvement in hospital admissions system is considered as an important factor in controlling the costs, and increasing the effectiveness of the medical care provided. The handling of such problem is difficult because hospital administration has little information about the demand for services, and the duration of service. The flow of patients should be predicted and controlled to match the human and material resources available in the near future.

Since it is extremely difficult to examine the system in all its complexity by means of analytical methods alone, a discrete-event simulation is proposed. The aim of this simulation is tree-fold. Firstly, it attempts to analyze alternative scheduling policies. Secondly, it seeks to examine possible ways to improve the quality of the attendance. Thirdly, it allows examination of the response of the system to the introduction of additional modules. The simulation described here is fed with empirical data selected from the hospital's database, and the effectiveness of the admission system is measured by the quality of the service. IDT believes that social quality is achieved, when the focus is on the final user as the center of the attention.

2.1 The 3D Scenery

The project of implementation of the new building is progressive and modular in order to avoid interference in the work routine of the areas in operation. The original plant of one of the sectors was kindly given by the director of the implementation committee. Figure 1 shows the studied sector. It is located in the 3rd floor of the new building. One can see details of the layout: (A) the waiting room, (B) reception desk, (C) and (D) corridor and (E) to (H) four consulting rooms. In the constructions of the scenario, facilities were proposed for the final service user, objects such as the furniture and other created detail [15].

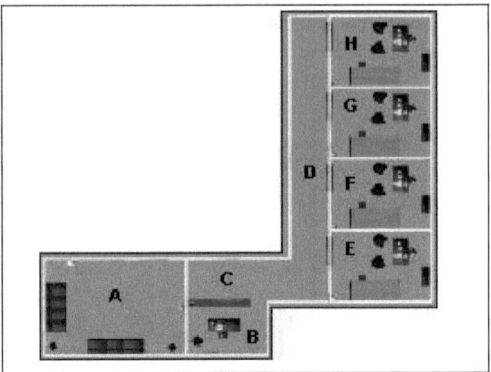

Figure 1: The 3D Scenario

3 Simulation

In many textbooks on simulation modeling, the simulation process is described as follows. There is a real world problem. This problem is formulated as a logical model. There are a variety of ways to represent the logic of a formulated problem. The next step is to convert the logical model in a computer model. This computer model is verified and tested to see if it is doing what the analyst wants it to do. The model is used as an operational model to produce some results, or some conclusions, or for implementation after the operational model has been validated against the real world.

Because of the complexity of the problem, formulation is a very difficult task. The construction of the logical model representing the formulation of the problem is, in many instances, the most difficult aspect of the modeling. In fact, understanding what the problem is may be the object of the whole exercise. One should be prepared to constantly undertake reformulation to obtain a common understanding of the problem as part of the modeling process. In many instances, the function that the computer model serves, is to perform a medium of communication for the structuring of the problem for all participants in the decision making process.

A discrete-event simulation is concerned with systems in which changes of state take place at particular points in time. Logical rules, or random events, generate the times at which changes occur. A simulation model can be considered to be composed of entities, things or components whose behavior one wishes to describe. These entities may have attributes and states, which distinguish and describe them in more details. The entities interact with specific activities of the world consistent with certain rules or conditions, which determine the sequence of changes. These changes are regarded as events of the system. As the simulated time advances entities can be active or idle. When an entity is active it is involved in an activity and when it is idle it is waiting in a queue. The models used here are concerned with the transfer of entities between queues rather than the alteration of the values of variables in expressions. The suggested simulation model is of probabilistic nature. Therefore, to accomplish the model it is necessary to generate a group or sequence of random numbers.

A simulation model of the admission system is designed, here, in order to identify the major congestion points, analyze alternative admission policies and investigate different ways of undertake the problem. The layout of the emergency department is utilized and the main parameters of the simulation model are estimated by sampling procedures. The hospital administrator is very interested in the proposal of investigating alternative policies by simulation because it would permit a series of experiments, with very little interference on the daily routine of the department.

The formulation cycle provides a good understand of what the problem is, and produces the logical and the computer model. The simulation is extensively used to verify the effect of a different combination of parameters in the system's performance. The visual simulation is the final step of the modeling process. One needs to create the 3D scenario and all the entities (objects) involved. The best results are then transferred into the 3D scenario. A complete description of this platform has been publishing elsewhere [14]. The 3D visual simulation enables one to "see" the results.

4 Visual Simulation

One of the most important areas of the current technology development is visualization. This is, basically, a method of computer graphics that transforms the symbolic in the geometric, allowing users to "see" the results of its simulation experiment. It enables one to observe data, simulations and models in a more elegant and significant way [15]. The graphic visualization enables the existent scientific methods and interacts with its data [17].

Animation improves the capability to present a simulation model [18]. It possesses the following characteristics:
• Refines the simulation presentation;
• Suggests improvements in the operational procedure or logical control of the system.

The animation also shows certain disadvantages. In particular, it does not substitute the careful statistical analysis of simulation results and it does not allow the user to take decisions about the model validity [15]. Changes in the logic of the problem are not interactive. For a visual simulation it is necessary to change the correspondence among elements of the model and those elements described visually in the computer screen [15].

5 Methodology

This work is based upon an existing simulation platform [4] divided in a series of modules that helps the OR analyst. It is composed of:
- Formulation;
- Discrete-event simulation;
- Building of the 3D model;
- Visual simulation.

In this work, programs were used for the generation of the formulation module and simulation. The conditions assumed in the development of the model are [15]:
- Simulate the attendance towards social quality target;Environment: patients, receptionist and physician (patient already registered);
- Hypotheses: patient's arrival is independent from the systems situation;
- All patients have the same length stay distribution;
- Distributions: Poisson (arrival rates and exit rates), Exponential (attendance).

It proposes medical attendance12 hours a day distributed in 3 shifts.

5.1 The Formulation Module

Formulation is the most important and difficult step of the simulation modeling. The first component of this module helps the user to create the relevant elements of the simulation program that is the entities involved. The component allows easy input parameters for the construction of the life cycle of each existing entity [4], [14]. The most important entity in this problem is the patient. The life cycle of the patient is basically its flow inside the hospital. In simulation terms the flow is an alternated succession of queues and activities. Arrival, reception, consultation and exit are example of activities. The model requires a closed life cycle, that is the entire final and the initial queue is necessarily the same. The simulator selects "patients" from an initial queue called "outside world".

The next step is to create the other entities involved in the simulation. The receptionist, the door and the doctor are example of entities involved in the life cycle of the patient. The same process accomplished for the main entity is repeated for the other entities. Figure 2 shows a window with a simple example of the life cycle of the entity "patient". It can be seen that the patients arrives, waits for reception, goes through the activity reception, waits to see the doctor before consultation and exits to the outside world.

The queues are passive states where the entities should wait until all the necessary conditions for the start of the next activity. For example, the activity "reception" can only start if there are a "patient" and a "receptionist" available. Otherwise, either the patient or the receptionist should wait. The queue component module is projected to analyze all queues that belong to the life cycle of the existing entities. The user is able to set the initial conditions and priorities of the queues. Figure 3 shows the window of this component.

```
Arquivo   Ediçao   Simulaçao   MultiSim

 Linha 1    Coluna 1   Insere
*CICLO PACIENTE
FILA ME
ATIV ENTRAR
FILA ESP_RECEP
ATIV RECEPCAO
FILA ESP_C
ATIV CONSULTA
FILA ESP_SAIR
ATIV SAIR
FILA ME
```

Figure 2: Patient's Life Cycle

Arquivo Ediçao Simulaçao MultiSim			
CICLO ENTIDADE	NOME da FILA	DISCIP	QTD
PACIENTE	ESP_SAIR	FIFO	0
	ESP_C	FIFO	0
	ESP_RECEP	FIFO	0
	ME	FIFO	6
PORTA	ESP_PACE	LIFO	1
RECEPCIONISTA	ESP_PAC	LIFO	1
MEDICO	ESP_P	LIFO	1
SAIDA	ESP_PSA	LIFO	1

Figure 3: Queue Component Window

The activity component uses all the information provided by the entity component and lets the user insert details of each activity such as the duration of time, requirements, priorities and so on. It shows for each activity, the entities involved and the flow. The program is interactive and keeps all the details inserted by the user in the entity module. Figure 4 shows the output of this component. It can be seen, for each activity, all the entities involved and details of the preceding and succeeding queues in the flow of each entity that participates in the particular activity.

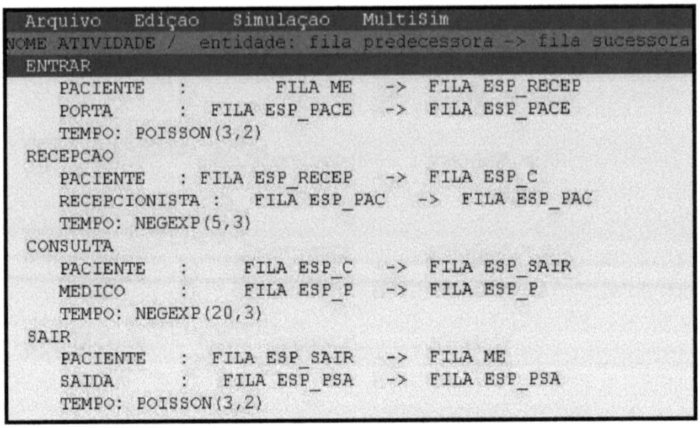

```
Arquivo  Ediçao  Simulaçao  MultiSim
NOME ATIVIDADE /  entidade: fila predecessora -> fila sucessora
ENTRAR
    PACIENTE    :        FILA ME    ->  FILA ESP_RECEP
    PORTA       : FILA ESP_PACE     ->  FILA ESP_PACE
    TEMPO: POISSON(3,2)
RECEPCAO
    PACIENTE    : FILA ESP_RECEP    ->  FILA ESP_C
    RECEPCIONISTA :   FILA ESP_PAC  ->  FILA ESP_PAC
    TEMPO: NEGEXP(5,3)
CONSULTA
    PACIENTE    :        FILA ESP_C ->  FILA ESP_SAIR
    MEDICO      :        FILA ESP_P ->  FILA ESP_P
    TEMPO: NEGEXP(20,3)
SAIR
    PACIENTE    : FILA ESP_SAIR     ->  FILA ME
    SAIDA       :  FILA ESP_PSA     ->  FILA ESP_PSA
    TEMPO: POISSON(3,2)
```

Figure 4: Activity Component Window

The module generates a computer code in Pascal, which is the logic of the model. The code is, in fact, an interface between the simulator and the formulation routines.

5.2 Simulation Module

There are several methods to execute a discrete- event simulation [18]. The use of the platform described above facilitates the fast development of simulation program, through a defined structure pattern. The simulator used here is basically a library of routines that execute the computer codes generated by the formulation module structured according to the three-phase method [19].

5.3 Interface Between The Discrete Simulation and Visual Simulation

The generation of the interface between the discrete event simulation and the visual simulation may be done using spreadsheet [17] or using a type of simulator as was done in this study. However, regardless of the manner done, the transition of the data requires setting up of specific positions for the principal entity being simulated. Such positions were acquired by being read directly from the data output of the simulation generated. Thus, starting at the interface, one may construct the trajectory of patients throughout the simulation.

5.4 3D Visual Model

The construction of a prototype of the section was made in agreement with the specifications of the plan and the environment considered. The software used in this paper for the visual representation is the used 3DS Max[1] [20], which facilitates the creation of a graphic interface that enables the analyst (or user) to observe the results of the simulation in a 3D fashion [15]. The steps for a visual model are:

- Creation and composition of objects in a scene;
- Lights and cameras;
- Application of textures;
- Render;
- Animation.

In the construction of the scenery, some objects of other libraries are imported [21,22]. The visual scenery modeled can be seen in Figures 5 to 10. It is shown details of the scenery: patients, reception, medical and waiting rooms.

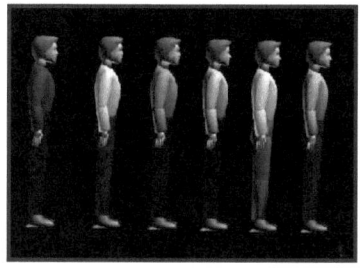

Figure 5: Patients   **Figure 6:** Medical Room

Figure 7: Reception   **Figure 8:** Waiting Room

---

[1]3DS Max is registered mark of AutoDesk, Inc.

Figure 9: Receptionist View   **Figure 10:** Top View

6 Conclusions

The study accomplished in this work show that is possible to represent the results of a formal discrete-event simulation model visually. The proposed method produces a visual model that is able to represent the complex project of the modules of a new hospital sector. The most important contribution made by this method is to point out a serious restriction in the existing project: there will be flow problems in the narrow corridor between the attendance room and the consulting room.

The used methodology offers a user friendly and flexible formulation module, which is able to define and make fast changes in the life cycle of the entities. The input data for the visual simulation are obtained directly from the simulation experiment, while preserving the integrity of the discrete-event simulation. In agreement with the presented results, it can be seen clearly that the 3D visual model do contribute to the analysis of several important factors that affect the system that otherwise could not be noticed by conventional spreadsheet simulation.

The layout of the visual model does represent one of the modules of the new IDT. From a simple study of "patients" trajectory in the 3D scenery one is able to "see" that an entirely new option for admission system is necessary to overcome difficulties with the flow of patients, medical staff, equipment and goods in the hospital corridors. The visual model can be used to implement new solutions that may contribute to improve the quality of attention and comfort for the patients and staff within the hospital facilities.

References

[1]   M. Lagergren, Modeling as a tool to assist in managing problems in health care, In: D. Boldy, J. Braithwaite and I. Forbes (Eds.), *Evidence Based Management in Health Care: The Role of Decision Support Systems*, Australian Studies in Health Service Administration, 92, (2002) 17-36.

[2]   J.C. Tuniclife-Wilson, Review of population health care problems tackled by computer simulation, *Public Health 94*, (1980) 174-82.

[3]   J.C. Bennett, *A flexible approach to improving outpatient clinic organization*, Paper presented at 20th meeting of the Working Group OR Applied to Health Services, 31, July-4, August, Chania, Greece, (1994).

[4]   M.J.F. De Oliveira, *A patient-oriented modeling of the emergency admission system of a Brazilian hospital*, Paper presented at EURO XIII, Glasgow, July 19-22, (1994).

[5]   J. Hershley, W. Pierskalla and S. Wandell, Nurse staffing management, In: D. Boldy (Ed.), Operational Research Applied to Health Services. *London, Croom Helm*, (1981).

[6]   P.C. O'Kane, *A heuristic approach to design efficient nurse rotas*, Paper presented to the 10th Annual Meeting of EURO Working Group on Operations Research Applied to Health Services, Altavilla, Italy, June, (1984).

[7]   C. Sapontzis, *Mathematical programming models in allocating units of blood to hospital blood banks*, Paper presented at EURO XII, Glasgow, 19-22 July, (1994).

[8]   G.G. Van Medode, A. Hasman, J. Derks, H.M.J. Goldsmith, B. Schoenmaller and M. Oosten, Decision support for clinical capacity planning, *International Journal of Bio-Medical Computing*, 38, (1995) 75-87.

[9]   N. Bailey, Queuing for medical care, *Appl. Statistics*, 3, (1954) 137-145.

[10] J.L. Balintfy, A stochastic model for the analysis and prediction of admission and discharges in hospitals, *Manag. Sci, Models and Techniques*, 2, (1960) 272-285.

[11] O. Balci, Requirements for model development environments, *Computers & Operations Research*, 13, (1986) 53-67.

[12] L.M. Jones and A.J. Hirst, Visual simulation in hospitals: A managerial or political tool? *European Journal of Operational Research*, 29, (1987) 167-77.

[13] J. Riley, Visual interactive simulation of accident and emergency departments, In: A. Kastelein, J. Vissers, G.G. Van Merode, and L. Delesie (Eds.), *Managing Health Care under Resource Constraints*, Proceedings of the 21st annual meeting of the ORAHS- EURO Working group, Eindhoven University Press, Eindhoven, NL, (1966).

[14] M.J.F. De Oliveira, 3D visual simulation platform for the project of a new hospital facility, Monitoring, Evaluating, and Planning Health Services: ORAHS'98, Singapore, *World Scientific Publishing Co. Pte. Ltd.*, (1999) 39-52.

[15] L. Gabcan, *Representação visual 3D de um setor para a nova unidade do Instituto de Doenças do Tórax (IDT)*, M. Sc. Thesis, COPPE/UFRJ, (2000).

[16] Comissão Especial de Implantação, Plano Diretor – *Instituto de Doenças do Tórax, IDT/UFRJ*, (1999).

[17] N.B. Gaspar, *Representação visual de modelos de fila de espera*, M. Sc. Thesis, COPPE/UFRJ, (1998).

[18] A.M. Law and W.D. Kelton, Simulation modeling and analysis, Singapore, 2° Ed, *McGraw-Hill*, (1991).

[19] E. Saliby and M. Pimentel, Simul: Um Sistema Computacional para a Simulação a Eventos Discretos em Turbo-Pascal, Rel, *COPPEAD*, Rio de Janeiro, (1991).

[20] M.T. Peterson, Fundamentos do 3D Studio Max, Rio de Janeiro, *Ed. Campus*, (1998).

[21] Mister Collection CD-Rom – Modelos para 3D Studio n°6, *Raven Multimídia*, Brasil.

[22] Products of the Platinum Technology Inc., http://www.platinum.com.

A MULTI-USER SIMULATION OF A HOSPITAL QUEUE

ADRIANA B. MORAES, MARIO J.F. DE OLIVEIRA,
SHEILA M. ESPOSITO, SIMONE M. BORDALO
Federal University of Rio de Janeiro, Brazil

Abstract

The recent advances in the information technology make it possible people in different places access, trough the Internet, a virtual environment and interact with other people. The simulation technique has evolved sufficiently in the last years and nowadays it is possible to visualize the results of a simulation model combined with sound, objects movement and in a way that approaches the reality. This article presents a contribution to the field of multi-user simulation. An application of a typical Brazilian public hospital queue is developed in a virtual space, where users have the chance to interact with each other. The main objective of this experiment is to let the users have a sensation of being in a hospital queue. One expects that this paper will bring a contribution to furthering understanding of this chronic and complex problem that occurs in Brazilian hospitals.

Key words: 3D visual simulation, hospital admission systems, multi-user virtual environments, emergency

1 Introduction

The 1988 federal constitution of Brazil mentions health as a social right and as an obligation of the state. It establishes, for the first time in its history, that all Brazilians have the right to public health care without any kind of discrimination. Unfortunately, after more than 10 years of its promulgation, there are still problems with the accessibility and quality of health care. Most public hospitals show long waiting lines, lack of doctors and medicines, not very good service, inappropriate buildings, obsolete technologies, etc. This situation is even worse in big cities like Rio de Janeiro, where most of the public hospitals are not capable of taking care of the demand for medical service [1].

Models of in the health and care systems operation have been proposed with the objective to improve performance by offering techniques for analyzing how existing resources could be managed in a more efficient way. Traditionally this kind of approach has been used to investigate administrative issues, such as appointment systems and waiting line management [2]. Modeling is one of the basic knowledge-building processes and simulation is a knowledge-evaluation technique, which enables one to explore the possibility of knowledge and the limits of this possibility. 3D Visual Simulation models are proposed to study the interaction and joint impact of several different factors of importance for the planning of admissions to a major public hospital in the city of Rio de Janeiro [3]. An early study evaluates the value of the visual representation of several queuing models and how it can be applied to the study of the hospital admission systems [4].

This article presents a proposal for a new type of simulation of queues that are developed in a collaborative computational environment, in which the user has the chance to explore and to interact with objects and people of this virtual environment. This simulation model is implemented with the C language and later on in the appearance-interactive animation, made over the Internet network through one "visual chat environment". The model discussed here follows an application of a hospital admission process presented in 28th meeting of the ORAHS.

2 Queuing Models

The mathematical models for the queuing theory started in Denmark, at the beginning of the last century. K. Erlang developed the first models, when working for a telephone company studying the problem of congestion, traffic and telephone exchanges. However, the theory was only applied to other hospital queuing problems, after the Second World War. With the development of the computers, the queuing models could also be analyzed by simulation, in order to overcome the difficulty to manipulate the appropriate mathematical formulas to study the functioning of complex queuing systems.

The basic assumption for the majority of hospital queuing models is that patients requiring services are generated in time by a "source of arrival", which is also called the potential population. Patients wait for the attendance in a queue and the waiting time depends, among other things, on the type of service. At certain times, an element of the queue is selected to be taken care of according to a previously defined rule, known as the queue discipline. The service is an activity that requires a determined time and is carried out by a particular entity involved in the process. After the attendance, the patient leaves the system.

The model used in this article is called M/M/1. This is a queue system where the arrivals are exponentially distributed according to a Poisson process with parameter λ. The service time is exponentially distributed with parameter μ, and there is only one attendant. The capacity of the system is considered unlimited and the discipline of the attendance is "First-In-First-Out" (FIFO) type. The average time between arrivals and service time is given by the inverse of these taxes, respectively, $1/\lambda$ and $1/\mu$. It is important to remember that this type of queue is very common in the admission of patients (selection) of the Brazilian public hospitals. A study on the complexity of the queues in hospitals is presented in [5].

3 The Simulation Model

This paper concentrates on discrete event computer-based simulation modeling. In many textbooks on simulation modeling, the simulation process is described as follows: There is the real world problem, which is formulated as a logical model (there are a variety of ways to represent the logic of formulated problem). The next step is to convert the logical model into a computer model, which is then verified and tested to see if it is doing what the analyst wants it to do. The model is used as an operational model to produce some results, or some conclusions and is implemented after validation with the real world.

Because of the problem studied here is complex, formulation is a very difficult task. The construction of the logical model representing the formulation of the problem is, in many instances, the most difficult aspect of the modeling. In fact, understanding what the problem is may be the object of the whole exercise. One should be prepared to constantly undertake reformulation to obtain a common understanding of the problem as part of the modeling process. In many instances, the function that the computer model serves is to perform a medium of communication for the structuring of the problem for all participants in the decision-making process [3].

For this study, mechanisms capable of simulating a M/M/1 queue are created and data are produced to make an interactive animation that visually represents a queue of a Brazilian public hospital. One can thus "see" a series of problems that occur during the simulation, contributing for a better understanding of the functioning of this complex system. Spreadsheets are created with a data generation program written in the C language. The entrance of values is shown in Figure 1. To get the data, that is, the values used for the simulation, it is necessary in the first place to generate pseudo-random numbers to create the time intervals between patient's arrival and departure. The average time for the patient's arrivals is denoted by λ and the service time is denoted by μ.

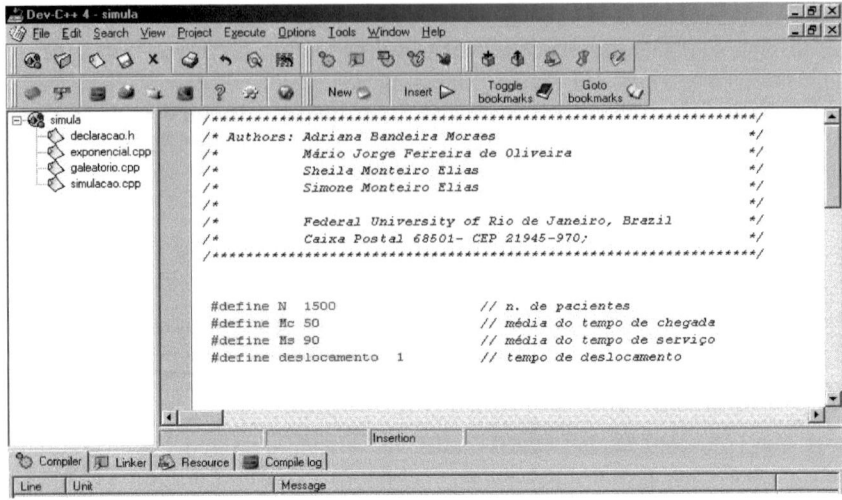

Figure 1: Entrance of values for generation of data

The data generation program uses the Wichmann-Hill method [6] to provide the interval between arrivals and the duration of attendance. The method generates the vector of pseudo-random numbers R from which it is possible to calculate for n patients [4] the following values:

$$TC(i) = -\lambda * \ln(R(i))$$

$$TS(i) = -\mu * \ln(R(i))$$

$$IC(i) = \sum_{k=1}^{i} TC(k)$$

$$IS(i) = \begin{cases} IC(i) + TD & , i = 1 \\ IC(i) + TD & , IC(i) > FS(i-1) \text{ e } i > 1 \\ FS(i-1) + TD & , IC(i) \le FS(i-1) \text{ e } i > 1 \end{cases}$$

$$FS(i) = IS(i) + TS(i)$$

$$TO(i) = \begin{cases} IS(i) & , i = 1 \\ IS(i) - FS(i-1) & , i > 1 \end{cases}$$

$$TF(i) = \begin{cases} 0 & , i = 1 \\ IS(i) - IC(i) - TD & , i > 1 \end{cases}$$

Where:
TC(i) = interval before the arrival of the patient i;
TS(i) = duration of the attendance of the patient i;
IC(i) = instant of arrival of the patient i;
IS(i) = instant of the beginning of the attendance of the patient i;
FS(i) = instant of the end of the attendance of the patient i;
TO(i) = idle time during the attendance of the patient i;
TF(i) = queuing time of the patient i;
TD = time between displacement and beginning of the attendance.

The chi-square test is used to verify if the intervals between arrivals and the duration of attendance follow an exponential distribution. The test shows that the distribution of the number of arrivals and the attendance time, in a certain time interval, follow the Poisson distribution. This is an indication that arrivals and attendance are exponentially distributed.

We considered the data of a major Brazilian public hospital that takes care of 1500 patient per day, between 8 a.m. and 8 p.m. The average times between arrivals and attendance are 50 and 90 seconds, respectively, with displacement time equals to 1 second. Table1, below, shows the values generated for the first five participants:

I	TC(i)	TS(i)	IC(i)	IS(i)	330FS(i)	TO(i)	TF(i)
1	16	5	16	17	22	17	0
2	21	268	37	38	306	16	0
3	0	22	37	307		1	269
4	84	53	121	331	384	1	209
5	20	230	141	385	615	1	243

Table 1: Output of data for 5 patients

For example, patient 4 arrives 121 seconds after the beginning of the simulation, that is IC(4)=16+21+0+84=121. The attendance starts in instant IS(4)=330+1=331 seconds and finishes in instant FS(4)=331+53=384 seconds. The idle time of the attendant is of TO(4)=331-330=1 second. That is, by the way, equal to the displacement time t TD=1 second. The patient's waiting time in the queue is almost 4 minutes, that is TF(4)=331-121-1=209 seconds.

For the chi-square test, we consider k as the number of arrivals (or attendance) in the time interval of 60 seconds, where O(k) is the observed number of values k, E(k) is the expected number of values k and $\alpha=0,01$ is the level of significance. The following table presents the values:

	Number of arrivals			Number of attendances		
	O(k)	E(k)	$(O(k) - E(k))^2/E(k)$	O(k)	E(k)	$(O(k) - E(k))^2/E(k)$
0	354,00	369,87	0,68	1149,00	1132,92	0,23
1	465,00	443,84	1,01	731,00	759,06	1,04
2	252,00	266,30	0,77	251,00	254,28	0,04
3	114,00	106,52	0,53	69,00	56,79	2,63
4	29,00	31,96	0,27	10,00	9,51	0,02
5	11,00	7,67	1,45	4,00	1,27	5,83
6	3,00	1,53	1,40	-	-	-
Total			6,10			9,78

Table 2: Data for the Chi-Square test

As the totals (6,10 and 9,78) are less than $\chi^2_{5,0,99}=15,086$ and $\chi^2_{4,0,99}=13,277$, respectively, the hypothesis that these distributions are Poisson is accepted. This result is confirmed by Figure 2, which presents the relative frequency graph of the number of arrivals (a) and attendance (b). It can be seeing that the relative frequency of the observed number of arrivals and attendance (hatched line) is similar to the expected relative frequencies (continuous line).

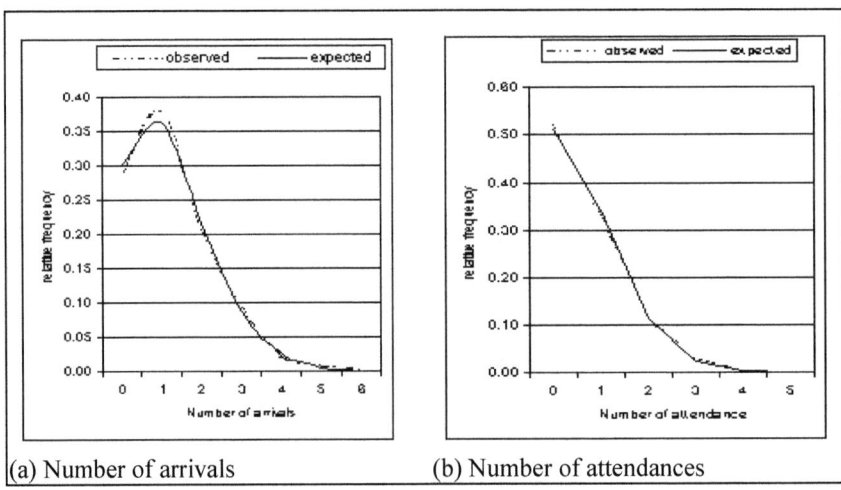

(a) Number of arrivals   (b) Number of attendances

Figure 2: Distributions of frequency

4 Visual Interactive Modeling and Simulation

Visual Interactive Modeling (VIM) as a managerial problem solving technique is about twenty years old, and owes its existence to the coming together of ideas from management sciences, Operational Research (OR) and management of information systems with the development of computers. A special issue of the European Journal of Operational Research publishes some results of the first international conference devoted exclusively to VIM. This conference is about combining user-friendly interactive interfaces, computer-generated visual displays of model status, and mathematical or symbolic models of problems or processes into systems to aid decision-making. The conceptual foundations of VIM and reviews of important recent developments can be found elsewhere [7,8,9].

Visual Interactive Simulation (VIS) is the method whereby a discrete simulation model drives a display that represents the dynamic workings of the simulation, and a user can interact with the model so as to view statistics, tries different experiments, etc. VIS is firmly established as a successful OR tool and many writers have discussed the praises of VIS over traditional simulation methods [10,11,12].

The Visual Simulation Environment (VSE) has been studied for over a decade and enables discrete- event, picture-based, visual simulation model development and execution for solving complex models. Guided by the fundamental requirements identified, incremental development and some prototyping approaches have been used to develop a Simulation Model Development Environment (SMDE). The VSE technology has led to the creation of a 2D model [13].

5 The 3D Visual Simulation

The 3D visual simulation is a method originally proposed by De Oliveira [3]. The method enables one to actually "see" the results of a simulation model in a 3D environment. The method is designed to run the simulation in four steps. The first step is to produce the simulation in a spreadsheet. The second step is to build the scenario where the animation is going to happen. The third step is to create and define the position of all objects, which will compose the scenes and the final step is to provide the animation. The production of the animation comprises the creation of the objects, the construction of the scene, rendering and showing the actual animation of the proposed simulation in a 3D environment.

The animation is basically the exhibition, in a certain speed, of a series of frames, where objects change their position in the scene. The example of simple queuing model is presented in Figure 3, below, with the objective of understanding the dynamic of the flow of patients. The model represents a M/M/1 system based upon the admission sector layout of the studied hospital. The main parameters of the model have been estimated by sampling procedures.

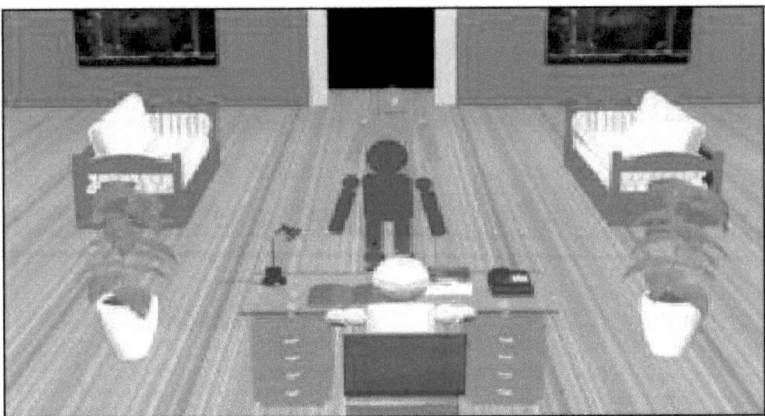

Figure 3: 3D model queue

The 3D visual simulation platform above described is proven to be a powerful tool to ease the plan of new hospital facility [14]. It provides means to think about several important points in the planning. The physical layout, the admission system, the flow of patients, the human and material resources and the flow of information are examples of some points that can be analyzed through the platform. The outcome of the exercise produces results that could be used to support other decisions. One's experiences in the hospital context show that patients, doctors, nurses and the administrators accept well this approach because they are able to "see" the simulation and reflect about their role in the process. The good point out of this experience is that "while the simulation program is running, one has time and opportunity to reflect about the 'reality' represented by the model" [3].

6 Virtual Environments

There are many definitions of Virtual Environment (VE). The most usual is: "A virtual environment is an interactive, immersive, multisensory, 3D synthetic environment" [15]. Out of this definition, the most interesting points are the interactivity and the immersion. The interactivity is interesting because one is able to monitor the entrances of a particular group of users, instantly modify the virtual world and evaluate the impact of the user actions on it. The immersion is interesting because it has the power to make the user feel the sensation of presence in the artificial world. An interactive environment can be immersive or not immersive [17]. An immersive virtual environment is either based on the use of helmets or projections rooms on the walls. The non-immersive virtual environment is based upon the use of monitors [16]. Normally, people are captivated when seeing the scenes changes associated with their commands.

One of the oldest virtual environment systems was originated with the development of flight simulators by the American military after Second World War. Many other applications have been made, mainly from the 80's by the military, academic and entertainment areas [17]. The existing relation among the areas of simulation, virtual environment and computer games is shown in Figure 4, where it is observed that the current applications of simulation incorporate totally the virtual environments area and partially the computer games area.

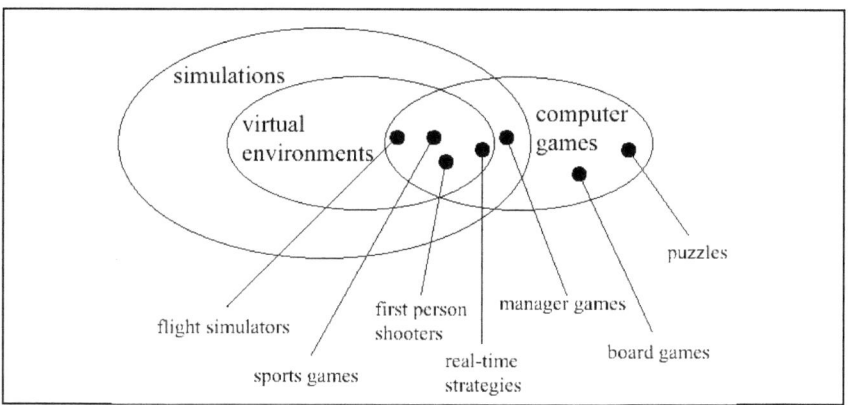

Figure 4: Relation between computer environments

The contributions of VE in the health field are noticeable. Amongst the most interesting applications are those involving surgical procedures, medical therapy, education, training, skill enhancement and rehabilitation and also architectural design of in the health-care facilities [16].

7 Multi-user Virtual Environment

Multi-User Virtual Environment (MUVE) is a new area of applications that incorporate computer graphics, sound and networks to simulate the real-time interaction between multiple users in a shared three-dimensional virtual world. Each user runs an interactive interface program on a "client" computer connected to a wide-area network. The interface program simulates the experience of immersion in a virtual environment as perceived from the user's simulated viewpoint [18].

In this kind of environment, the user can interact with other users through his virtual representation called "avatar". In some cases, the user can also find an agent or a virtual robot (bot), which has its behavior defined by the software. MUVE uses the metaphor of physical space, describing position and informal communication styles in order to create the illusion of being in the company of other people. In this environment, it is possible to exchange messages with other users and to move from place to place within the environment.

8 Multi-User Simulation

This section presents a new model, which is suitable to produce a visual representation of this queuing situation that is very common in Brazilian hospitals. It is argued that this approach would contribute to create a virtual scenario that can be used by hospital managers to underderstand this chronic problem. The model uses a MUVE to simulate a typical hospital queue with the objective of let the user have a sensation to be in the waiting line.

The multi-user simulation experiment was made with the help of users located in different points of the city of Rio de Janeiro. The users are expected to join a particular Internet site in a fixed day and time. A public announcement with an invitation to hospital managers to participate of the experiment has been sent out by electronic mail in august, 2002. The document included a brief description of the exercise, the rules and objectives with emphasis on its scientifically relevance.

After the potential users returned the e-mail showing interest and the intention to participate of the experiment, the organizing team provided further assistance. It included full instructions and guided visits to the site, prior to the experiment. This action was necessary to overcome possible difficulties to access the site, avoiding technical problems during the actual experiment. Moreover, the participants are supposed to be familiar with the environment and to be able to create and manipulate the entities involved in the simulation. The users are, in technical terms, called avatars.

The avatars do interact with each other users in the virtual environment, being able to move through the rooms and also exchange messages like in a chat room. The site is actually a virtual environment, which represents the hospital admission system of a well-known public hospital. The experiment tries to simulate the situations found in the real admission sector of hospital studied.

Forty people have agreed to participate of the experiment, acting as patients of the virtual hospital. Two of the organizers have also participated of the exercise. One of them plays the role of the attendant and the other controls the access of the participants. The data generation program described in section 3 provides the data used to control the experiment. The arrival of every participant was previously defined and checked by the controller. All participants were advised to connect with the system 5 minutes before the scheduled time to prevent possible delays.

The most interesting moments in the attendance of the 5 first patients are in the Figure 5, where:

- The Figure (a) shows the arrival of the first patient to the attendance desk 16 seconds after the beginning of the simulation;
- The Figure (b) shows the moment of the end of the first attendance and the exit of the first patient 22 seconds after the beginning of the simulation;
- The attendance of the second patient that happened 38 seconds after the beginning of the simulation can be seen the Figure (c);
- The Figure (d) shows a small queue with 3 patients that happened during the attendance of the second patient, 121 seconds after the beginning of the simulation. It is interesting to notice that the participants are able to communicate with each other by means of chat messages.

It is important to notice that the user is considered to participate of the simulation only after passing the entrance of the virtual hospital. The experiment shows that the forth and fifth participants were visiting other rooms of the virtual environment before joining the waiting line that can be seen in the Figure (d).

(a) Arrival of the first patient   (b) Exit of the first patient

Figure 5: Visual multi-user simulation of a queue (a and b)

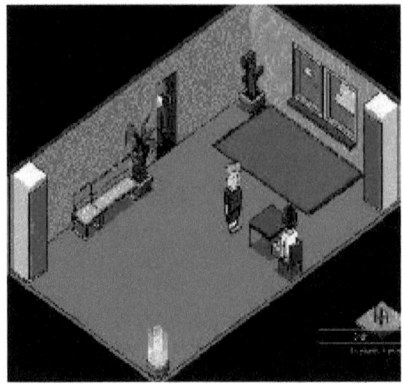 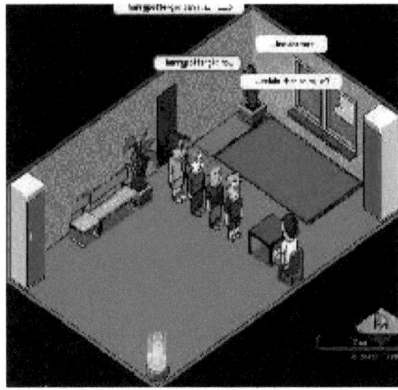

(c) Attendance of the second patient   (d) Formation of a small queue

Figure 5: Visual multi-user simulation of a queue (c and d)

Although was not done question to the participants about the experiment, some had revealed enthusiasm with the study and the virtual environment used. Evidently, the fact of the participants were not really sick, influenced in its interaction with objects and people of the space, which revealed less dense and worried that the one found in the real hospital. However, as well as in a real queue, they had had claims regarding the attendance time, which was expressed in questions made to the attendant.

9 Directions for Future Developers of The Model

Nowadays, the technological progress in computer hardware and software allows increased developments in the area of modeling. The advances in computer graphics and on the computer languages enable the production of new graphical libraries, which can be used to produce complex models. "Virtual" models can be made more accurate and new possibilities of practical application in several areas arise. However, one must draw the line of division between virtual and "reality".

For the accomplishment of the animations it was first necessary create a data worksheet in a platform that is not directly linked to the conversational site used for the multi-user simulation. The idea is create a conversational site that is integrated to the model of simulation of queues. This is necessary in order to automate the control on the entrance times, exit and attendance of the participants that at this work were all controlled manually by the authors. An option would be to use the language Virtual Reality Modeling Language (VRML) to create this platform.

Another point to be developed is that the used conversational site in this work is in the truth a rudimentary form of virtual reality; therefore it is a 2D environment that tries to recreate a 3D environment. The simulation was made in this environment, due to the difficulty in the visualization of three-dimensional environment in some computers. However, the methodology applied in this study can be applied in any conversational site in 3D. Truly, the ideal was that this simulation was made in an immersive environment; therefore it would be possible to have an idea of what really happens in the studied queue. Unfortunately, this type of simulation is still very expensive.

The main contribution of this work is the visual representation of queues models, by means of a virtual environment, were people could participate interactively of the simulation, what until then it was not implemented. Also an easy use program in C language was created, where it is possible to carry through simulation of the queues models and to generate the necessary parameters for the confection of the animations.

References

[1] M.J.F De Oliveira and L.N.P Toscano, Emergency information support system for Brazilian public hospital, in: M.S. Rauner, K. Heidenberger, (Eds), Quantitative Approaches in Health Care Management, *Peter Lang*, Germany, (2003) 235-251.

[2] M.J.F De Oliveira, A patient-oriented modeling of the emergency admission systems of a Brazilian Hospital, Paper presented at *EURO XIII*, Glasgow, July, (1994) 19-22.

[3] M.J.F De Oliveira, 3D Visual simulation platform for the project of a new hospital facility, in: V. de Angelis, N. Ricciardi & G. Storchi (Eds.), Monitoring, Evaluating and Planning Health Services, *World Scientific Publishing Co. Pte. Ltd.*, (1998) 39-52.

[4] N.B. Gaspar, *Representação visual de modelos de fila de espera*, Msc. Thesis, Production Engineering Department, Federal University of Rio de Janeiro, (1998).

[5]   J. Vissers, H. Bil and R. Kusters, Towards decision support for waiting lists: an operations management view, Evidence based management in health care: The role of decision support systems, *Australian Studies in Health Service Administration*, 92, (2002) 69-91.

[6]   J.N.W. Dachs, Estatística Computacional: Uma introdução em Turbo Pascal, *Editora LTC*, (1998) 33.

[7]   P.C. Bell, Visual interactive modeling: The past, the present, and the prospects, *European Journal of Operational Research*, 54 (1991) 274-286.

[8]   P.C. Bell, Visual interactive modeling in operational research: Successes and opportunities, *Journal of the Operational Research Society*, 36, (1985) 975-982.

[9]   P.C. Bell and R.M. O'Keefe, Visual interactive simulation – history, recent developments and major issues, *Simulation*, 3, (1987) 109-116.

[10] R.D. Hurrion and R.J.R Secker, Visual interactive simulation: an aid to decision-making, Omega, 6, (1978) 419-426.

[11] J. Riley, Visual interactive simulation of accident and emergency departments, in: A. Kastelein, J.Vissers, G.G. van Merode, L. Delesie (Eds), *Proceedings of the XXI ORAHS*, Maastrick, The Netherlands, (1995) 135-141.

[12] J.B. Macintosh, R.W. Hawkins and C.J. Shepard, Simulation on microcomputers - The development of a visual interactive modeling philosophy, *Proceedings of the Winter Simulation Conference*, IEEE, NJ, USA, (1984).

[13] O. Balci et all, The visual simulation environment, *Proceedings of the XI European Simulation Multiconference*, SCS, San Diego, CA, (1997) 61-68.

[14] M.J.F. De Oliveira, 3D Visual Simulation of Hospital Admissions, In: J.Riley (Editor) *Proceedings of the 26th meeting of the ORAHS Working Group*, Glasgow Caledonian University, (2000) 77-96.

[15] M. Matijasevic, A review of Networked multi-user virtual environments, Course EECE 619, *Advanced Topics in Computer Science/Engineering*, Section 8, (1997).

[16] J. Moqueue, Virtual environments for health care: A white paper for the Advanced Technology Program (ATP), *National Institute of Standards and Technology*, site http://ovrt.nist.gov/projects/health/vr-envir.htm (1995).

[17] J. Smed, T. Kaukoranta and H. Hakonen, A review on networking and multiplayer computer games, Turku Centre for Computer Science, *TUCS Technical Report*, (2002) 454.

[18] T.A. Funkhouser, Network services for multi-user environments, *Proceeding of the IEEE Network Realities '95*, Boston, MA, (1995).

INFORMATION SYSTEMS

DEVELOPING ELECTRONIC PATIENT RECORDS: EMPLOYING INTERACTIVE METHODS TO ENSURE PATIENT INVOLVEMENT

KEVIN LEONARD, WARREN WINKELMAN
University of Toronto, Canada

Abstract

The perceptions of the role of an Electronic Patient Record (EPR) vary widely with many of the stakeholder groups focusing on the provider needs for information sharing and knowledge management. Often lost in this focus is the perspective and needs of the patient in managing their medical condition and care. The overall goal of this paper is to improve patient education and to enhance the patient experience through the use of information technology (IT) in order to facilitate the sharing of information between providers and their patients. This research project took place at University Health Network (UHN) in Toronto (Canada), which is a large teaching hospital with multiple hospital sites in the city. In this process, we first examined the literature to investigate the human factors issues related to healthcare as well as other settings. Subsequently, we interviewed a number of interested stakeholders from two groups: the physicians (both family and attending) and the patients themselves. Finally, using a written survey, we explored the content that UHN lung-transplant patients would be interested in having within their EPR.

Key words: health information systems, patient decision-making, system design

1 Background

In recent years there has been an increased move towards an electronic patient record (EPR). The possibility of instant, universal access to up-to-the-minute, accurate patient information is a goal that is actively sought throughout health services organizations. In their review of the medical literature, Jerant and Hill [5] showed that the use of electronic medical records is associated with improved surrogate outpatient care outcomes.

Patients are becoming more active participants in the decision making process for medical care and more medical decisions are becoming the result of a shared process between the patient and health care provider [4, 17]. An integral part of this process is the sharing of information between health care providers and patients. Interactive multimedia has the potential to improve communication of the risks involved in medical decision-making and has been used to assist patients in making treatment decisions [1, 10, 13].

As the patient becomes a more active participant in the decision-making process, it is increasing demand for access to personal health information [15]. Patients' desire to find medical information from electronic resources, particularly the Internet, is well documented [3]. In addition, studies have found that patients are willing to use electronic media for education, assistance in decision-making and as a source of personal health information.

In an effort to improve communication in the patient care process, we have put forward the concept of transferring patient information from the medical record (paper-based and electronic) to a read-only compact disc (CD). This portable physical medium would be available to and usable not only by, patients but also attending physicians, primary care physicians and other allied health care workers caring for patients who are associated with one particular healthcare provider organization. It is our hypothesis that the use of a CD technology will overcome many of the security and data issues while simultaneously illustrating the benefits of electronic patient records.

Many benefits of an EPR can be summarized as follows:
- Data amalgamation and prompt data retrieval;
- Simultaneous and remote access;
- Legibility;
- Confidentiality;
- Flexible and tailored layout;
- Integration with other information sources;
- Data incorporation;
- Continuous data-processing;
- Assisted search;
- Greater range of output methods;
- Tailored output - Displays and printed reports can include many fonts, colors, still and moving images [14].

Unfortunately, there are many disadvantages associated with the EPR. They include:
- Layout not intuitive;
- Need for structured, coded data;
- Temptation to "stamp collect" everything;
- Temptation to embellish data;

- Loss of design control and flexibility;
- Costs;
- Adverse response from patients;
- Reliance on hardware;
- Reliance on software.

Our hypothesis is that patients, once exposed to the benefits of the EPR, will be one of the strongest advocates for change – and will work with their healthcare providers to overcome the drawbacks in order to access the benefits. From a patient perspective some of the direct benefits are:

- Availability when live instructors are busy or absent;
- Consistency and patience in gathering and dispensing information;
- Customized instruction;
- Patient privacy and avoidance of embarrassment;
- Apt use of feedback and reinforcement;
- Precise documentation of the learning processes and outcome.

Patients must have a comprehensive understanding of all benefits if they support the use of an EPR. As such, efforts should be made to comply with design principles based on human-computer interaction research. Poor design can complicate the navigational process for patients (and clinicians) and increase demands on their attention, perception, language and memory. By acknowledging these constraints, the structural design of the EPR CD should aim to match existing user workflow, follow established standards, accommodate flexibility and recognize human limits. Well-designed EPR should focus the viewer's attention on the data. The information should be presented in an easily navigable structure and comprehensible format.

As a result, in this paper our principal objective is to document the research findings pertaining to the design and layout of an electronic patient record. Based on our empirical evidence (from surveying and interviewing stakeholders) and incorporating literature from other areas of computer systems design, we will describe the critical success factors pertaining to EPR development and implementation. Further, we describe a research project where one large Academic Health Center in Toronto, Canada (University Health Network – UHN) has developed an EPR prototype using compact disc (CD) technology. It is hoped that this technology will not only address some of the limiting issues within the EPR but also expose the patient to the inherent value that lies within their health record – value for both themselves and other patients.

2 Rationale for CD Technology

The primary reason to move to CD technology was to overcome the restrictive issues of the EPR while at the same time illustrating to patients the value of information inherent in their health records – valuable to both their own health management as well as that of others. Two of the restrictive issues in using the EPR are data consistency and security. First, the development of the EPR CD at UHN was facilitated by the previous investment in developing a comprehensive organization-wide health record. Most departments and programs had already addressed significant data consistency issues.

The option to include data from computer systems (and organizations) outside of UHN was not considered. Second, by using a CD, patients perceived the medium to be highly secured. In essence, only one copy of their file was in use outside of their healthcare provider. The fear of someone accessing their information (e.g., over the Internet) was now no longer an issue. Being one of the first projects to develop an information system for patients, however, issues around exposing patients to computer interface design escalated in their importance. The following are some examples of these issues.

2.1 Structure

User-interface design is a key component of any system. Having a wealth of data is not useful if the pertinent information is not easily accessible to the stakeholders. Issues such as how data can be better organized within a record and on a document page and how computers can be used to enhance data interpretation are critical. They include:

- Navigation - Unambiguous and user-friendly point-and-click interface;
- Mode of information display - visual, symbol- and color-coded for fast and easy interpretation and comprehension;
- Multi-media - information presented in pictures, sounds, videos, instead of texts;
- Format of data – not static but dynamic and query-able;
- Graphic content (radiology and other imaging results) - possible diagnostic quality;
- Language - technical terms made understandable to patients with hyper-linked glossary.

2.2 Security

Security measures must balance the risks of providing access with the need to view valuable data. Canadian privacy and confidentiality laws ensure that personal health information is protected and exchanged between health care workers and patients for medical purposes only. Methods to make personal health information electronically accessible to patients and relevant health care workers in a CD format while protecting privacy were investigated through interviews and questionnaires. Analysis of current data security measures and technologies will be presented.

2.3 Internet – Web-Based Patient Record

There are very few examples in the literature of the patients holding the necessary information to allow physicians to make optimal therapeutic and diagnostic decisions. Most of these concern either their use in ambulatory care settings or with chronic diseases entailing a multi-disciplinary approach to patient care. Several Internet electronic medical services have been started in recent months. The web sites are not uniform. Some allow patient input of information, while others rely on doctors, but they provide emergency access to a patient's information. While many in the medical community have embraced the service, concerns over security still linger.

The field is so new that no standards exist for how online record services operate. The early entrants vary widely in how much and what kind of information they collect, what purpose the information is intended to serve, how it can be accessed, and whether physicians or patients maintain the record. Furthermore, principles of user-interface design are negligible. In addition, fundamental questions about Internet security and reliability remain, despite the sites' claims that it is easier for some unauthorized person to fish your medical record out of a storage room than out of a web site.

3 Review of Stakeholder Needs

Interviewing various stakeholders within UHN carried out the need analysis. These included attending physicians, family physicians and patients. When the initial survey of patients found that many patients were not computer literate, we interviewed patients selected because they would likely be early adopters of the CD.

Most of the research suggests that physician groups are certain to show the most resistance to change. Leonard [7] reports that a reason for this is that nearly all physician systems developed have made the work of the physician more cumbersome as well as there be insignificant financial incentives for physicians to use such systems. Lorenzi and Riley [9] found that technology is perceived to interfere with the traditional role of the physician. Conversely, other research reports that physicians are content with patient health information programs because they result in higher patient satisfaction and compliance, and more legible and accessible patient records [12].

A survey conducted found that 80 percent of the physicians would use information technology if it helped improve management of patient records and diagnostics. Finally, literature on physician acceptance of new medical information systems is beginning to develop. Treister [16] gives eleven reasons why physicians fail to accept new systems.

Among these is the failure to begin with an adequate:
- Physician base of support;
- Lack of user-friendly interfaces;
- Concern regarding the information collected;
- Failure to collect the most important information;
- Physician "techno" phobia;
- Exclusion of physician involvement in the financial analysis;
- Failure to include marketing to physicians in the implementation plan;
- Inadequate training of physicians to use the system;
- Lack of strong, centralized IS leadership respected by physicians;
- Lack of control by the organization over physician practices.

In summary, it is clear that physician resistance is high when an EPR system creates no added value to the physicians work. If it enhances the relationship with the patient and is not cumbersome to use, there will be little or no resistance [2].

3.1 Survey of Physicians

Responses were received from only 20 physicians in total (4 attending, 6 family and 10 residents in internal medicine). All surveyed felt that the care of patients would be improved if the patients or their family physicians had more relevant information. All, except one, felt that the referring physicians do not receive sufficient information on their patients' hospital stays. The entire physician group felt that the information was not received in a timely fashion. Table 1 summarizes the types of information that those surveyed felt that they and/or their patients should have access to on the CD.

Information	Physician Group	Patient
Discharge Summary	19	10
Lab Tests	20	5
X-ray Results	20	6
Medications	20	15
Self-Care Instructions	18	20
Future Appointments	19	20
Operative Notes	19	5

Table 1: Physician's perspective on who should have access to information

Across all physicians, only two expressed concern that the confidentiality of patients could be violated. In particular, one physician stated that her patients did not always reveal their entire medical history to all of their doctors. Two expressed concerns about the possible misinterpretation of technical information and comments in medical notes.

One physician felt that the discharge summary would need to be customized for patients, such that potentially offensive statements should be removed. All surveyed felt that the CD should include illness-specific information to educate the patient. All physicians felt that the CD should be password-protected. Four physicians felt that the CD would increase patient satisfaction and enhance patient's perception of communication, while two did not. On the subject of patient compliance, two physicians felt that patients do not carry out appropriate self-care and often require readmission to hospital; two felt that this occurs sometimes, and one did not answer the question.

3.2 Survey of Patients

The literature suggests that patients are willing to embrace technologies that allow them to manage their health, given that the information is dynamic (i.e. multimedia, sound etc) and easy to use. Kreider and Haselton [6] found that technology-based patient management programs could reduce the length of time required for conventional (i.e. via physician) patient education without compromising quality. Patients that used such programs felt well informed about the decisions that they faced, and were more satisfied with their overall care. Weed [18] found that generic and static (i.e. Pamphlets, Charts etc) patient education tools provide minute benefits to the patient due to their impersonal nature. Hence, patient education software should be dynamic and contain pertinent medical information.

In the literature, patients were positive about having an electronic medical record. Confidentiality was not a major concern of patients. However, other studies have shown drawbacks from patients because they felt that the EPR infringed upon their personal privacy. As an illustration, patients from an academic general practice, a private group practice and a solo practice were randomized into the experimental and control group. Patients withdrew from the study because they were sensitive to the nature of the information in the record and because of crises in psychosocial circumstance [8]. In summary, patients will use media that will improve their health given that they are dynamic and easy to use. However, patients welcome computer-assisted care as an augmentation and not a replacement of individualized health care. Patient acceptance of this technology is high and spans through all age, education, and socio-economic boundary [11].

In our study, ten patients completed the survey. They can be best described as "early adopters". They were all between ages 20 - 40, had access to computers with CD drives and Internet connections, would like more information about their hospital say after discharge, and would use the proposed CD program for the management of their health. Table 2 summarizes the types of information that those surveyed would like to be able to review them, and would like their physicians to have access to review on the CD.

Information	Self	Physician
Discharge Summary	9	10
Lab Tests	9	10
X-ray Results	9	10
Medications	9	10
Self-Care Instructions	9	9
Future Appointments	9	9
Operative Notes	8	9

Table 2: Patient's perspective

Almost all expressed interest to have more information on their medication, including an explanation of their purpose, warnings on drug interactions, and possible side effects and their symptoms. There was also a strong interest to have more information about their illnesses (severity, length, and course). Some would like to see on the CD their medical history and their physicians' suggestions.

4 Second Level Study

At this stage, we proceeded to delve deeper into one specific patient group in order to get their contribution to the design and development of a CD EPR. The primary research instrument used to interview was a written survey administered to UHN lung transplant patients. The survey was divided into three sections – demographic profile, computer use profile and information profile - and was designed to address three main questions:

1. What is the level of computer readiness and accessibility among lung patients?

2. Are lung transplant patients' interested in the concept of an EPR?

3. What type of content would lung transplant patients' like to see in an EPR?

4.1 Response Rate and Limitations

The written surveys were distributed in-person by team members at the lung transplant clinics on March 5, 12 and 19, 2001. Respondents were invited to return the questionnaire directly to the team member or to place them in a secure box provided by UHN. A total of 30 surveys were returned. The total UHN post-lung transplant (living) population is estimated to be approximately only 75 individuals. As a result, with the sample size of 30, tentative generalizations to the UHN lung transplant population might be made. The results cannot be generalized to the broader UHN transplant program or the UHN outpatient population.

4.2 Survey Construction

The survey was, in general, well received. Over 80% of patients approached agreed to fill out the survey. The main reason patients declined to complete the survey was poor health at the time of the survey. In general the majority of respondents answered most questions.

4.3 Demographic Profile

A total of 30 post-lung transplant patients responded to the survey. Six questions on the survey assessed the demographic characteristics of respondents. 60% of the respondents were female and 40% of respondents were male. The largest group of respondents (23%) was between the ages of 46 to 55. The second largest group (20%) was between the ages of 56-65. The level of education among the respondents ranged from a Master's degree (3%) to completing some grade school (3%). 57% of respondents had attended some level of post-secondary education. All of the respondents were receiving care from the multi organ transplant program, however, 70% of respondents also received care from a family physician and 30% of respondents received care from another lung specialist.

4.4 Computer Use Profile

Seven questions on the survey were designed to measure the level of computer readiness and accessibility among the lung transplant sample. Respondents were asked to rate themselves on their knowledge of computers. In this self-assessment 40% of respondents felt they had "beginner" knowledge of computers, while 30% of respondents had "moderate" knowledge of computers. Just less than one-quarter (23%) respondents had no knowledge of computers. Sixty percent of respondents stated that they had a CD in their computer and 57% of respondents had access to the Internet. Over half (53%) of respondents had access to the Internet at home while only 3% reported they had Internet access at work. Twenty-three percent of respondents indicated they did not use the Internet. Of those using the Internet, usage ranges between 1-2 hours up to 8-10 hours per week.

4.5 Information Profile

The questions contained in the information profile section of the survey were designed to address the two key questions: Are lung transplant patients interested in the concept of a EPR, and, if yes, then what type of content might they want to see in a EPR? The survey gauged patients' interest in their medical record. Sixty-three percent of patients have seen some part of their medical record. Blood work and x-rays were the most common aspects of a medical record that patients had seen. Over 60% of patients believe that having access to information about the medical care that they receive would help in managing their care at home.

Next, we asked patients what they believe would be the most valuable aspect of having access to their medical information. Respondents were encouraged to check all that apply:
- 57% of patients believe that access to their medical information would help enhance their understanding of their medical condition;
- 12% of patients indicated that access to their medical information would help ensure the information was available to their family doctor;

- 12% of patients felt access to this information was important in case of an emergency.

Patients were asked if they received enough information about their condition upon discharge from the hospital. Seventy-seven percent of patients believed they received enough information. Of the 20% of patients, who did not believe they received enough information, the majority wanted more information about necessary follows up care. Forty percent of patients did not believe that having medical information about their stay in hospital would affect their health at the time of discharge from hospital.

However, as previously discussed, over 60% of patients believe that having access to information about the medical care that they receive would help in managing their health care while at home. The difference in the phrasing of each question may illustrate the importance patients' place on information necessary for self-management over information about their hospital stay. Sixty percent of patients believe that if they were provided with their medical record, they themselves and their family physician would use it the most. Related to the use of the patient's medical record, 73% of respondents did not have any concerns about a family physician, family members or other medical specialists having access to their record.

Patients were also given the chance to choose what type of information from the hospital they would find useful to help manage their care at home The most popular choice was the lab test and results (67%) followed by a summary of active diseases (53%). Given a choice, 63% of patients would want this information as a paper copy. Other preferences included CD (13%), secure Internet (13%), and floppy disk (10%). Forty-seven percent of respondents indicated that they would find it useful to have the UHN lung transplant manual in an electronic format.

4.6 Discussion

The survey showed an approximately equal distribution of male and female respondents and covered a wide range of age groups with 75% falling between 26–65 years of age. Approximately 60% of respondents had engaged in some type of post-secondary education. The majority of the patients had access to the Internet from home. Overall the sample group can be described as young, educated, computer literate and Internet-accessible.

Almost two-thirds of patients (63%) had seen some portion of their medical record (most commonly blood work or x-ray results) and a similar percentage believed a personal medical record would help them manage their personal health care. The most common reason respondents wanted access to their medical chart was to enhance their understanding of their medical condition. This desire to have further access to personal medical information was expressed despite a comprehensive patient education program provided by the transplant program and despite the fact a high degree of patients felt they were provided with an adequate degree of information upon discharge from hospital (77%). As a whole, the sample group appears to have a high level of interest in their medical information and can be described as active participants in their care.

When given a choice of formats the majority of patients (63% of all respondents) expressed a preference for a paper copy of their medical chart. Other choices, such as CD, Internet or floppy disk were far less preferred - 13% of all respondents selected an Internet access, 13% preferred a CD and 10% selected a floppy disk. The specific information that patients identified as most likely to help them manage their care at home was lab results, a summary of their medical history, medication information (history and current), contact information (specialists and emergency contacts) and blood pressure/ temperature charts. Family and personal history and height/weight charts were not strongly endorsed. Only 17% of all respondents felt the inclusion of an allergy history was necessary in their personal health record. It is hypothesized a survey of health care providers would produce a different response as this information is crucial to providers when considering medications.

The reason behind patient preference for paper versus electronic formats of their health information was not explored in the survey conducted in our study. The literature would suggest the majority of patients who want a paper copy of their medical record rather than electronic copies do so because of concerns regarding security. In our study only 13% of patients would prefer a copy of their health record on a secure Web site but a further 23% selected either a CD or a floppy disk. It is hypothesized the CD and floppy disk are not considered as high risk regarding invasion of privacy. In contrast approximately half of the patients would find an electronic copy of a lung transplant manual helpful.

Further explanation for the preference of paper format may be the familiarity with hard copy and therefore patients can conceptualize what their personal health information might look like on paper. It may be more difficult for them to conceptualize how health information would be presented and navigated in an electronic format. The desire for personal health information is reflected in our study where almost 2/3 of respondents felt that access to their medical record would help them manage their health care at home. Our study did not specifically address the issue of e-mail connectivity with health care providers.

5 Conclusions

The results of this study demonstrate a desire on the part of some patients to have access to personal medical information. This desire stems from increased self-reliance in the management of personal health and the desire to take a more active role in the medical decision-making process. While the effect that this information may have on patient health outcomes is not clear, access to personal health information is associated with improved patient satisfaction. As patients move to a more self-reliant role in the management of their health the demand for personalized information will increase and the health care industry has to be prepared to meet this new consumer demand.

The survey conducted in this study indicates that lung transplant patients at UHN are interested in accessing their personal health information to support their health management. Over half of the total sample group is connected to the Internet and according to the literature it can be expected they are accessing health information through that medium. The preferred format for a copy of a personal health record is on paper although over a third of the information-seekers sub-group also endorsed some type of electronic format.

In addition to the survey of lung transplant patients, a prototype electronic patient record was developed as means of bringing to life some of the recommendations of the previous student group and the survey results of the current study. This prototype could be used to further explore the acceptability of personal electronic health records among UHN patients. The prototype could also be used in a focus group format with a variety of different patient populations to refine the tool and determine the best way to deliver customized medical information to patients. This prototype does not contain specific patient information for a variety of reasons. However, it would provide patients with a concrete tool by which to envision the possibilities of an electronic patient health record. Reaching beyond the lung transplant population, additional patient groups need to be targeted to see how well the results of this study reflect the level of interest and desired specific content of other patient groups.

A further possible area of study is that of security and regulation of health information. As discussed, concerns about inappropriate access to health information continues to be a significant issue amongst the public, even with those described as on-line users of health information. Future study groups may consider a more in-depth analysis of the technical solutions to security concerns as well as attempting to ascertain the level of concern about security among the hospital patient population.

A final area of future study is specific to providers and could address the key steps necessary for further development of an EPR. Future steps would include the analysis of the technical requirements and implications of developing an EPR and would require an in-depth review of system compatibility. Consequently, we must address any issues around legal and ethical implications of releasing hospital information to patients in an electronic format. Finally, hospitals must consider an internally focused strategy to gain the support of their own healthcare professionals to the concept of the electronic patient record.

Acknowledgements

The authors would like to thank the following contributors to our research program: Roslyn Devlin, George Tolomiczenko, Mowafa Househ, Jean Liao, Jason Lin, Shiran Isaacksz, Aaron Pollett, Jennifer Rodgers, Shalimar Santos-Comia, Matthew Anderson, Colin Smith.

References

[1] M.J. Barry, D.C. Cherkin, Y. Chang, F.J. Fowler and S. Skates, A randomized trial of a multimedia shared decision-making program for men facing a treatment decision for benign prosthetic hyperplasia, *Disease Management and Clinical Outcomes*; 1(1), (1997) 5-14.

[2] L.P. Drazen et al. Patient care information systems: Successful design and implementation, *Springer-Verlag*, New York, (1995) 32.

[3] H. Eliasoph, E-health consumer: A diminishing tolerance of hospitals, *Hospital Quarterly*, (Winter), (2000/2001) 30-34.

[4] I. Iakovidis, Towards personal health record: current situation, obstacles and trends in implementation of electronic healthcare record in Europe, *Int J Med Inf* 52(1-3), (1998) 105-15.

[5] A.F. Jerant and D.B. Hill, Does the use of electronic medical records improve surrogate patient outcomes in outpatient settings? *Journal of Family Practice*, 49, (2000) 349-357.

[6] A. Kreider and N. Haselton, "The systems challenge" *Chicago: American Hospital Publishing*, (1997) 95.

[7]   K.J. Leonard, Information systems for healthcare: Why we have not had more success – the Top 15 Reasons. *Healthcare Management Forum*, 13 (3), (2000) 45-51.

[8]   S.T. Liaw, A.J. Radford and I. Maddocks. The impact of a computer generated patient held health record, *Aust. Fam. Physician,* 27: (Suppl 1), (1998) S39-S43.

[9]   N.M. Lorenzi and T. Riley, Organizational aspects of health informatics: Managing technological change, Springer-Verlag, New York, (1995) 224.

[10] S. Molenaar et al. Decision support for patients with early-stage breast cancer: Effects of an interactive breast cancer CDROM on treatment decision, satisfaction, and quality of life, *J Clin Oncol.*, 19(6), (2001) 1676.

[11] A. Osheroff. Jerome et al. Computers in clinical practice: Managing patients, information, and communication, *Amer. College of Physicians*, (1995) 94-99.

[12] M. Ruffin, Digital doctors, *Hillsboro Printing Co.*, Florida, (1998) 189.

[13] V.J. Strecher, T. Greenwood, C. Wang and D. Dumont, Interactive multimedia and risk communication, *J. Natl. Cancer Inst.* Monogr., 25, (1999) 134-9.

[14] F. Sullivan and E. Mitchell, Has general practitioner computing made a difference to patient care? A systematic review of published reports, *BMJ*, 311, (1995) 848-52.

[15] P.C. Tang and C. Newcomb, Informing patients: A guide for providing patient health information. *J. Am. Med. Infrm. Assoc.*, 5(6), (1998) 563-70.

[16] N.W. Treister, Physician acceptance of new medical information systems: The field of dreams, *Physician Executive*, Vol 24 (3), June (1998) 20-4.

[17] K. Walsh-Burke and C. Marcusen, Self-advocacy training for cancer survivors: The cancer survival toolbox. *Cancer Practice*; 7(6), (1999) 297-301.

LOGISTICS INFORMATION SYSTEMS IN HOSPITALS: A CASE STUDY IN BRAZIL

ROBERTO M. PROTIL, LUIZ C. DUCLÓS, VILMAR R. MOREIRA
Pontifícia Universidade Católica do Paraná, Brazil

Abstract

Hospital administration, using logistics approach, shows some characteristics that are of different complexity compared to the administration of other kinds of organizations. This case study consists of four hospitals, a medicine distribution center and a health insurance called "Aliança Saúde-PUCPR". It shows an organizational structure where planning, coordination and integration of different physical, human, financial and informational flow present a non-trivial problem to be solved. Due to the inherent complexity of hospital administration and the characteristics of the case reported, it is verified that the use of an information system and simulations is a way to support the system management and the logistics involved. This article shows the importance of information and the role it plays in the logistics process. Logistics concepts and the modeling and simulation of processes, as an alternative to better understand and identify restrictions of complex processes like logistics systems, are also shown.

Key words: information system, logistics, simulation, hospital management

1 Introduction

Hospital services present basic differences if compared to other types of activities, especially those regarding complexity. The main purpose of hospital services is to preserve human life. Based on this fact, quality assurance is required to demonstrate efficiency in all kinds of demands – always taking into consideration the resources and the precious social role hospitals play. The complex organizational structure, the nature of services rendered and the increasing cost retention of sponsors contribute to make hospital management more difficult [15], [10].

Hospital services can be defined as a group of processes focused on the reestablishment and maintenance of people's health. In comparison to other productive processes, support activities represent a considerable part of the global cost of a hospital. For this reason the rationalization of resources and the optimization of the supply logistics of a hospital is highly relevant, especially in the Brazilian context, where the public health system is very poor regarding its administration. Despite the difficulties found in the health system, the awareness of the public is translated into demand for quality services with lower costs. This has forced the health sector to search for new techniques and methodologies to minimize complexities regarding hospital administration [14].

The use of traditional planning techniques, programming and production control is not boldly adapted to the hospital context if some basic perspectives and features are not taken into consideration [11]. Some of these features, which are specific to hospital and differentiate them from general manufacturing, are:

- The approach of the manufacturing production control is based on good flow controls. In hospitals, the main focus of its activities is the flow of patients, not always well defined and predictable, while the concern with the flow of materials is considered secondary;
- Complete and explicit specifications of final product requirements, as well as distribution, are essential for manufacturing production control. These aspects present considerable deficiencies within hospital systems;
- In hospitals there is no simplified command structure, but a delicate power balance structure among different groups (managers, doctors, nurses, etc). Due to this problem there is no general consensus regarding the targets to be reached for improving production performance;
- Basically, whoever improves hospital production (i.e., doctors through service requirements), is also responsible for providing it;
- Hospital care is not considered a commodity that can be stored. Hospitals are organizations driven by resources.

2 Logistics and Information Technology

Entrepreneurial logistics is the activity that deals with profitability and efficiency of services for supporting and distributing production, retail and services. Planning, organization and effective control of acquisition activities, material transportation, storage and the flow of information involved in these processes are attributes specific to the logistics department of a company [3].

According to P.F. Fleury et al. [13]: "Logistics is a real paradox. It is, at the same time, one of the most ancient economic activities and a state-of-the-art management concept". This can be explained, in part, because until the 80's the main concern of companies was manufacturing and selling [12]. The strategically importance of logistics used to be left behind. However, when production and commercialization efficiency regarding products was achieved, companies searched for other kinds of competitive features, for the reduction of production and commercialization costs was close to its limits. Within this context the focus was driven towards optimization of logistics costs and from this point on, logistics efficiency has become a strategically target. A. G. Novaes [20] highlights production cost as the "hard" dollar for the price composition of a product. A product released from a plant costing a dollar ended up being sold for four dollars at retail stores. However, reducing production costs has become an almost impossible task. For this reason, focusing on a reduction effort of three remaining dollars, considered as the "soft" ones – part of the total cost involved in all levels of distribution and commercialization chain – is extremely important.

Further than the competitive differentiation provided by the reduction of global cost, companies also had to adjust to consumer requirements. That demanded better products and service quality. This was also important to highlight the strategically importance of logistics [13,20].

Within the hospital context, characterized by a diversity of human, physical and informational flows, the strategically importance of logistics becomes evident. Hospitals are provided with two alternatives to improve their clients' expectations; that is, improve the available capacity or the existing system productivity [9]. The first alternative faces the department's current cost retention and the lack of resources. This way, the increase in productivity of the existing system that is based on the reduction of costs, along with the increase of logistics efficiency, seems to be the best alternative to be followed. W. Daniel [8] came to the conclusion that, for each dollar spent in the acquisition of supplies, there is an additional cost of US$ 0.70 to US$ 1.00 in distribution logistics. This reinforces the need of hospitals to reduce this additional cost through the incorporation of modern logistics management techniques.

R.Y. Akikubo et al [1] emphasize that the amount of information and the number of executed processes in daily tasks of a hospital makes necessary reliable and flexible controls in order to avoid repetition of tasks and losses caused by the lack of rationalization. They also argue that adequate process information to the organization – supported mainly by the information systems – is helpful for the planning, organization, coordination and control of it. A. G. Novaes [20] highlights that the modern management techniques, integrated with well-defined information systems, are necessary tools for supporting management and logistics decision-making systems. A hospital unit can be described as a complex logistics system, where human, physical and informational resources need to be coordinated and integrated. Due to this system's complexity, integration and coordination could be possible, in an efficient way, only through the incorporation of an information system for management processing [2].

2.1 Supplying Logistics

Logistics concerns are production support through availability of material at the right time and in the right place. The distribution of finished goods at sales stations is mostly close to clients [3,6]. The purpose of integrating all these activities is to reduce costs and improve efficiency through a closer relation with suppliers and clients. Basically, the production support activity, also known as material administration, consists of acquisition, storage and inner distribution of materials and is the main purpose of supplying logistics.

2.1.1 Purchasing

The supplying logistics process, also known as acquisition is responsible for the purchase of supplies for production or service. The purchase process takes into consideration several aspects such as the relationship with suppliers, flexible deadlines, delivery dates and planning, with the main purpose of reducing cost [12].

The financial efficiency of the purchase process is directly dependent on the stock activities. That is why programmed purchases and the set up of lots are influenced by demand information and safety stocks are originated at the stock department [3].

2.1.2 Inventory

The inventory presents two main features: first, it works as a shock absorber that guarantees oscillations between production and demand regarding its purpose of storing finished goods. That is the case of manufacturing and sales stations. Second, it guarantees the supplying of material necessary for the production of goods or servicing [12].

As far as the supplying of material necessary for the production of goods or services are concerned, the inventory department must plan and control the necessary amount of material in order to guarantee its availability when the production of goods or services are needed. Several techniques to help planning and controlling inventory were developed through the years. They originated from the application of production engineering and were extended to other types of activities, including services. These are, basically statistics and operational research methods which guarantee availability of material, taking into consideration storage costs, the re-supplying time and the impact caused by the lack of material at the time when they are needed [3].

Companies also apply other management systems with control sub-systems, which present different levels of complexity. Two management policies for elaborating control systems are usually adopted: The Just-in-Case (JIC) in western countries and the Just-in-Time (JIT) in eastern countries. The JIC uses a centralized Planning, Programming and Control system of Production (PPCP) based on the principle of pushing the production. In this PPCP system, production programming is done through the use of a series of procedures and rules based on Manufacture Resource Planning (MRP) logic. On the other hand, the JIT policy incorporates a PPCP de-centralized system, based on a principle of pushing the production, called Kanban, characterized by signaling cards that are used to elaborate production programming [7,3].

The JIC policy mostly determines a minimum safety inventory level, which must guarantee availability of material within a pre-established period of time to make the purchasing process and supplying possible. The JIT is based on the premise that stocked material is a synonym of idle financial resources. Its main purpose is to provide automatic re-supplying of existing material at the exact moment when they are needed. This requires, consequently, more acquaintance with suppliers and a faster purchasing process.

With regards to hospital management, the inventory department must guarantee availability of medicine and material at a specific time and place. In this particular area, the effective and efficient stock control plays a special role that is, in a certain way, important for manufactures and retail stores. In specific situations, the lack of medicine and/or material directly interferes with the specific activities of the hospital and may result in unsuccessful medical intervention, with direct consequences to health and/or survival of patients. It is possible, in certain cases, to mix JIC and JIT in order to rationalize stock management controls within a hospital [8].

2.1.3 Internal Distribution

The internal distribution process refers to transportation of material between stocks and production stations, or service. There are several techniques to determine the best ways to distribute material, taking transportation and rationalization of resources into account [3]. The hospital distribution logistic must ensure the delivery of material at the right time and right place. However, the distribution flow is not usually well defined, and it is not always possible to safely provide all necessary material to a specific medical procedure. This lack of determination for distributing material results in some planning and controlling difficulties, which are not so sensitive in regular manufacturing [8].

2.1.4 Logistics Costs

The logistics management is focused on product flow, material and services with the purpose of integrating and rationalizing resources along the way, from suppliers to final clients. That is the reason why the evaluation of costs and the performance of this flow are highly desirable.

Thus, an integrated logistics approach and an efficient distribution management must take into consideration logistics costs as one of the main element [6]. Traditional calculation methods do not adequately apply to the complex activities of logistics flows [20,6]. That is why some cost calculation methodologies were developed and improved to provide support to logistics costs calculations such us Activity Based Costing (ABC).

The key for costs based on activity is the search for 'cost generators' through logistics flow because they require resources [6]. One of the purposes of the ABC method is to highlight, more intensively, the cost profiles of both the company and the supply chain [20]. Different from the traditional cost accounting vision that adopts the cost account/center approach, the vision of the ABC method is focused on processes/activities.

Thus, the ABC method is focused on the relations between resources used in several activities of the company. That is why the method identifies three basic elements involved in the composition of costs: activity, event and transaction. Every activity is originated in an event that generates a transaction, finally leading to the materialization of the first one [20].

2.2 The Importance of Information Technology in Logistics Processes

Basically, one of the most important elements in logistics operations is the flow of information involved. Clients and re-supplying requests, stock orders, storage house in-and-out flow, transportation documents and invoices are some of the most common ways to gather logistics information [13].

Through aspects pertaining to logistics management, with regards to involved information, information technology can provide effective and efficient control gains, follow-up and decision support. Among information technology tools, information systems may provide the necessary support for making information available regarding status of client's orders, stock control policy determination, control of internal material flow, efficient communication with suppliers and distributors, etc.

2.2.1 Information Systems

One of the greatest improvements that have resulted in significant efficiency gain in administrative processes is originated from the use of information systems. It includes all available tools to control and manage the information flows of a specific organization. Some authors also consider that equipment, procedures and personnel do create an information flow. That could be used in the daily operations of an organization and in the global planning and control of its activity [3]. The information systems used for these purposes are commonly called "corporate information systems".

The corporate information systems are classified as support systems for operations and management support systems [19]. The operation support systems, also known as transactional systems, are responsible for the processing of routine transactions and procedures. The management support systems, also known as management information systems, are responsible for the support provided to managers with the availability of relevant and processed information that may be useful to the decision-making process. There is a strong tendency, noticed in the past years, towards a more intimate integration of these two types of systems. This tendency, characterized mostly for the use of management-integrated systems, can improve efficiency and the applicability of information systems in the corporate environment.

2.2.2 Management of Integrated Systems

Management of integrated systems, also known as Enterprise Resource Planning (ERP), makes information integration possible (either transactional or manage mental) of the distinctive organizational areas, enabling integrated management. The main reason for choosing ERP is the dissemination of a totally integrated management of information avoiding the mixture of several systems, different suppliers, and various departments of an organization [13]. The implementation of an ERP system involves only two suppliers (could be possible with only one): the system supplier – most commonly the *software* developer; and a consulting company which helps in the implementation and re-definition of administrative processes aiming at re-utilization and organization of the way the system is used.

However, some ERP systems are destined almost exclusively for the transactional control of information. Decision support tools usually have to be acquired, or even conceived, so the information, stored and controlled in ERP, provide management subsidies regarding decision-making [13]. On the other hand, the use of an ERP system, with integration of logistics systems, may provide effective gains for controlling integrated value chain management.

Logistics information systems are sub-systems of management-integrated systems. As they are integrated to other sub-systems, the logistics information systems use the ERP system, with its transactional functions, to allow total integration of logistics information [13].

2.2.3 Logistics Information Systems

Logistics information systems are defined as sub-systems of management information systems, or management integrated systems, which provide all necessary information for the logistics activities of a specific organization [3], [13]. Logistics itself presents several elements in its structure, configuring an extensive flow of information [13]. In this flow, the analysis of transactions and logistics element history, along with structured techniques, allows the determination of important control features, such as the definition of stocks.

It is currently a fact that an integrated productive chain is one of the keys for competitive differentiation. In this context the logistics information systems provide the support necessary for tactic and operational control of the chain. Basically, a logistics information system, along with the management information system, is necessary for the definition and operation of modern Supply Chain Management (SCM) - concepts [13].

2.3 Modeling and Simulation

Modeling and simulation techniques were developed in the 50's. Due to new technology, they are being constantly used to solve complex logistics problems. According to P.F. Fleury et al. [13]: "It is true, logistics systems are complex dynamic systems that include several elements that interact among themselves and are influenced by random effects". Due to these features, logistics systems are natural candidates for the application of modeling and simulation techniques to support decision-making procedures.

Modeling consists of an abstract representation of a specific process of the real world expressed by physical, graphical or mathematical means [2,16]. According to C.J. Austin and S.B. Boxerman [2]: "Models necessarily simplify the representation of an operation, process or decision, and include only those aspects that are of primary importance regarding the problem being analyzed". Particularly in the context of modeling logistics processes, mathematical modeling techniques are frequently used, which can be experimented by computer through simulation.

Mathematical models represent a system with the use of logical and quantitative relationships. These relationships can be manipulated with the purpose of illustrating how the model reacts, or how it should react under specific circumstance [16]. Models can be deterministic or stochastic. Deterministic models are "predictable" and commonly used in cases in which decision-making does not involve uncertainty conditions. Stochastic models are employed to represent "uncertainty" conditions and for outgoing parameters, and are determined through statistical approaches [2].

The simulation is closely connected to a complex modeling system process and is the best tool for dealing with it. It is also a powerful support tool for decision-making. According to G.S. De Borba and L.H. Rodrigues [9]: "it allows the reduction of risks and costs involved in a changing process, since they can be pre-determined before the effective change occurs".

According to P.F. Fleury et al. [13]: "the simulation is the use of models for the study of real complex nature problems through computational experiment". According to R. Bowden et al. [5], with the purpose of reproducing operational behavior of dynamic systems, the simulation is: "the mimicking of dynamic systems with the use of a computational model for evaluating and improving system performance".

The simulation, in this case, provides a virtual mode for performing experiments in the system. Still according to G.S. Borba and L.H. Rodrigues [9]: "computational simulation is an operational research technique involving the creation of a computational program that represents some part of the real world, in a way that experiments in the original model predict what is going to happen in reality. Thus, the basic idea is to turn the model into a vehicle to introduce questions such as "what would happen if...?".

There are several types of software, which support computational modeling and simulation [13]. Among them is the ProModel platform, allowing a version, which is exclusively destined for simulation of processes in health systems. Health systems are natural candidates for simulation applications due to their features, especially regarding the great number and interdependency of variables in the processes involved [9].

3 PUCPR's Health System – Aliança Saúde

The "Pontifícia Universidade Católica do Paraná (PUCPR)" is in the health segment since 1959, when the incorporation of the "Faculdade de Ciências Médicas do Paraná" took place. In 1977 the "Hospital Cajuru" became part of PUCPR with the name "Hospital Universitário Cajuru". In 1999 the "Irmandade Santa Casa de Misericórdia de Curitiba (ISCMC)", a non-profit and philanthropic hospital network, handed over two of its hospitals and a health plan institution to PUCPR. A company named "Aliança Saúde" was then created with the responsibility to concentrate the system administration. In 2001 the control of another ISCMC hospital is handed over to the system. The structure of the PUCPR health system can be seen in Figure 1.

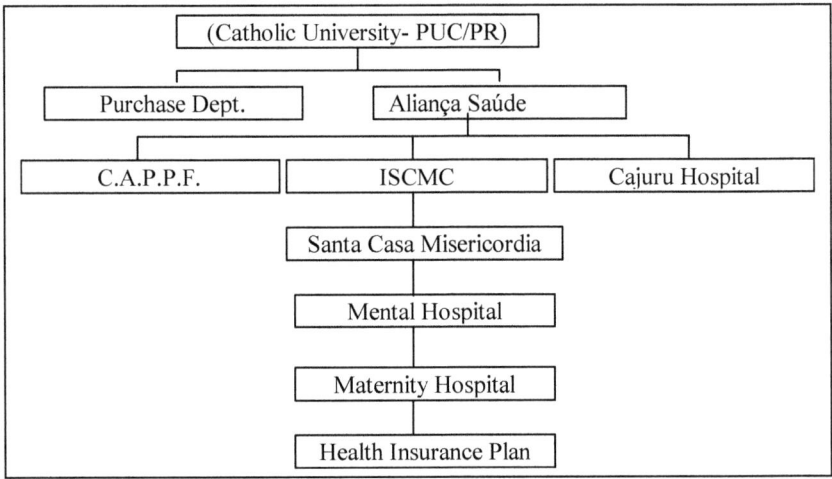

Figure 1: PUCPR's Health System

There are several different organizations among hospitals belonging to Aliança Saúde. Some difficulty to standardize and control administrative processes is experienced. Not all processes are in a data bank and, for those, which are, partially or totally, their information systems are not integrated through a network.

The Central Supplying And Processing of the Pharmaceutical Products unit (CAPPF) is also part of the health system – Aliança Saúde – that is known as a central laboratory. This company is responsible for the support provided to the supplying logistics of the Aliança Saúde's hospital network. Its main purpose is: to organize the medicine and material acquisition process through the supervision of orders and the control of standardization and necessities, periodically centralize and distribute medicine and material to hospitals.

The distribution work, executed by CAPPF to hospitals, is done on a weekly basis, except when there is an urgent need for medicines and material. The central stock is planned to supply the monthly needs of the hospital network. Orders are made on a monthly basis. The operational purpose of CAPPF is very important for the standardization and organization process of an integrated supplying logistics for the hospital network, allowing effective gains for the purchase, supervision and stock transfer processes among hospitals. However, there is no integrated information system able to provide support to its operations.

The department responsible for the negotiation and purchasing of medicines and material for the hospital network is part of PUCPR, which is also responsible for the general purchasing of supplies for the university. The information system, which provides support to purchasing, does not present specific characteristics for the selection of registered suppliers, as well as for the purchasing of medicines and health material. There is also no integrated and computerized information exchange system linking all hospitals, CAPPF and suppliers, with the purpose of checking stocks.

Each hospital is provided with two inventory centers. The first is a local central pharmaceutical unit for storage and internal distribution of medicines. The second is a central storage unit for keeping and distributing other material, necessary for hospital services (such as one-way material, surgery threads, X-ray material, etc), and supplying of general material for operational use in hospitals. There is no effective control of store up in inventory units. Emergency requirements for medicines and/or material lacking in stock are regularly issued. There is a great gap in relation to physical stock and the one registered, which compromises the determination of average demand for medicines/material in certain periods of time. There is no computerized control of stock, and is practically impossible to trace patients through the number of medicines/material lots used by them.

This deficiency of control has a great negative impact on CAPPF functions regarding control and determination of appropriate purchase lots. A negative impact is also felt in purchasing, since the negotiation with suppliers, through more expressive purchasing lots, is not possible. Regarding cost control, there are also large difficulties that make the application of some technical procedures, such as ABC, impossible.

Another determinant factor regarding supplying logistics optimization difficulties is the incompleteness of standards for medicines/material and suppliers. As each hospital has its own policy for selecting brands, the use of medicines and similar material and/or generic medicines is diminished according to doctors' preference, for these doctors are the ones who prescribe them. This situation also has a negative influence on the rationalization of costs and purchasing.

Based on this description it is possible to concise PUCPR's health system as follows:

- There are effective integration deficiencies among the several information systems of Aliança Saúde;
- The strategic and operational efficiency of CAPPF is prejudiced due to the lack of availability for obtaining quick and reliable information;
- The purchasing process is slow due to the several communication difficulties among suppliers, CAPPF and hospitals;
- The inventory control in hospitals is not practical and rational. That is why the purchasing process is prejudiced by constant emergency orders resulting from the lack of items in an existing safety stock;
- The standardization of medicines/material is desired, but this process had made difficult due to doctors preferences in each hospital;
- Decision-making, regarding the best procedures for an effective logistics supplying optimization in the hospital network, is prejudiced due to the deficiency of information and well-defined procedures.

4 Analyses and Discussion

However, due to the complexity of health systems, it becomes necessary to know more about the system dynamics, characterized by interdependent and random elements. In this case the only possible tool for acquiring more detailed knowledge about the system behavior and its inter-relations with its environment would be the use of computer simulation, according to what presented by G. S. De Borba and L. H. Rodrigues [9]. The simulation model allows the performance of experiments based on information of the real system, which leads to a better understanding of the real system behavior, further than experimentally determine the best configuration of the logistics information which is to be developed for PUCPR's hospital.

The "Aliança Saúde-PUCPR" logistic system has complex characteristics and lack of more accurate controls. The main goal is to maximize efficiency and minimize logistic costs. For this reason, some modern techniques and concepts of material administration and supply chain, like just-in-time, just-in-case and integrated management of supply chain, are possible ways of verification through computational simulation of the whole system.

Supported by computational simulation, PUCPR's health system is searching for better ways to improve inventory control, purchasing process, material distribution, cost determination policies and integrated information system in all levels of its logistic structure.

C.J. Austin and S.B. Boxerman [2] present four studies regarding situations in which inventory processes and logistics cost experienced a significant improvement through the use of the economic lot model. These studies were performed with a wholesale pharmacist, in a community hospital (non-profit), in a pediatric university hospital and in a special care hospital. These examples of analyzed cases, due to the nature of the people involved, show that the use of logistics control techniques in the PUCPR's health system can result in substantial efficiency gains.

Health performance improvement alternatives are using the integration power of based in Internet solutions. In this case SCM techniques are one of the most valuable instruments to apply just-in-time concepts to control hospital supplies. These techniques, used in production areas, make possible inventory costs reduction by its rationalization as well the upgrade of the whole system by the use of fundamentals concepts as the continuous improvement of supply chain.

Following studies will propose an effective integration for the whole supply chain, through SCM principles, connecting suppliers and hospitals in a reliable and automatic way. These plans include testing some retails techniques, which support automatic mechanisms of transference and supply necessities as implanted by Efficient Consumer Response (ECR). These techniques are shown major advance in cost rationalization between all the supply chains with big retails stores as the supermarkets [20].

5 Conclusion

This article is an analysis of the different aspects of supplying logistics for a health system. Specific features and intersections are presented among hospital management, supplying logistics and information technology. Through the study of the PUCPR's health system, problems and opportunities for improvement of decision-making and the possibility of developing logistics information systems are identified.

It is promising to notice that hospitals are complex logistics systems. The operational efficiency depends mainly on the support of well-structured information systems and it is possible to identify and eliminate barriers in existing flows. However, it is not possible to identify, in literature, detailed studies involving logistics and hospital information systems, which clearly show deficiencies in this area. In this study it is also clear the need for developing a simulating system, which produces knowledge about the dynamic behavior of decision-making processes and the relationship of information technology in the day-by-day activities of a hospital organization. This simulation model helps in the determination of a better architecture for the management information system to be applied within hospital logistics area. In the future this simulation should provide a way to determine new inventory policies, alternative distribution systems, rational allocation resources, among others possibilities.

References

[1]   R.Y. Akikubo et al, Informatização em hospitais de grande porte, *Revista de Administração em Saúde*, Vol: 4, 15, (2002) 17-24.

[2]   C.J. Austin and S.B. Boxerman, Quantative analysis for health services administration, *AUPHA Press / Health Administration Press*, Michigan, (1995).

[3]   R.H. Ballou, Logística empresarial, *Ed. Atlas*, São Paulo, (1993).

[4]   O.J.N. Bittar, Produtividade em hospitais de acordo com alguns indicadores hospitalares, *Revista Saúde Pública*, 30, (1996) 53-60.

[5]   R. Bowden, B.K. Ghosh and C. Harrell, Simulation using ProModel, *McGraw-Hill*, (2000).

[6]   M. Christopher, Logística e gerenciamento da cadeia de suprimentos, *Pioneira Thomson Learning*, São Paulo, (1997).

[7]   H.L. Corrêa and I.G.N. Gianesi, Just-in-time, MRP II e OPT: Um enfoque estratégico, *Ed. Atlas*, São Paulo, (1993).

[8]   W. Daniel, Applying just-in-time systems in health care, In: *IIE Solutions*, Vol: 29, 8, (1997) 32.

[9]   G.S. De Borba and L.H. Rodrigues, Simulação computacional aplicada a sistemas hospitalares, REAd - *Revista Eletrônica de Administração da UFRGS*, (1998), (http://read.adm.ufrgs.br/read08/artigo/borba2.doc).

255

[10] G.S. De Borba, *Desenvolvimento de uma abordagem para a inserção da simulação no setor hospitalar de Porto Alegre*, Dissertação – Universidade Federal do Rio Grande do Sul, Porto Alegre, (1998).

[11] G. De Vries, W.M. Bertrand and J.M.H. Vissers, Design requirements for health care production control systems, In: *Production Planning & Control*, Vol: 10, 6, (1999) 559-569.

[12] M.A.P. Dias, Administração de materiais: Edição compacta, São Paulo, *Ed. Atlas*, (1999).

[13] P.F. Fleury, P. Wanke and K.F. Figueiredo, Logística empresarial: a perspectiva brasileira, Coleção COPPEAD de Administração – Centro de estudos logísticos, São Paulo, *Ed. Atlas*, (2000).

[14] M.A. Jacobi, How to unlock the benefits of MRP II and Just-in-Time, In: *Hospital Material Management*, Vol: 15, (1994) 12-22.

[15] D.S.P. Hames, Productivity - enhancing work innovations: remedies for what ails hospitals, In: O.J.N. Bittar, Produtividade em hospitais de acordo com alguns indicadores hospitalares, *Revista Saúde Pública*; 30, (1996) 53-60.

[16] A.M. Law and W.D. Kelton, Simulation modeling & analysis, *McGraw-Hill*, NY, 2nd ed., (1991).

[17] J. March and M. Feldman, Information in organization as signal and symbol, In: *Administrative Science Quarterly*, Vol: 26, (1981) 171-186.

[18] J. March and H. Simon, Limites cognitivos da racionalidade, In: A teoria das organizações, Rio de Janeiro, *Fundação Getúlio Vargas*, (1966) 169-213.

[19] L.W. Martins, *Uma proposta de configuração de sistema de informações executivas para gestão universitária: o caso da universidade do oeste de Santa Catarina*, Dissertação, U.F.S.C, Florianópolis, (2001).

[20] A.G. Novaes, Logística e gerenciamento da cadeia de distribuição. Rio de Janeiro, *Ed. Campus*, (2001).

[21] H.A. Simon, Comportamento administrativo, *Fundação Getúlio Vargas*, 2nd ed. rev., Rio de Janeiro, (1970).

PERFORMANCE MEASUREMENTS

CHARACTERIZATION OF ANAEROBIC THRESHOLD IN DYNAMICAL PHYSICAL EXERCISE OF HEALTHY MEN

F.M.H.S.P. DA SILVA[1], A.C. SILVA FILHO[3], M.A.S. LAVRADOR[1],
V.R.F.S. MARÃES[4], M.S.A. MOURA[4], E. DA SILVA[4], A. M. CATAI[4],
B.C. MACIEL[2], L. GALLO JR[2]
[1,2]*Universidade de São Paulo,*
[3]*Universidade de Ribeirão Preto,*
[4]*Universidade Federal de São Carlos, Brazil*

Abstract

The main goal of the present work was to explore the possibility that the measure of some parameters usually applied in physical system in order to identify non-linear dynamics could also be used in Medicine in order to characterize the response changes of biological variables that, as it is well known, have non-linear components. During dynamic exercise there is a changing point in physiological state called Anaerobic Threshold (AT). Some respiratory and cardiovascular variables, including heart rate variability (HRV), experiment substantial changes at this point. We propose that the Kolmogorov-Sinai entropy applied to HRV may be used for detecting the Anaerobic Threshold in normal volunteers, with the advantage of being a non-invasive and fast procedure that requires low cost equipment.

Key words: time series, applied probability, Kolmogorov-Sinai entropy, non-linear programming, systems dynamics

1 Introduction

The integration among non-linear dynamics with experimental physiology and clinical cardiology can contribute for the understanding of very complex biological processes. As an example, the pacemaker intervals of healthy individuals show fluctuations that can result from unpredictable disturbances, or from a chaotic dynamics or both [1, 2, 3].

Dynamic exercise (DE) is the most common kind of effort used as a test of the cardio respiratory system. It is, also, used as therapeutic and preventive procedure in cardiology [4, 5].

Our objective has been to look for non-invasive low cost tools, in order to measure the Anaerobic Threshold (AT) during DE in men. AT is one of the best parameters to evaluate the cardio respiratory functional reserve, since it is able to quantify the O_2 transport in sub-maximal effort levels. Some ventilator variables, particularly the minute respiratory ventilation and the CO_2 production are usually used to identify the AT, since both exhibit at this point a fast response increase coincident with the increment of the blood lactic acid concentration [4].

Special emphasis has been given in the last few years to the heart rate variability modification that occurs during dynamic exercise. Close to AT (or in AT itself) there have been reported changes in the variability patterns of the R-R intervals of electrocardiogram (ECG). These changes have been detected by several statistical tests, like auto-regressive integrated moving average models (ARIMA) [6, 7, 8, 9].

2 Kolmogorov-Sinai Entropy

The general idea to be understood in the entropy concept is that it is impossible to use all the system energy involved in a work realization, because part of that energy is lost. Entropy is, in this sense, a measure of the inaccessible energy. The physicist Ludwig Boltzmann proposed a statistical entropy measure (H):

$$ H = - K \sum_{i=1}^{N_s} P_i \log (P_i) $$

Where K is the Boltzmann constant (only depending on the units used), and P_i is the ordinary probability of an element being in any one of the N_s phase space states. Shannon, particularly, reached to the same Boltzmann expression with K = 1. Kolmogorov and Sinai proposed, in 1959, to apply the Shannon entropy to dynamic systems.

The Grassberger-Procaccia algorithm uses the probability to quantify information [10]. The Takens theorem [11] allows the construction of m-dimensional vectors ξ_i (where m is the embedding dimension) from only one time variable $\{x_i\}$, where $x_i = x (t_i)$ and i = 1,2, N. In each vector ξ_i, $x (t_i)$ is its first coordinate, $x (t_{i+p})$ is the second coordinate and $x (t_{i+(m-1)p})$ is the last coordinate (p is the reconstruction step).

The correlation integral [12] is defined as a function of ε:

$$C(\varepsilon) = \lim_{N \to \infty} \frac{1}{N(N-1)} \left\{ \text{number of pairs i, j whose distance } |\vec{x}_i - \vec{x}_j| \text{ is less than } \varepsilon \right\} =$$

$$= \frac{1}{N(N-1)} \sum_{i=1}^{N} \sum_{j=1}^{N} \Theta \left[\varepsilon - |\vec{x}_i - \vec{x}_j| \right] \tag{1}$$

Where ε are radius of spheres needed to cover the whole set and $\Theta(y)$ is the Heaviside step function defined as:

$$\Theta(y) = \begin{cases} 1 \text{ if } y \geq 0 \\ 0 \text{ if } y < 0 \end{cases}$$

Grassberger and Procaccia [10] used the correlation integral values, C, obtained from the Takens reconstruction. The computed K-S (H_{KS}) can be interpreted as a loss (or gain) of information by the system, between the m.p and (m+1). p instants, where p is the reconstruction step.

$$H_{KS} = \lim_{\varepsilon \to 0} \lim_{m \to \infty} \frac{1}{p} \ln \frac{C_m(\varepsilon)}{C_{m+1}(\varepsilon)} \tag{2}$$

As m grows, the K_2 mean value defined as:

$$K_2 = \frac{1}{p} \ln \frac{C_m(\varepsilon)}{C_{m+1}(\varepsilon)} \tag{3}$$

Converges to H_{KS} (2). This mean value is plotted in a diagram as a function of m, for different values of ε, and we look for its asymptotic value.

3 Objective

The main goal of the present work is to evaluate the Kolmogorov-Sinai entropy potential tool when applied to R-R ECG series in different powers of dynamic exercise, in order to quantify the AT in healthy individuals.

4 Material and Methods

Ten healthy male volunteers have been studied: five young men (22 ± 1.5 years) and five middle-aged men (42 ± 2.5 years). They exhibited a sedentary life style. The dynamic exercises (discontinuous ones) were made with two experimental protocols, that is, progressive (EPI) and random (EPII) power levels, lasting fifteen minutes, with a rest period among them (Figure 1).

The DE, for the EPI power level, was made with progressively growing resistance in a cycle ergo meter (CORIVAL-400 model) with seated position (where the speed was around 60 rpm) and after 25 W we used increments of 10 and/or 5 W for 15 minutes. Between the different power levels there was a rest period in order to allow the cardiac frequency to return to its basal conditions.

The cardiac frequency values were visualized in a computer screen during the protocol. If a slow slope in the cardiac frequency plot were identified in a given power, between the first and the twelfth minute, a last session with a 5 W smaller power would be performed. This procedure aimed to increase the power resolution where could possibly be found the AT.

The DE, for the EPII power level, was made with the same equipment and experimental conditions of the EPI. The main difference was regarding the initial power level that was set to the value where it was found a slow slope in the cardiac frequency plot during the EPI protocol.

The R-R intervals have been measured, in seconds, from each one of the following situations: at rest, in supine and seated positions; in the last position during exercise, using an electromagnetic braked cycle-ergo meter at several power levels (Watts). The RR intervals were obtained using specific software to detect R waves of ECG signals and the respective periods [13].

For each one of the studied powers, the ARIMA model [6, 7] was used to analyze the cardiac frequency response and the Kolmogorov-Sinai entropy [1, 2, 3, 9] was used to analyze the R-R responses.

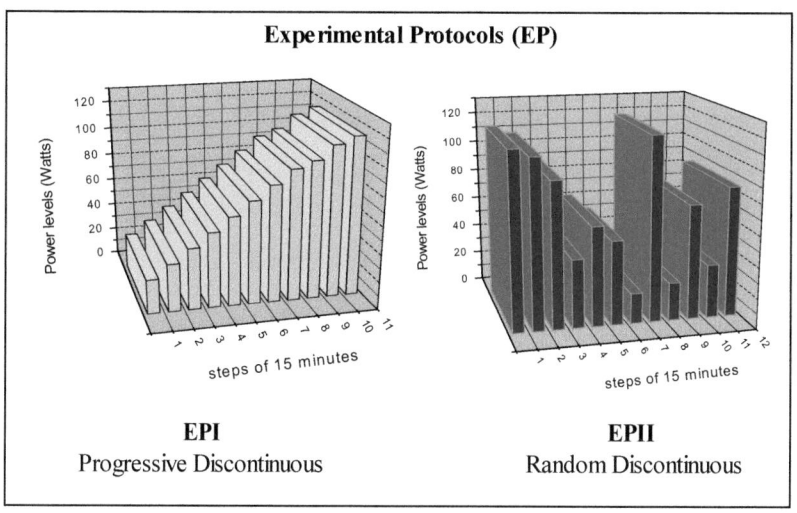

Figure 1: Experimental protocols for data acquisition

5 Results

In order to estimate the Kolmogorov-Sinai entropy for each set of data, we have plotted the values of K_2 against the embedding dimension m, m = 2, 3, ...30 and for different values of ε, where the values were obtained through the Grassberger-Procaccia algorithm [10]. Each RR-series was reconstructed with time-delay coordinates x(t), x(t+p), x(t+2p), ..., where the delay p was properly selected [1, 2, 3, 4, 5, 6, 7, 8, 9].

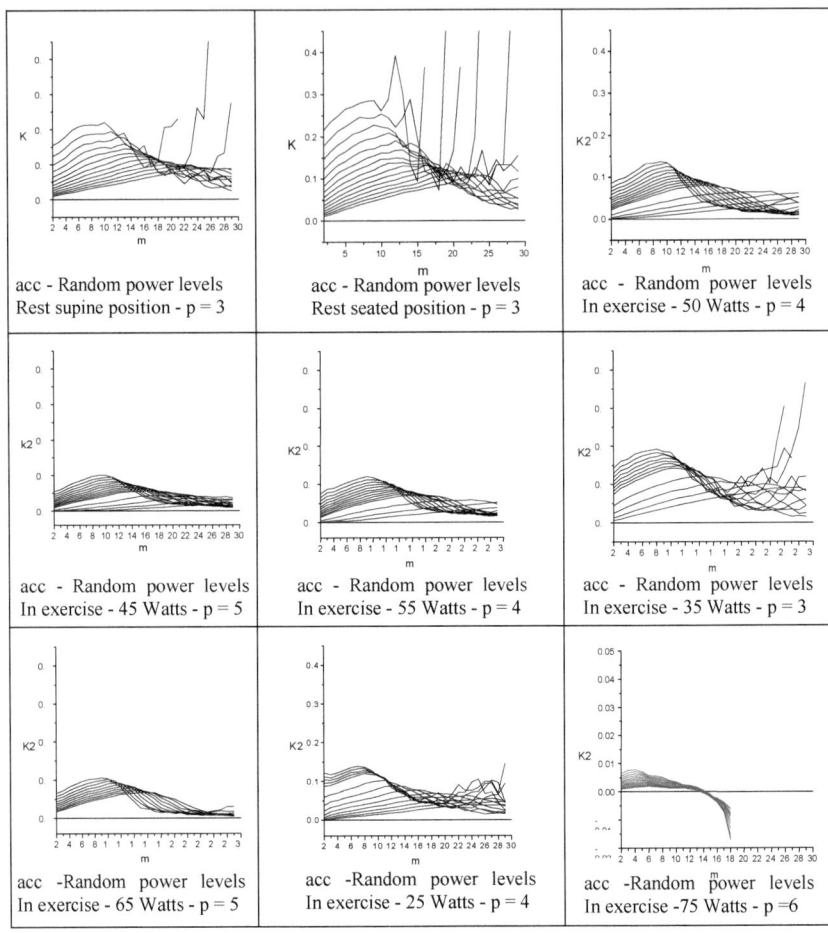

Figure 2: Diagrams of K_2 as function of m for one of the individuals (ACC)

The Kolmogorov-Sinai entropy (K-S) showed, in a phenomenological way, a very distinct change in the system response patterns at a specific power. The lines joined themselves and crossed the abscissa axis. This occurred in a power value, which corresponds to the AT. For one of the individuals (ACC), for instance, that power was found as 75 watts, represented as red lines in Figure 2. For the other power values, the lines do not cross the abscissa axis.

INDIVIDUAL	ARIMA – POWER (W)	K-S – POWER (W)
EFM(Prog)	90	90
FDM(Prog)	75	90
HBF(Prog)	75	*
MAN(Prog)	100	100
DB(Prog)	115	115
EFM(Rand)	90	90
FDM(Rand)	75	90
HBF(Rand)	75	*
MAN(Rand)	100	100
DB(Rand)	115	115
ADS(Prog)	55	65
ACC(Prog)	55	55
MAF(Prog)	85	85
MABC(Prog)	75	*
JAC(Prog)	75	75
ADS(Rand)	65	65
ACC(Rand)	75	75
MAF(Rand)	85	*
MABC(Rand)	75	*
JAC(Rand)	85	95

Table 1: Comparison between the power values

* No power could be assigned to AT by the method

We have organized the results in Table 1 in order to compare the power values associated to the AT by K-S entropy and ARIMA.

The AT values, obtained by K-S and ARIMA methods, usually corresponded to the same power values: Spearman rank correlation coefficient = 0.93 and p-value < 0.01, for N = 15 (Figure 3).

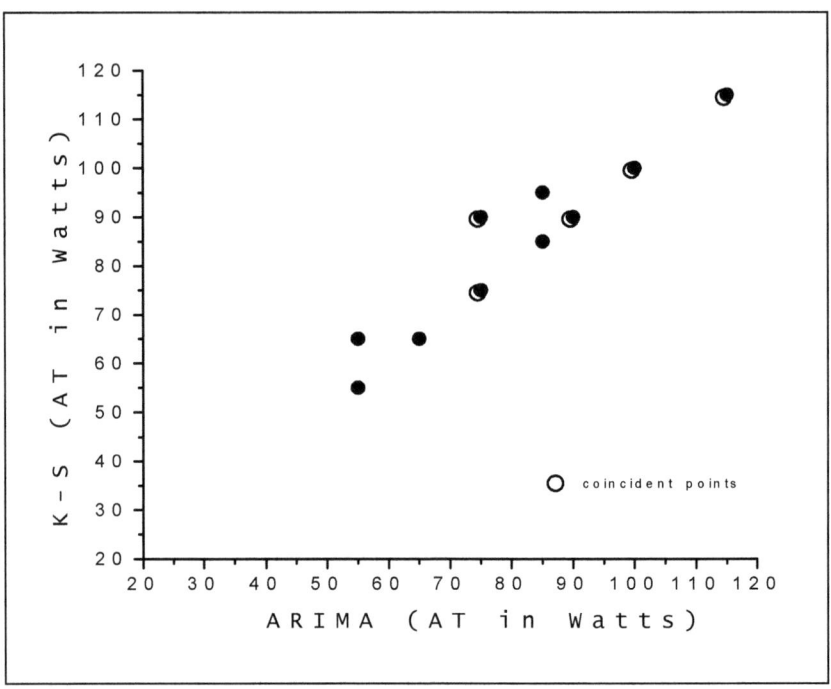

Figure 3: Correlation of AT values between both methods: K-S and ARIMA

6 Conclusions

We have described an alternative non-invasive way to obtain the Anaerobic Threshold. Our conclusions can be summarized as follows:

1. The Kolmogorov-Sinai entropy exhibited, in a phenomenological way, a drastic change in the system dynamics, showing a graphic pattern completely different from the others at power values that, invariably, agreed with the AT obtained from the ARIMA model.

2. The high linear correlation (r = 0.93), statistically significant at 1% level, between the ARIMA and Kolmogorov-Sinai entropy methods. It allows the conclusion that this last method can be used to obtain the AT, despite some problems that were expected like the data set size, different embedding dimensions and the reconstruction step size. The advantages of the Kolmogorov-Sinai entropy are: (1) it involves a fast computational procedure and (2) does not require elaborate statistical analysis. This implies that a physician can perform this test without the aid of a specialized staff.

Acknowledgement

Research support: CNPq (Proc. 300528/85-0)

References

[1]   A.A. Tsonis, Chaos: from theory to applications, *Plenum Press*, NY, (1992).

[2]   T. Elbert et al, Chaos and physiology: deterministic chaos in excitable cell assemblies, *Physiol. Rev.*, 74, (1994) 1-47.

[3]   G.P. Williams, Chaos theory tamed, *Taylor and Francis Pub.*, London, (1997).

[4]   K. Wasserman et al, Principles of exercise testing and interpretation, *Lippincott Williams and Wilkins*, 3rd ed., (1999).

[5]   L. Gallo Júnior et al, Control of heart rate during exercise in health and disease, *Braz. J. Med. Biol. Res.*, 28, (1995) 1179-1184.

[6]   G.E.P. Box and D.S. Pierce, Distribution of residual autocorrelations in autoregressive-integrated moving average time-series models, *J. Am. Statistical Assoc.*, 65, (1970) 1589-1526.

[7]   G.E.P. Box and G.M. Jenkins, Time series analysis: forecasting and control, *Holden- Day Pub. 1st ed.*, San Francisco, (1976).

[8]   V.R.F.S. Marães et al, The heart rate variability in dynamic exercise. Its possible role to signal anaerobic threshold, *The Physiologist*, 43, (2000) 339.

[9] F.M.H.S.P. Silva, *Aplicação da dinâmica não-linear no estudo da resposta dos intervalos R-R do eletrocardiograma durante o exercício físico dinâmico em indivíduos sadios*, Dsc Thesis, University of São Paulo, Brazil, (2001).

[10] P. Grassberger and I. Procaccia, Measuring the strangeness of strange attractors, *Physica 9D*, (1983) 189.

[11] F. Takens, Detecting strange attractors in turbulence. In: D.A. Rand; L.S. Young (Ed.). Dynamical systems and turbulence, (Springer lecture notes in mathematics) *Springer-Verlag*, Vol: 898, (1981).

[12] H.G. Schuster, Deterministic chaos: an introduction, *Verlagsgesellschaft*, (1981).

[13] E. Silva et al, Design of a computerized system to evaluate the cardiac function during dynamic exercise, *Phy. Med. Biol.*, 33, (1994) 409.

CLINICAL ENGINEERING AS A SOURCE OF INPUT VALUES TO THE MANAGEMENT EQUATION METHODOLOGY

LEILA C.N. GOMES, PAULO R.T. DALCOL

Pontifical Catholic University of Rio de Janeiro, Brazil

Abstract

One of the main issues concerning medical equipment refers to the several levels of maintenance services that can be applied. Clinical engineering activities can be extremely useful in helping managers to decide which maintenance level – local, central or outsourcing – to be used for each device implemented in a given hospital unit. This paper describes how clinical engineering can contribute in the identification of the most appropriate and cost-effective decisions in a specific institution based on a very useful methodology known as management equation, since its activities can provide precise values to the indicators of this equation. The three maintenance levels identified in Brazilian healthcare institutions and the institutional difficulties in implementing each level will also be described in an attempt to offer managers subsidies to take decisions, especially about which kind of equipment should employ the outsource level because of its complexity.

Key words: clinical engineering, management equation methodology, equipment, maintenance

1 Introduction

An extremely important and central issue concerning the healthcare sector refers to the maintenance of technology employed in both public and private institutions. Medical technology is a major component of the healthcare system, accounting for something around 15% to 40% of its cost. Thus, each technological device in a hospital unit should be capable of serving patients as well as improving, even more, the level of the services offered for diagnosis and treatment [4].

When establishing a maintenance system for medical equipment, it is necessary to consider the importance of the service to be executed and, especially, the way of managing such execution. Therefore, one must be aware of the level of importance of each device in clinical procedures or in the support activities for such procedures.

Another requirement is to possess information on the device's history. It includes equipment group or family, the average useful life, the obsolescence level, building characteristics and the possibility of replacement during maintenance. That is, everything that refers to each specific device and may somehow back up the maintenance service with the purpose of providing optimal security and quality to the task.

All of such information is useful for analyzing failures, establishing priorities in the performance of a service, setting up a preventive maintenance routine and reaching the level of security required, since inadequate maintenance might represent life risks for patients.

Clinical institutions that deal with specific areas of clinical engineering are intensely employing the activities of this field of study to identify issues concerning maintenance procedures, obtaining great results. This field may be the largest data provider concerning all the related technology.

A very common classification referring to the maintenance of medical equipment is to identify three different levels of the services to be executed. Levels classified as local and central are options for simpler, less complex maintenance tasks that do not require great amounts of intervention and specialization, and therefore can be carried out internally. On the other hand, maintenance services classified as outsourcing may represent complex interventions, requiring specific tools and abilities, and often highly specialized work. The characteristics of each level will be detailed further in this paper.

The correct determination of these levels is essential to yield better results along the life cycle of a new technology. Therefore, the results of the whole process to provide adequate maintenance services may be identified in the obtainment of the goals established by the institution and in the offer of high-quality services to the patients. This is especially important in relation to the great technological variety that exists in healthcare sector.

Obviously, each of these levels presents specific and characteristic advantages and difficulties, and it is important that managers are able to identify all these particularities in order to take their decisions. Besides, aiming to reach the results established by the institutions, it is crucial that managers employ specific methodologies to select the maintenance levels and work jointly with the clinical engineering sector, which is the main responsible for obtaining data and information on medical equipment.

One of such methodologies is the management equation methodology. It relates the values attributed to three important issues:
- Function values (therapy, diagnosis, analysis and support);
- Risk values (patient death, injury, wrong diagnosis or treatment and no risk);
- Maintenance values (frequent, regular and rare) required by the equipment.

According to this methodology, the set of values established could be used to identify the level of importance and maintenance required by the devices, and clinical engineering can be a strategic source of such value [3].

The purpose of the present paper is to show how the knowledge and practice of clinical engineering may provide support to managers in their decisions about the maintenance levels to be employed per device, applying the management equation methodology. Figure 1 presents the integration cycle among clinical engineering, this methodology and the maintenance levels. In the specific case of medical imaging equipment, the use of such methodology is highly significant, especially due to the complexity and cost of such equipment.

Clinical engineering, with its specific programs and activities, as illustrated in Figure 2, is able to supply very useful data and information for the constant improvement of the quality of the healthcare services provided, by means of monitoring and managing medical equipment installed in hospital units.

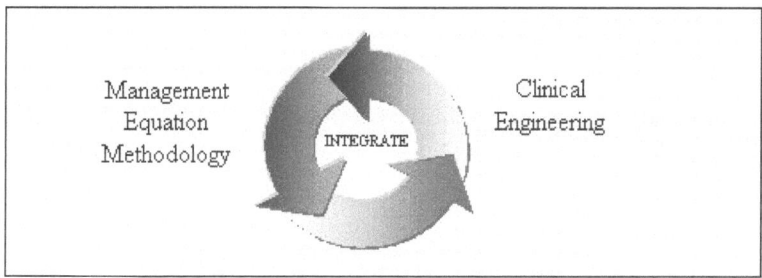

Figure 1: Integration cycle among clinical engineering, the management equation and the maintenance levels

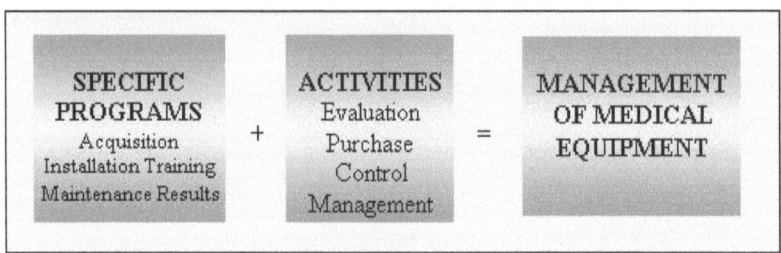

Figure 2: Structure of clinical engineering

2 Medical Equipment: Relevant Aspects

In terms of the physical structure, a hospital unit consists of its building (physical installation) and its technological property (equipment). However, is crucial to evaluate the costs relative to the acquisition of equipment by healthcare institution, in order to understand the importance of correctly choosing the maintenance services.

Table 1 presents some indicators relative to setting up hospitals and the amounts spent with equipment. The values shown clearly demonstrate the importance of the maintenance services to the best conservation of all technological resources, assuring their optimal performance.

Hospital Unit	Construction Costs (U$) (1)	Equipment Costs (U$) (2)	Proportion (2) / (1)	Set Up Year	Location
Beth Israel Hospital/ Children's Hospital Medical Care Center	5.498.000	2.900.000	53%	1993	Massachusetts
University of Washington Medical Center	16.813.000	7.390.000	44%	1994	Washington
Roanoke Memorial Hospital South Pavilion	43.563.497	19.000.000	44%	1994	Virginia
FHP Medical Campus	32.398.531	19.518.084	60%	1993	Utah
Memorial Hospital Addition	10.177.000	5.581.000	55%	1993	Indiana

Table 1: Relative costs of installation and medical equipment in some hospital units [5]

According to Cohen [2], medical equipment can be grouped into six categories, as follows:

1. Laboratory apparatus: devices used in the preparation, storage and analysis of in-vitro patient specimens, such as centrifuges, lab analyzers and lab refrigeration equipment;

2. Imaging and radiation therapy: devices used to image patient anatomy, such as X-ray, CT, MRI, ultrasound, nuclear medicine and radiation therapy equipment;

3. Patient diagnostic: devices connected to the patient, used to collect, record and analyze patient information, such as physiologic monitors, spirometers and endoscopes;

4. Life support and therapeutic: life-support equipment and devices that apply energy to the patient, such as anesthesia machines, ventilators, lasers, electro-surgical units and powered surgical instruments;

5. Patient environmental and transport: patient beds and other equipment whose purpose is the transportation of patients or enhancement of the patient environment, such as wheelchairs, gurneys, beds, exam lights and patient room furniture;

6. Other medical equipment: medical equipment not included in the above categories, such as sterilized.

The purpose of understanding to which of the above categories a given medical device belongs is to evaluate the specific requirements of the device and its relevance to the patient's health. This leads to the constant development of tools that allow managers to reduce costs with corrective maintenance by means of preventive and calibration maintenance procedures.

As already mentioned, medical imaging equipment constitutes a group with very specific characteristics, especially due to its complexity. It is possible to evaluate this fact by means of the maintenance expenses presented in Figure 3, extracted from a study carried out in seven hospital units (A, …, G) by Cohen [2].

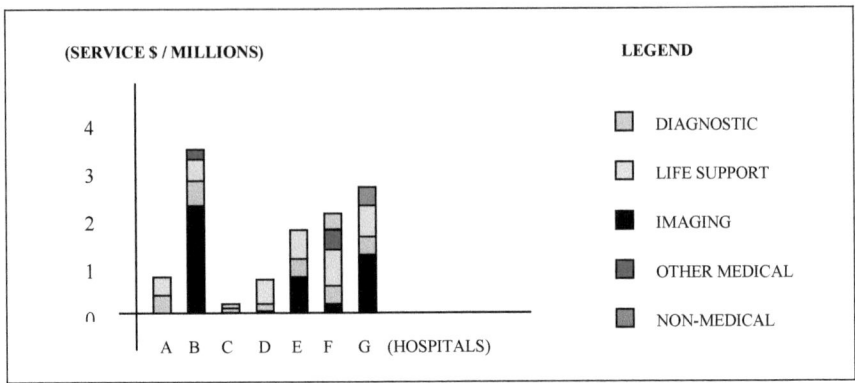

Figure 3: Costs with maintenance services per category of equipment

Imaging equipment such as traditional X-ray instrumentation, nuclear imaging, ultrasound devices, CT scanners, magnetic resonance imaging (MRI) and digital radiography is highly differentiated in various dimensions, and each of these technologies has a unique set of characteristics [6].

Given the substantial performance variation among these technologies and the fact that large price differences continue both within and across these technologies, it is not surprising that performance attributes are of central importance and that maintenance is the most important issue related to it [6].

3 Maintenance Levels

It is often impossible for a maintenance team to provide support to all the equipment in a hospital internally. Hospital units tend to require outsource services for equipment maintenance, especially those with greater electronic complexity, by means of specific agreement [1].

In Brazil, such agreements are usually related to equipment of high and medium complexity, which can represent around 4% to 10% of all equipment installed in the hospital unit, in quantitative terms, but whose set-up costs may account for 30% to 60% of the total cost [1].

To decide between internal or outsource maintenance, several aspects must be considered [1]:

- Existence of trained personnel for the maintenance of each specific type and model of equipment;
- Existence of technical documentation relative to each device to receive internal maintenance – according to the purchase agreement/call, such documentation should be provided with every device;
- Existence of testing and calibration equipment for evaluation after the maintenance, as several devices, especially those that represent risks to patients (resolution SVS/SAS n.1 of January 23, 1996, issued by the health department), require security and/or calibration tests soon after preventive or corrective maintenance;
- Proximity to the device manufacturer/technical representative in function of the transportation conditions available, which can sometimes represent very high costs for the maintenance procedures;
- Possibility of acquiring original parts.

The frequency with which maintenance must be executed is another important factor to be considered in the decisions concerning levels of maintenance. Such frequency relates to several other aspects, as can be seen in Table 2.

All of such information demonstrates the importance of establishing an adequate maintenance service, especially in function of the cost of technological resources.

Therefore, some methodologies can be applied to help managers take decisions about which level of maintenance to be implemented in their hospital unit and provide access to every particularity, allowing them to choose the most cost-effective option and obtain the best possible results from maintenance services [3].

Following, the three maintenance levels mentioned – local, central and outsourcing – would be described, with their specific characteristics and particularities.

3.1 Local Level

The first level to be analyzed is the local level, also called field service. Its execution is the responsibility of an internal hospital team, installed in offices equipped with proper tools and instruments. Since the services must be fast and with good quality, the technicians are more generalists, repairing several problems of average complexity.

Around 80% of the problems that occur in hospital units have simple causes and can be solved by this internal team.

Equipment such as some specific models of beds, sphygmomanometers, laryngoscopes, lamps in video devices and other similar ones can be repaired in this level, especially since they do not require very complex parts and accessories for their maintenance.

The greatest problem presented in this level is its installation itself in the hospital sector, first because of the physical space required for the repair area and stock of basic parts and working tools, and second because of the training that should be provided to those who will take part in the maintenance team and deal with a large variety of equipment.

EQUIPMENT CATEGORY	GENERAL INTERVALS AND CRITERIA
Electrical-powered equipment	Yearly interval: broad Preventive Maintenance (PM) should include visual verification. The yearly specific PM should include the verification of electric security (required by some norms).
Battery-powered equipment	Same procedures as for electrical-powered equipment, with the addition of battery capacity or voltage tests at each broad or specific PM. Some batteries require a discharge/charge cycle to increase performance and useful life. To minimize emergency calls and possible deactivations, the possibility of periodically replacing the batteries, based on their average useful life, should be considered.
Equipment controlled or fed by mechanical, electromechanical, pneumatic or fluid systems	Intervals of six or three months. PM instructions should include visual verification, electrical and performance security tests, cleaning, lubrication. The execution of a broad or specific PM will depend on the type of equipment.

EQUIPMENT CATEGORY	GENERAL INTERVALS AND CRITERIA
Resurrection of life-support equipment	Intervals of six or three months. Due to the critical nature of such devices and the bad use to which they are exposed, they require more frequent checks. They should be verified at least half-yearly.
Equipment located in areas of special care	Just like the previous category, this equipment may require more frequent verifications. However, its presence or use in areas of special care does not mean that there is a need to increase PM frequency.
Critical-monitoring equipment	Intervals of six months or one year. While failures in this equipment may have adverse consequences, experience shows that most component failures are random, and PM frequency has little or no effect in their occurrence.

Table 2: Intervals of Preventive Maintenance applicable to equipment [1]

3.2 Central Level

The second level is the central level, in which a more complex maintenance is to be executed. This service should be performed by more specialized personnel, with specific tools and more precise instruments.

The best results in this level are identified in equipment that compose the structure related to patient and transport control, pulmonary ventilators and other support devices. Here, it is possible to identify a larger stock of parts and accessories, usually acquired directly from representatives and/or manufacturers, such as Philips, General Electric, Siemens, Kodak, etc.

Obviously, infrastructure costs to set up this level in a hospital unit are considerably higher that those of setting up a local level. This is why this level is more frequent in healthcare networks of health departments, private hospital groups, state consortiums and other, more complex, healthcare structures.

3.3 Outsourcing Level

When a hospital unit or network has no local or central structures to fulfill its maintenance requirements, such services must be outsource. Hiring a third-party service constitutes the third level of maintenance for medical equipment.

In this level, the managers' attention should focus on monitoring, controlling and managing the outsource services. Inadequate management of such external services may represent losses for the unit of up to 30% of the annual budget for the equipment maintenance sector, apart from exposing the unit's technologic property to early deterioration.

Despite higher costs, there are some clear advantages in this structure. The main one refers to the warranties given by the companies that provide the services. This solution is ideal for highly complex devices that demand, more than just technicians executing the services, professionals usually with a degree on Electrical or Electronic Engineering. This is the case of medical imaging equipment such as CT, MRI and X-ray devices.

It must be noticed that the main purpose of the present paper is not to evaluate the best option for a hospital unit in terms of selecting its maintenance levels, but which maintenance level is the most adequate for each specific type of equipment.

Thus, in the following sections, a methodology will be described that might provide great help, combined with contributions in the field of clinical engineering, to choose optimal maintenance solutions.

4 Management Equation Methodology

The complexity of the clinical environment and the growing need for managing the technology involved in all this structure have taken managers to ponder on the maintenance level to be employed in each specific device in the institution.

The main reason for focusing on this issue is the need to reach organizational goals and the best results along the technologies' life cycle. In order to obtain such results, the applications of an adequate methodology and joint work with the area of clinical engineering are essential, as will be shown next.

One of such methodologies is the management equation methodology, which associates the equipment's function, risk and the required maintenance [3]. This methodology covers a set of established values that can be used to identify the level of importance and maintenance required by certain equipment, as shown in Tables 3, 4 and 5.

Equipment's Function	Values
Therapy	8, 9, 10
Diagnosis	6, 7
Analysis	5, 4, 3
Support	2

Table 3: Equipment's function values [3]

Equipment's Risk	Values
Patient death	5
Patient or operator injury	4
Wrong diagnosis or treatment	3, 2
No risk	1

Table 4: Equipment's risk values [3]

Equipment's Required Maintenance	Values
Frequent (daily, weekly)	5, 4
Regular (monthly, bimonthly)	3, 2
Rare (half-yearly, yearly)	1

Table 5: Equipment's required maintenance values [3]

By applying this methodology, clinical engineering is able to identify the complexity of each device by adding the attributed values:

$$ME = F + R + RM$$

Where:

    ME = Management Equation
    F = Function (Table 3)
    R = Risk (Table 4)
    RM = Required Maintenance (Table 5)

The values used in the analysis and selection of the maintenance level required by the medical equipment can be considered according to the values presented in Table 6, mostly composed by indicators obtained in clinical engineering.

Maintenance Level	ME Values
Outsource (high complexity)	[13,20]
Central (average complexity)	[8,12]
Local (simple complexity)	[4,7]

Table 6: Indices proposed base on data observed by clinical engineering

Thus, with routine information obtained from clinical engineering activities, this evaluation of the maintenance levels required by medical equipment can prove very practical in the effective execution of such maintenance.

5 Conclusion

The purpose of this paper was to show know the knowledge of the clinical engineering field can support decision taking on the maintenance levels to be applied to specific categories of medical equipment, especially in relation to the indicators manipulated by such field.

Concerning such indicators, it is important that very precise values are used, so that the decisions taken are based on real data. The strict control of the equipment's history, effectively carried out by clinical engineering, can provide such data to a hospital unit's management staff.

By means of programs executed by clinical engineering – acquisition, installation, training, maintenance and results – the complete control of the hospital's technological property is the responsibility of this area. The contribution of such programs is greatly relevant to determine the maintenance levels required by medical equipment, especially the results program, whose main function is to control the results obtained in certain periods of time, issuing periodical performance reports of the hospital unit and generating performance indices [5].

The main procedure of this program is to provide reports on the economy and cost-effectiveness achieved. Indices informing the average time of unused devices, time spent in maintenance, costs with training, costs with spare parts, number of intervention per devices, failures, etc., are extremely important [5].

Several indicators provided by the program, such as these indices, can support an evaluation of the results, demonstrating precisely if the choices made were satisfactory in terms of the applied maintenance levels.

As well as the results program, all other programs that constitute the clinical engineering field are important in the identification of such options. A good example is the imaging diagnosis equipment sector, which presents several peculiarities. In this case, the contribution of clinical engineering can be definitive.

Therefore, clinical engineering can be a great ally in the determination of the best maintenance options required by medical equipment and in the evaluation of the maintenance levels established in healthcare institutions.

Combining such knowledge with the support provided by methodologies such as the one here described – management equation methodology – hospital units can constantly enhance their choices and options in terms of maintenance.

References

[1]   S.J. Calil and M.S. Teixeira, Gerenciamento de manutenção de equipamentos hospitalares, *Fundação Peirópolis Ltda*, São Paulo, Brazil, (1998).

[2]   T. Cohen, Validating medical equipment repair and maintenance metrics: A progress report, *Biomedical Instrumentation & Technology*, January/February, (1997).

[3]   Fiocruz, Gestão operacional de sistemas e serviços de saúde, Vol: 3, *Editora Fundação Instituto Osvaldo Cruz*, Rio de Janeiro, Brazil, (1998).

[4]   E. Geisler and O. Heller, Management of medical technology – Theory, practice and cases, *Kluwer Academic Publishers*, Massachusetts, (1998).

[5]   L.C.N. Gomes, *Gestão tecnológica em unidades hospitalares: Um estudo sobre a gerência de equipamentos médicos*, Msc Thesis, Pontifícia Universidade Católica do Rio de Janeiro, Brazil, (2000).

[6]   C. Pleatsikas and D. Teece, The analysis of market definition and market power in the context of rapid innovation, *International Journal of Industrial Organization*, Vol: 19, Elsevier Science B.V., (2001).

CORRESPONDING AUTHOR'S ADDRESSES

*Duncan P. Boldy, Shu-Chiung Chou
and Andy H. Lee*
Curtin University of Technology
Centre for Research into Aged Care Services
and School of Public Health
GPO Box U1987 - Perth WA 6845
Australia
Fax: + 61 8 9266 2508
Phone: + 61 8 9266 7942
Email: d.boldy@curtin.edu.au

*Vanda De Angelis, Giovanni Felici
and Giovanni Storchi*
Università degli Studi di Roma "La Sapienza"
Dip. Statistica, Probabilita' e Statistiche
Piazzale Aldo Moro, 5
00184 Rome - Italy
Fax: +39 06 4959241
Phone: +39 06 4880411
Email: vanda.deangelis@uniroma.it

*Sérgio L. Hoeflich, Luiz R.T.A. Costa
and, Rogério A.C. Penna*
COPPE – Programa de Engenharia Oceânica
Cidade Universitária - Centro deTecnologia,
Bloco C - Sala 203 - CEP: 21931-010
Rio de Janeiro - RJ- Brazil
Fax: +55 21 22906626
Phone: +55 21 25607143
Email: hoeflish@radnet.com.br

Maria H. Brachowicz and *Cesar das Neves*
725 Westbrook Avenue
Brandon, FL 33511
United States of America
Phone: +1 813 6574355
Email: mbrachowicz@yahoo.es

Marten Lagergren
Stockholm Gerontology Research Centre
Box 6401
113 82 Stockholm - Sweden
Fax: +46 8 335275
Phone: +46 8 6905812
Email:
marten.lagergren@aldrecentrum.se

Lupe N. P. Toscano
Universidad Nacional de Ingeniería
Lima - Perú
Apartado Postal No. 1301
Email: lpizan@yahoo.com

Martin Dlouhý
University of Economics
Department of Econometrics
W. Churchill Sq 4
130 67 Prague 3
Czech Republic
Phone: +421 2 24095443
Email: dlouhy@vse.cz

*Marcos P.E. Lins, Antonio C.Gonçalves,
Eliane G. Gomes and Angela C.M. da
Silva*
Universidade Federal do Rio de Janeiro
Cidade Universitaria,
Caixa Postal 68507
CEP: 21945-970
Rio de Janeiro - RJ - Brazil
Phone: +55 21 2562 8245
Email: lins@pep.ufrj.br

Santiago S.R. Carvajal
Av. Cel. Luiz de Oliveira Sampaio 369
ap. 201
Ilha do Governador
CEP: 21931-010
Rio de Janeiro - RJ - Brazil
Fax: +55 21 2562-7403
Phone: +55 21 3396-3209
Email: sramirez@skydome.net

Rosimary T. Almeida, *Rafael M. Gênova
and Maria Inês Gadelha*
Universidade Federal do Rio de Janeiro
Cidade Universitaria, Centro de Tecnologia,
Bloco H sala 327
Caixa Postal 68510 - CEP: 21945-970
Rio de Janeiro - Brazil
Fax: +55 21 2562 8591
Phone: +55 21 2562 8630
Email: rosal@peb.ufrj.br

Jaime G. Bellido
Universidade Federal do Rio de Janeiro
Cidade Universitaria, Centro de Tecnologia,
Caixa Postal 68507
CEP: 21945-970
Rio de Janeiro - RJ - Brazil
Phone: +55 21 25628285
Email: bellido@pep.ufrj.br

Ludmila Gabcan *and Mario J.F. De Oliveira*
Universidade Federal do Rio de Janeiro
Cidade Universitária, Centro de Tecnologia,
Bloco F sala 105 - Caixa Postal 68507
CEP: 21945-970
Rio de Janeiro - Brazil
Fax: +55 21 22807438
Phone: +55 21 22250070
Email: gabcan@lamce.ufrj.br

Marco. A. S. Lavrador
Universidade de São Paulo
Fac.Ciências Farmacêuticas de Ribeirão
Preto
Departamento de Física e Química
Via do Café s/n - CEP: 14040-903
Ribeirão Preto - SP - Brazil
Fax: +55 16 6332960
Phone: +55 16 6024176
Email: lavrador@usp.br

Antônio A. Gonçalves
Av. Atlântica, 2440 - Apt. 503
Copacabana
CEP: 22041-001
Rio de Janeiro - RJ - Brazil
Phone: +55 21 9156 5178
Email: augusto@inca.org.br

Jan M.H. Vissers
Eindhoven University of Technology
Department of Technology Management
P.O.Box 513
5600 MB Eindhoven - The Netherlands
Fax: +31 40 2464596
Phone: +31 40 2463937
Email: j.m.h.vissers@tm.tue.nl

Adriana B. Moraes, *Sheila M. Esposito
and Simone M. Bordalo*
Rua Arruda Negreiros, 1430
Austin - Nova Iguaçu
CEP: 26000-000
Rio de Janeiro - RJ - Brazil
Phone: +55 21 2763 5154
Email: adrianabandeira@ibge.gov.br

Kevin J. Leonard and *Warren Winkelman*
Dept of Health Policy, Mgmt and Eval
University of Toronto
12 Queens Park Cres. West, 2nd Floor
McMurrich
Toronto, Ontário - M5S 1A8 - CANADA
Fax: 4168611281
Phone: 41 69788364
Email: k.leonard@utoronto.ca

Roberto M. Protil, *Luiz C. Duclós*
and Vilmar R. Moreira
Pontifícia Universidade Católica do
Paraná
Centro de Ciências Sociais Aplicadas
Programa de Pós-Graduação em
Administração
Rua Imaculada Conceição, 1155 - Prado
Velho CEP: 80215-901
Curitiba – Paraná - Brazil
Fax: +5541 3323323
Phone: +55 41 33011634
Email: protil@ppgia.pucpr.br

Fátima M. H. S. P. da Silva, *Antônio C. Silva*
Filho, Vera R. F. S. Marães, Maria S. A.
Moura, Ester da Silva, Aparecida M. Catai,
Benedito C. Maciel and Lourenço Gallo Jr
Universidade de São Paulo
Fac.Ciências Farmacêuticas de Ribeirão Preto
Departamento de Física e Química
Via do Café s/n - CEP: 14040-903
Ribeirão Preto - SP - Brazil
Fax: +55 16 6332960
Phone: +55 16 6024176
Email: fsimoes@fcfrp.usp.br

Leila Gomes and *Paulo R.T. Dalcol*
Pontifícia Universidade Católica do R.J.
Rua Sorocaba 756 C/04, Botafogo
CEP: 22271-110
Rio de Janeiro R.J - Brazil
Phone: +55 21 25272044
Email: foccus@openlink.com.br

PUBLISHED PROCEEDINGS FROM PREVIOUS MEETINGS

- M. Kulej, M. Lubicz, B. Mielczareck and Z. Krokosz-Krynke (Eds.) Operational Research Applied to Health Services, Proceedings of the 16th Annual Meeting of the EURO Working Group on Operational Research Applied to Health Services, Conference Series, vol. 20, Wydawnictwo Politechniki Wroclawskiej, Wroclaw, Poland, 1991.

- Kastelein., J. Vissers, G.G van Merode and L. Delesie (Eds.) Managing Health Care Under Resource Constraints, Proceedings of the 21st Annual Meeting of the EURO Working Group on Operational Research Applied to Health Services, Eindhoven University Press, Eindhoven, The Netherlands, 1996.

- E. Matson (Ed.). Operational Research Applied to Health Services, Proceedings of the 23rd Annual Meeting of the EURO Working Group on Operational Research Applied to Health Services, Norwegian University of Science and Technology, Trondheim, Norway, 1997.

- V. de Angelis, N. Ricciardi and G. Storchi (Eds.) Monitoring, Evaluating, Planning Health Services, Proceedings of the 24th Annual Meeting of the EURO Working Group on Operational Research Applied to Health Services, World Scientific, Singapore-New Jersey-London-Hong Kong, Singapore, 1999.

- E. Mikitis (Ed.) Information, Management and Planning of Health Services, Proceedings of the 25th Annual Meeting of the EURO Working Group on Operational Research Applied to Health Services, Health Statistics and Medical Technology Agency, Riga, Latvia, 2000.

- J. Riley (Ed.) Planning for the Future: Health Service Quality and Emergency Accessibility, Proceedings of the 26th Annual Meeting of the EURO Working Group on Operational Research Applied to Health Services, Caledonian University Press, Glasgow, Great Britain, 2001.

- M. Rauner and K. Heidenberger (Eds.) Quantitative Approaches in Health Care Management, Proceedings of the 27th Annual Meeting of the EURO Working Group on Operational Research Applied to Health Services (ORAHS), Peter Lang, Frankfurt am Main-Berlin-Bruxelles-New York-Wien, 2003.

Marion Sabine Rauner / Kurt Heidenberger (eds.)

Quantitative Approaches in Health Care Management

Proceedings of the 27th Meeting of the European Working Group on Operational Research Applied to Health Services (ORAHS), Vienna, Austria, July 30–August 4, 2001

Frankfurt am Main, Berlin, Bern, Bruxelles, New York, Oxford, Wien, 2003.
307 pp., num. fig. and tab.
ISBN 3-631-39009-2 / US-ISBN 0-8204-5470-2 · pb. € 45.50*

Health care policy makers are facing the problem of limited expenditures and growing demand. Thus, quantitative approaches can help solve this urging issue. For this reason, the EURO Working Group on Operational Research Applied to Health Services (ORAHS) was formed in 1975. The objectives of the group are communication of ideas, knowledge and experience concerning the application of Operational Research approaches and methods to problems in the health services area, mutual assistance among members, co-operation on joint projects, inspiration with regard to approaches and attitudes in this field. The 27th meeting of this group was hosted by the University of Vienna, Austria, 2001. This books covers a selection of 18 papers presented at this conference.

Contents: Quantitative Approaches in Health Care Management: General Strategies, Health Services Planning, Hospital Planning Models, Decision Support Systems, Prevention and Health Promotion

Frankfurt am Main · Berlin · Bern · Bruxelles · New York · Oxford · Wien
Distribution: Verlag Peter Lang AG
Moosstr. 1, CH-2542 Pieterlen
Telefax 00 41 (0) 32 / 376 17 27

*The €-price includes German tax rate
Prices are subject to change without notice
Homepage http://www.peterlang.de

Peter Lang · Europäischer Verlag der Wissenschaften